Better Health Economics

Better Health Economics

An Introduction for Everyone

TAL GROSS AND
MATTHEW J. NOTOWIDIGDO

The University of Chicago Press
Chicago and London

The University of Chicago Press, Chicago 60637
The University of Chicago Press, Ltd., London
© 2024 by The University of Chicago
Published 2024
Printed in the United States of America

33 32 31 30 29 28 27 26 25 24   1 2 3 4 5

ISBN-13: 978-0-226-82029-3 (cloth)
ISBN-13: 978-0-226-82033-0 (paper)
ISBN-13: 978-0-226-82030-9 (e-book)
DOI: https://doi.org/10.7208/chicago/9780226820309.001.0001

Library of Congress Cataloging-in-Publication Data

Names: Gross, Tal, author. | Notowidigdo, Matt, 1981– author.
Title: Better health economics : an introduction for everyone / Tal Gross and
    Matthew J. Notowidigdo.
Description: Chicago : The University of Chicago Press, 2024. | Includes
    bibliographical references and index.
Identifiers: LCCN 2023017134 | ISBN 9780226820293 (cloth) | ISBN 9780226820330
    (paperback) | ISBN 9780226820309 (ebook)
Subjects: LCSH: Medical economics—United States. | Medical care, Cost
    of—United States.
Classification: LCC RA410.53 .G748 2024 | DDC 338.4/73621—dc23/eng/20230527
LC record available at https://lccn.loc.gov/2023017134

Contents

Introduction

What Do Health Economists Do?

At cocktail parties, we introduce ourselves as health economists. Most people we meet smile and then find someone else to talk to.

After all, what even is a health economist? And why does the world need an entire species of economists dedicated to health? What's next—shoelace economists? Pavement economists?

The world needs health economists because healthcare is different from every other part of the economy. Most transactions outside of healthcare are relatively straightforward. For example, a farmer sells heirloom tomatoes to a customer at a green market. Everyone knows what they're getting—there are no surprises, no complications. The customer can reach out and feel the tomatoes—she might even ask for a sample.

In contrast, imagine a doctor selling annual physicals. Suddenly, things are much more complicated.

- The doctor can be paid a fee for each annual physical she provides, or a lump-sum fee for each patient she covers each year, or the doctor might be salaried. It's not obvious which option is best. (Chapter 8)
- The customer is no longer the one paying—typically a health insurance company is footing most of the bill. (Chapter 4)
- Customers do not even know how much healthcare they need. Everyone knows how many tomatoes they want to buy, but if a doctor recommends an extra blood test or two, most patients just have to trust them. (Chapter 7)
- A farmer doesn't care who buys his tomatoes. By contrast, doctors (and insurers) care deeply about which people they treat. Some people will always be unprofitable for insurers and sometimes doctors face incentives to avoid certain types of patients. (Chapter 2)

- No farmer is required to give away his tomatoes, but healthcare organizations are often required by law to provide free care. (Chapter 3)
- Whether my neighbor buys tomatoes or not is his business—it doesn't affect me. But in healthcare, my neighbor's decisions can sometimes affect my health through contagion. (Chapter 13)

All of which is to say that healthcare really is different. And that is why health economists exist. The tools that economists have developed to understand agriculture—or telecommunications, or real estate—are different from the tools necessary to understand healthcare.

Dolphins and Tuna

One of our thesis advisers in graduate school, Jon Gruber, used a "dolphins-and-tuna" metaphor as a way to talk about the broader issues in health policy.

Dolphins and tuna often swim together in the ocean. The two are very different: dolphins are mammals that hold their breath to swim underwater, and tuna are fish. For reasons that are not completely clear, eating dolphin is seen as deeply offensive, while tuna is one of the world's most commonly eaten fish.[1]

In the 1980s, people became concerned that tuna fishermen were accidentally killing dolphins. The dolphins would get caught in the nets meant for tuna and then drown. The technical term is that the dolphin had become a "bycatch." Through the 1990s, regulators developed standards that were meant to prevent dolphins from dying this way. Americans adopted the "Dolphin Safe" label to reassure concerned consumers that no dolphins were harmed in the production of their tuna.

So: we want to catch the tuna but leave the dolphins in the ocean. We often face the same problems in healthcare. We want to prevent wasteful healthcare spending but preserve important healthcare. When it comes to the pharmaceutical industry, for instance, we want to pay much less for the drugs that exist, but we also want the drug industry to continue to develop new drugs. Or, in another context, we want to reward high-quality hospitals but also help low-quality hospitals improve. All of these are examples of the tuna-dolphin challenge: we want to cut out bad healthcare—that is, yank the tuna out of the water—but we don't want to limit good healthcare—we want the dolphins to happily swim away.

This book is something of a tour of health economics, and maybe by the end you'll see how regulating the healthcare sector is an endless series of dolphin-tuna challenges. What we hope to do in this book is explain why.

Who We Are

For nearly twenty years, ever since we met as graduate students at MIT, we've worked as health economists. We've written half-a-dozen papers together and a couple dozen papers with other coauthors. We've taught courses on health economics. One of us, Tal Gross (hereafter "Tal"), taught health economics to students getting master's degrees in public health at the Mailman School of Public Health at Columbia University, and then to students getting a master's in business administration at the Questrom School of Business at Boston University. The other, Matt Notowidigdo (hereafter "Noto"), taught health economics to undergraduate students at Northwestern and later to students getting their master's in business administration at the Booth School of Business at the University of Chicago.

Those courses are a tour of health economics—how to think about health insurance, healthcare delivery, and the life-sciences industry. Our notes for these courses would collectively fill a giant three-ring binder: materials for class, summaries of research, exhibits.

If we could, we would drag that three-ring binder to every cocktail party to which we are invited. And then, when people ask us what it is that we do for a living, what health economists actually *do*, we would pull out that binder and walk them through it.

But it's a party, not a deposition. And while some eccentricities are socially acceptable, pulling out a binder in the middle of a party is not.

And so, instead, we have turned that three-ring binder into this book. This book is an answer to all of the people who wonder what it is that health economists do. It's a summary of our health economics courses, a summary of what we believe our field has accomplished in the fifty-odd years that it's existed.[2]

PART I

Demand

What Does Health Insurance Do?

To many people, health insurance is boring. It's a matter of faxed paperwork and deductibles and "your call is very important to us, please stay on the line." Health insurance is a *financial* product: it determines who pays for your healthcare. For most people, that's about as thrilling as filing their taxes.

But in the United States, unlike every other wealthy country, not everyone is lucky enough to have health insurance. About 50 million people were uninsured a few years before the Affordable Care Act—also known as Obamacare—was implemented in 2014, and about 25 million people were still uninsured a few years later. In other words, let's ask the most *American* of questions: "What does health insurance do?"

The Fundamental Purpose of Health Insurance: A Red Sox Parable

In the fall of 2007, we were graduate students at MIT. Jenny, Noto's then girlfriend and now wife, bought a dining room table. The table was solid cherry and expensive: it cost a thousand dollars. We, being graduate students, couldn't afford a $1000 table, but there were a couple factors that brought that $1000 table into Noto and Jenny's apartment. At the time, Jenny was a software engineer and she spent her weekends decorating her and Noto's Cambridge apartment. Even if Noto couldn't afford the table, she could.

But there was something else that made the table more affordable that fall. Jenny bought the table from a large Boston chain called Jordan's Furniture. And that fall, Jordan's Furniture ran a promotion. If the Red Sox won the World Series, then all of the furniture they sold would be free.

So Jenny bought the table and then happily explained to Noto the price. Yes, it cost a thousand dollars. But if the Red Sox won, they would get the money back. The Red Sox had previously won the World Series in 2004, the first time they'd done so since 1918. In the minds of Boston's fundamentalist sports fans, the 2004 victory ushered in a new era in which the Red Sox would probably win the World Series every year. By 2007, when Noto and Jenny bought the table, the team seemed downright overdue.

Noto recognized right away that he and Jenny faced a very particular form of uncertainty. In one timeline they would get a thousand dollars and a free table—in the other, they would get nothing and would have bought a very expensive piece of midcentury-modern furniture (table 1.1).

Most people detest uncertainty, and because Noto is an economist, he detests it even more. So Noto came up with a scheme that would eliminate the uncertainty. At the time, a popular website, Tradesports.com, made it easy to bet on sports teams. Noto used the website to place a $500 bet *against* the Red Sox.[1] If the Red Sox lost the World Series, the bet would pay out $1,000.

Why did Noto do this? Well, think about the two possible outcomes here as two different timelines: one in which the Red Sox win the World Series, the other in which the Red Sox do not win the World Series (table 1.2).

Noto used the bet as a way to transfer resources across two hypothetical timelines. The bet let him move $500 from the timeline in which the Red Sox won to the timeline in which the Red Sox lost. And that transfer of resources eliminated the uncertainty that he and Jenny faced: once Noto made the bet, she would be up $500 regardless of who won the World Series.[2] But to enjoy that certainty, Noto had to pay $500 for the bet.

Insurance, at its core, offers the same service. Insurance allows people to transfer resources across timelines.[3] After all, think about car insurance. One

TABLE 1.1. Uncertainty Jenny Faced

Timeline	Consequences
The Red Sox win the World Series.	Jordan's Furniture sends Jenny a check for $1,000.
The Red Sox lose the World Series.	They keep the table but do not receive the $1,000.

TABLE 1.2. Jenny's Situation after the Bet

Timeline	Consequences	Net costs
The Red Sox win the World Series.	Jordan's Furniture sends Jenny a check for $1,000, but Noto paid $500 for a bet that, in this case, would not pay out.	On net, Jenny and Noto have paid $500 for the table.
The Red Sox lose the World Series.	Jordan's Furniture doesn't send any money, but Noto's bet pays off. He paid $500 to place the bet, and it pays out $1,000.	On net, Jenny and Noto have paid $500 for the table.

day, you park your car and run inside a store for an errand. While your beloved car is just sitting in the parking lot, another driver plows into it, causing thousands of dollars' worth of damage. That's one timeline, and a pretty bad one. The other timeline is realized all other days, when your car is *not* damaged. Without insurance, you would face uncertainty: either you're going to pay a mechanic thousands of dollars tomorrow or you'll have no need for a mechanic. Either you'll spend a lot of money, or you'll spend nothing. Car insurance reduces that uncertainty: each month you pay a set premium rather than facing the risk of thousands of dollars in repairs.

Health insurance is similar. If we become ill, health insurance allows us to receive thousands of dollars in medical care for a fraction of the cost. The primary purpose of health insurance is to resolve that uncertainty, to be there in case we get ill or injured, by committing to the fixed cost of a health insurance plan. This leads to a textbook answer to the question "What does health insurance do?"

> Health insurance allows risk-averse individuals to transfer resources across states and thus smooth their consumption in the face of unanticipated, out-of-pocket medical expenses.[4]

"Risk averse individuals"—people who prefer to avoid risk—is key. Without aversion to risk, there would be no demand for insurance.

For decades, policymakers have struggled to get all Americans covered by health insurance. President Roosevelt tried and failed in 1939, President Nixon tried and failed in 1974, and President Clinton tried and failed in 1993. Why, for so long, have American politicians spent scarce political capital in the hopes of getting all Americans on a health insurance plan?

Sometimes, politicians would link the effort directly to risk aversion. When signing Medicare into law in 1965, President Johnson declared, "No longer will illness crush and destroy the savings that [Americans] have so carefully put away over a lifetime." President Obama also emphasized the financial security provided by the Affordable Care Act.

Given that definition, you might assume that economists have been studying the financial consequences of health insurance for decades. But when we started graduate school, there had been very little work on health insurance's *financial* effects. Most of the research we read studied the effect of health insurance on healthcare and health-related outcomes: Did having health insurance lead to more doctor's visits? More preventive care? Those are certainly interesting questions, but we start first by focusing on the financial effects of health insurance. We do so because health insurance is, first and foremost, a tool for handling financial risk.

The Effect of Health Insurance on *Financial* Health

Noto used online gambling as a financial product to reduce the uncertainty he and Jenny faced.[5] Health insurance is also a financial product: it primarily determines who pays for your medical care. And so the first effect of health insurance we examine is its financial impact.

We have been interested in the financial effects of health insurance since 2006. That year, we were both graduate students in the economics department at MIT. And we were *struggling* graduate students, struggling with a fundamental challenge that faces graduate students in economics. Doctoral programs in economics require a couple years of classes—exams, problem sets—and then several years of research. The transition between those two pieces is often difficult. For a couple years, a graduate student is handed well-defined, concrete problems to solve. And then, all of a sudden, the student is told: you are a researcher now. Come up with a paper on your own. Find a way to impress the entire field of economics: we're done teaching you—now you teach us.

And so, for months, we stared at blank sheets of paper. Occasionally, we would come up with an idea to research.[6] We would bring the idea back to our thesis advisers, only to be told that it wasn't good enough, had already been published, or was too ambitious. This was a slog.

We would occasionally meet for lunch and commiserate. For us, one image sums up the student-researcher transition: the two of us eating overpriced sandwiches at a depressing chain restaurant in Kendall Square. Noto, for some reason, would always buy a VitaminWater. Tal would order a tuna salad sandwich. And we would show each other notebooks filled with failed ideas, potential research topics that our advisers told us were not good enough.

Eventually, during one of those lunches, the sun started to shine. We started talking about bankruptcy. Bankruptcy is a legal procedure that allows Americans who are overwhelmed by their debts to get a fresh start.[7] Those considering bankruptcy are typically in dire straits. Perhaps their small business has failed, or perhaps they've recently been laid off. Bill collectors are constantly calling. Their credit cards are maxed out. And then they find a bankruptcy attorney. For a fee, the attorney files paperwork on their behalf, and a judge reviews the case. Sometimes, the judge will require some assets to be sold and the proceeds distributed to creditors. But, usually, after a lot of paperwork, all of the person's debt is wiped away, and they get a fresh start. (At the same time, their credit scores plummet and don't recover for years.)

We started to wonder whether health insurance might play a role in all of this. In fact, there had been some discussion among law scholars as to how much healthcare costs might drive Americans to bankruptcy.[8] Over lunch, we discussed those papers, and then we had an idea. What if we could somehow test whether health insurance coverage affects the risk of bankruptcy?

That day in Kendall Square, we discussed a particular thought experiment. Imagine that we took thousands of Americans and randomly selected some to be covered by Medicaid. Then we took thousands of others and made them uninsured. Those covered by Medicaid would face few medical bills. Medicaid in the United States is publicly provided health insurance for low-income households. There are few copayments and no deductibles. Meanwhile, the uninsured face the full price of healthcare. If they visit an emergency room, the hospital will often send them a bill for thousands of dollars.

We discussed the idea at length. And then we asked our thesis advisers what they thought. To our surprise, they thought we were on the right track. Jon Gruber, an MIT health economist, was especially encouraging. He sent us an e-mail. "There are about 1 million bankruptcies per year. So you would need a pretty big change in medical expenditure risk to see a measurable effect on bankruptcies. The only really good candidate here is Medicaid expansions. You could see whether Medicaid expansions lowered bankruptcy."

And with that encouragement, we started to poke around. Medicaid programs began in the 1960s and originally only provided coverage to very young children and pregnant mothers. Over time, though, states gradually expanded who was eligible. In the 1990s, states started to allow low-income parents onto Medicaid and also older children. We collected data on state-level expansions of Medicaid in the 1990s. Some states were especially aggressive in expanding Medicaid: California and Missouri, for instance, made large shares of their populations eligible for Medicaid during that time. Meanwhile, other states—for instance, Texas and South Carolina—were much slower to expand coverage.

We then compared bankruptcy rates across states. Nearly all states expanded Medicaid in the 1990s, and nearly all states saw an increase in bankruptcy rates during that time due to broader trends in the economy. But the states that expanded Medicaid the most saw the smallest increases in bankruptcy rates. We then dug in and analyzed the relationship between Medicaid expansions and bankruptcies in various ways. In all cases, we found a robust negative relationship: Medicaid expansion seemed to lower the number of bankruptcies. If a state expanded Medicaid eligibility to cover an additional 10 percent of the population, our results suggested this would reduce the consumer bankruptcy rate by 8 percent.[9]

We wrote this all up and eventually published it in the *Journal of Public Economics* as one of our first papers. As of this writing, the paper has been cited over 250 times, which is not a bad outcome for two depressed graduate students sadly sipping VitaminWater and eating overpriced tuna salad sandwiches.

What's more, this basic finding has been replicated and demonstrated by other researchers. Bhash Mazumder and Sarah Miller studied the Massachusetts health insurance expansion of 2006. In that year, Massachusetts enacted healthcare reform with the goal of achieving universal coverage. The policy was, eventually, the inspiration for Obamacare. All Massachusetts residents were compelled to purchase health insurance—those who did not would face tax penalties. And, indeed, over just a few years, the uninsured all but disappeared in Massachusetts.

Mazumder and Miller studied the effects of the Massachusetts reform in credit bureau data. They found a very clear relationship: the more Massachusetts residents who gained coverage, the fewer bankruptcies they observed. What's more, Mazumder and Miller looked at all of the other markers of financial distress beyond bankruptcy. As more people gained coverage there were reductions in the amount of debt that was past due, higher credit scores, and fewer third-party collections.[10] Gains in insurance coverage led to drops in all of those bad financial outcomes. That study by Mazumder and Miller, and our own prior work on bankruptcy, demonstrated a relationship between expansions of health insurance and a reduction in financial distress.

Researchers have also studied how health insurance helps those dealing with severe bouts of illness or injury. Noto wrote a paper with three coauthors—Carlos Dobkin, Amy Finkelstein, and Ray Kluender—that studied the effect of health insurance on people in crisis. The team linked data covering almost every hospitalization in California over four years to each patient's credit report. Every American who has ever taken out a loan has a credit report—it lists their balances on all accounts and also their credit score, a measure of the chance that they'll default on another loan. Then they focused on California residents who suddenly appear in the hospital for the first time. Most of those people were dealing with a first heart attack or stroke: they were suddenly grappling with a new health crisis. What did that crisis do to their credit report?

For those who had health insurance, the sudden hospitalizations barely affected their credit records. But for those who came into the hospital uninsured, things were much different. Figure 1.1 shows that, on average, a hospitalization leads to about $6,000 in unpaid medical bills for people who are uninsured. And this average, as one might expect, conceals a lot of variation at the extremes. About 10 percent of the uninsured who are hospitalized end up with over $18,000 in unpaid medical bills. By contrast, for those

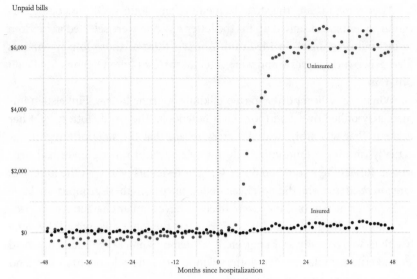

FIGURE 1.1. The impact of a hospitalization on unpaid bills for uninsured and insured adults. The data link consumer credit reports to all non-pregnancy-related hospitalizations in California between 2003 and 2007, limited to adults ages 25–64. The horizontal axis plots the months relative to the hospital admission.

with health insurance, a hospitalization leads to a tiny increase in unpaid medical bills.[11]

To date, many other researchers have written similar studies.[12] At this point, the evidence is very clear. Health insurance leads to lower out-of-pocket medical costs. Those lower out-of-pocket medical costs lead, in turn, to reduced financial distress. In other words, more health insurance means fewer bankruptcies, defaults, and delinquencies. Health insurance is good for people's finances.

What Does Health Insurance Do to *Healthcare*?

Around the time that we were sitting down for lunch in Kendall Square, another research project was just getting off the ground. Finkelstein, at the time, was an assistant professor at MIT and just making her name as an up-and-coming star in economics. One day, she was driving to work and, like all professors, listening to NPR on her car radio. That day, the reporters were discussing a story out of Oregon. The state of Oregon had decided to expand Medicaid, but it had a problem. In 2008, funding was sufficient to add 10,000 new Oregon residents to Medicaid, but many more than 10,000 people were interested.

After some debate, the state decided to run a lottery. Of the 90,000 Oregon residents who signed up for the lottery, 35,000 were selected at random to be invited to enroll in Medicaid. About a third of those lottery winners filed paperwork properly and were actually enrolled onto Oregon's Medicaid program.

When the NPR reporter started talking about the lottery, Finkelstein immediately pulled over and took out a notebook. The word "lottery" got her excited. That was a big deal. A lottery meant that the state of Oregon was actually running a randomized clinical trial, even if no one there had realized it. Researchers could compare Oregon residents who won the lottery to Oregon residents who did not. Even better, since both these groups were large and selected at random, they were likely to have similar characteristics: people who won the lottery and people who lost the lottery likely had the same health factors (obesity, smoking, etc.) and demographics (age, race, etc.). And so Finkelstein could compare lottery winners to lottery losers to understand how health insurance affects behavior.

When the NPR story was over, Finkelstein finished scribbling in her notebook and drove the rest of the way to work. As soon as she got to her office, she started making calls. Would the state of Oregon allow her to study the effects of the lottery?

It took years, but Finkelstein eventually teamed up with a group of researchers who were as excited about the lottery as she was. She joined forces with Heidi Allen, Kate Baicker, Sarah Taubman, and Bill Wright. The team matched Oregon's records on lottery numbers to records from local hospitals on ER visits. And that allowed Finkelstein and her coauthors to use the lottery as a way to test how Medicaid coverage affects the degree to which Americans use the healthcare system.

What did they find? Oregon residents who won the lottery were more likely to consume healthcare—all types of healthcare. They were more likely to visit the emergency room, more likely to have an outpatient visit, more likely to be hospitalized, and more likely to pick up prescription medications (fig. 1.2). The results were clear: having health insurance leads to more healthcare.

Before the study was complete, some experts expected a different outcome.[13] There's a stereotype about the uninsured in the United States, that the uninsured do not visit doctors and so instead end up in the emergency room. It is thought that they end up in the emergency room for conditions that could be better treated in an outpatient setting.

The research in Oregon invalidated that view. Finkelstein and her coauthors found that Oregon residents who won the lottery were more likely to consume *all* types of healthcare, including emergency room visits. When you

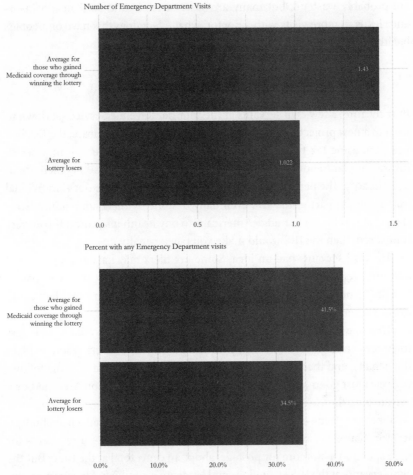

FIGURE 1.2. The effect of Medicaid coverage on emergency room (ER) visits using data from the Oregon Health Insurance Experiment. The first panel shows the effect of gaining Medicaid coverage on the number of ER visits by comparing the average number of ER visits for those who gained Medicaid coverage through Oregon's Medicaid lottery to the average number of ER visits for those who did not win the lottery and ended up in the control group. It shows an increase in ER visits of about 0.4 visits per year, or about a 40 percent increase over the average number of visits for the lottery losers. The second panel reports results for the share of the population with an ER visit (rather than the average number of visits). Gaining Medicaid coverage through the lottery increased the share with an ER visit by about 7 percentage points.

give uninsured Americans health insurance coverage, it seems, they are more likely to visit doctors everywhere.

It is this effect of health insurance that raises a natural question. The Oregon study demonstrated that having health insurance leads to an increase in healthcare utilization, that is, to more visits with a doctor. Some of those visits are probably wasteful, but many are surely useful. And so if health insurance leads to more visits with a doctor, what effect does this have on people's health?

What Does Health Insurance Do to *Health*?

In early 2016, a few civil servants at the Internal Revenue Service sat down to discuss a new project. Beginning with the passage of Obamacare, the IRS had been imposing tax penalties on Americans who failed to enroll in a health insurance plan: about $100 in 2014 for every uninsured adult, then about $300 in 2015. The penalties were part of the Affordable Care Act's "individual mandate": the part of the law, eventually undone by the Trump administration, that was meant to nudge Americans to buy health insurance. If you were uninsured, then the IRS would make you pay a penalty.

The civil servants had an idea. Some tax filers may have been penalized and not even realized it. Why not tell those taxpayers that they had paid a penalty? And while they were at it, why not also tell them how they could avoid a penalty the following year?

That one meeting led to a simple plan. Staff at the IRS would send letters to American taxpayers who had paid the penalty. The letters would explain the penalty, and then explain how the filers could avoid a penalty the following year: just go to healthcare.gov to figure out how to get on Medicaid or a private plan there.

Like everything else in Washington, this new program had a fixed budget. It's not that expensive to print out a letter and send it out—a few cents for the paper and a bit more for postage, about 49 cents total at the time. But the civil servants at the IRS wanted to send letters to 4.5 million American households. That's a lot of letters and a lot of postage. So the civil servants decided to randomize who received a letter.

There are certain phrases that excite a certain kind of professional. Say the words "900 horsepower" to a race car driver and see what happens. Try saying "meringue" to a pastry chef. You can get the same reaction if you lean up against a health economist and whisper one word in her ear: "randomization."

The randomization meant that the letters were no longer just another bit of paperwork at the IRS—they were a randomized controlled trial, an "RCT." Researchers could compare American households that received a letter to American households that did not receive a letter and then see what the letters did. If the letters convinced some Americans to sign up for health insurance, then the whole episode could be used to study the effects of health insurance.

Let us pause to describe the value of randomization and why health economists are so excited whenever something is randomized. When studying health insurance, one could always compare people who have health insurance to people who do not. The problem, though, is that people with health insurance are pretty different from people who lack health insurance. The uninsured tend to have lower incomes and they also tend to be younger. More importantly, people who don't have health insurance tend to be relatively healthy. As a result, simple comparisons of the insured to the uninsured do not isolate the effect of health insurance but rather reflect many other differences between the two groups.

One approach is to try and adjust for differences between the insured and uninsured, adjusting for differences in age, income, gender, and race. But such an approach is typically imperfect. You can never adjust for every factor, only the few factors that you actually observe. Randomized trials, in contrast, allow researchers to difference out those other factors and isolate the effect of the one factor that's been randomized.

OK, so back to the IRS. Three researchers—Jacob Goldin, Ithai Lurie, and Janet McCubbin—sought to evaluate the effects of the letters. They waited a year after the letters had gone out, and then they ran the numbers, comparing American households that were randomly assigned to receive a letter to similar American households that were randomly assigned not to receive one.

Sure enough, the letters worked. Americans who received a letter were 1 percent more likely to be covered by insurance the following year. That 1 percent increase sounds like a small change.[14] But remember: it's just a letter. Surely, many of the letters ended up unread and at the bottom of a recycling bin. What's more, because nearly 4 million Americans were randomized into the experiment, the researchers could be highly confident that the 1 percent increase was caused by the experiment rather than some other confounding factor.

OK, so far so good. Sending people letters suggesting that they sign up for health insurance leads them to—sign up for health insurance. It's what the researchers found next that staggered them.

The IRS keeps detailed death records. (After all, the agency needs to know who isn't paying their taxes because they are breaking the rules, and who isn't paying their taxes because they have passed away.) So the researchers used the IRS death records to study the mortality differences between people who received letters and people who did not. Americans who received one of these letters faced a risk of death that was about half-a-percent lower than those who did not (fig. 1.3). Half-a-percent may not sound like a big effect, but it is.

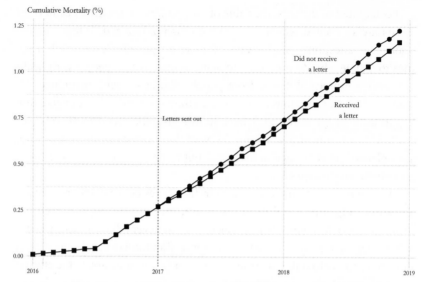

FIGURE 1.3. Cumulative mortality from January 2016 through December 2018, comparing the Americans who were randomized into receiving a letter from the IRS to those who did not receive a letter.

The authors estimated that the average mortality rate of the individuals who gained health insurance coverage from receiving the letter from the IRS was about 1.8 percent over the twenty-four-month study period, so the mortality rate decline of a half-a-percent translates into a 28 percent reduction in mortality. (By comparison, COVID-19 increased the American age-adjusted death rate by about 16 percent [Ahmad et al. 2021].) The story here, it turns out, is that having health insurance in America lowers your risk of death. The letters from the IRS got some people to enroll in a health insurance plan, and then, being insured, made them less likely to die.

There's a technical term that health economists use for such a finding: a "really big deal." An effect of health insurance on mortality means that getting people on health insurance plans leads to fewer heart attacks, fewer strokes, and fewer terminal cancer cases. The authors could only study mortality, not all of the other markers of bad health, but a drop in mortality suggests that health insurance also leads to many other happy consequences. These insured Americans, who were now utilizing more healthcare, were getting their blood pressure under control, taking necessary medications, sitting down for talk therapy, and so on. A drop in mortality suggests a myriad of ways in which health insurance was, behind the scenes, making lives better.

If it feels like a leap to imagine that health insurance affects health, let's consider how it actually works in practice. Let's make this visceral: it's the middle of the night, and you wake up in pain. It's like the world's worst acid reflux: burning pain that radiates out from your sternum. You can't catch your breath, and you realize that you've sweated through your pajamas. Your wheezing wakes up your spouse, who takes one look at you—you who are blue, and sweating, and out of breath—and then calls 911. The doctors in the emergency room admit you to the hospital, and you spend ten days there, recuperating.

As health economists, we are not so interested in the *medicine* involved: the medications given to you in the ER, the procedures performed on you in the hospital. Instead, we are more interested in another aspect of all of this: How does such an event differ for those who do not have health insurance?

Health insurance makes it more likely that you will survive such a midnight healthcare crisis. The IRS study confirmed this. So did another study focused on the effect of health insurance coverage on precisely these types of emergencies. David Card, Carlos Dobkin, and Nicole Maestas studied a particular aspect of the American healthcare system: millions of uninsured Americans gain health insurance through Medicare when they turn sixty-five.

What the researchers realized was that that arrangement leads to a particular natural experiment. Americans who are just younger than age sixty-five are somewhat likely to be uninsured, and Americans who are just older than age sixty-five are highly unlikely to be uninsured. But those two groups are otherwise very similar: one is only a few months older than the other. The two groups do not differ when it comes to smoking rates, obesity, preexisting conditions, or other medical concerns.

So the team performed a simple analysis. They studied a large sample of Americans who experience a sudden healthcare emergency. Among those unfortunate Americans, the team tested how being just older than age sixty-five affected survival rates. They found a striking difference. Those just older than age sixty-five had seven-day mortality rates that were 1 percentage point lower than those just younger than age sixty-five.

The authors could not pin down precisely *how* Medicare coverage lowers mortality rates for Americans in crisis. It seems as though Medicare coverage increases the number of procedures performed in the hospital. Somehow, it seems, American hospitals are more willing to perform procedures when the patient is covered by health insurance. But, at the end of the day, they had to conclude that the "actual mechanism for this effect is unclear."

So if you are unlucky enough to be rushed to the hospital in the middle of the night, you are more likely to survive if you are lucky enough to be insured, even if we don't exactly know why.

The Bottom Line

The movie *Animal House* was set on the campus of the fictional Faber College. And the motto of Faber College: "Knowledge Is Good." We borrow from Faber College here: Health Insurance Is Good.

We have, after all, evidence that health insurance saves lives. If you have health insurance coverage, you are less likely to die. We know that having health insurance reduces the risk of financial distress. Bill collectors are less likely to show up, unannounced, and tow away your Honda Civic. When you try to buy a new Civic, if you've been covered by health insurance, your credit score is likely higher, and so the dealer is less likely to recommend a "special" loan. We know that health insurance increases medical utilization. If you have health insurance, you're more likely to see a doctor. So you find a fuzzy mole on your back, or you wonder why a flight of stairs is suddenly making you wheeze, or you wake up in the middle of the night with the weight of an oversized pickup truck compressing your rib cage into a pancake—if you're covered by health insurance, you are more likely to seek professional help.

OK, health insurance is good for you. But does that mean that everyone should have health insurance? After all, lots of things are good for you. Broccoli is good for you. Should we force everyone to eat broccoli?

Just because health insurance is good for you does not, necessarily, mean that everyone should have it. People should be free to make their own decisions. While health insurance seems to extend people's lives, so does eating broccoli. And yet, no one suggests that the government force everyone to stock up on broccoli.

That said, there is a reason why health insurance is different from broccoli. There exists an economic argument as to why all Americans should be forced to buy health insurance. It's not just that health insurance is good—there's more to it than that. We turn to that argument next.

References

Ahmad, Farida B., Jodi A. Cisewski, Arialdi Miniño, and Robert N. Anderson. "Provisional Mortality Data—United States, 2020." *Morbidity and Mortality Weekly Report* 70, no. 14 (2021): 519.

Anderson, Michael L., Carlos Dobkin, and Tal Gross. "The Effect of Health Insurance Coverage on the Use of Medical Services." *American Economic Journal: Economic Policy* 4, no. 1 (2012): 1–27.

———. "The Effect of Health Insurance on Emergency Department Visits: Evidence from an Age-Based Eligibility Threshold." *Review of Economics and Statistics* 96, no. 1 (2014): 189–95.

Armour, Philip. "The Role of Information in Disability Insurance Application: An Analysis of the Social Security Statement Phase-In." *American Economic Journal: Economic Policy* 10, no. 3 (2018): 1–41.

Barr, Andrew, and Sarah Turner. "A Letter and Encouragement: Does Information Increase Postsecondary Enrollment of UI Recipients?" *American Economic Journal: Economic Policy* 10, no. 3 (2018): 42–68.

Bettinger, Eric P., Bridget Terry Long, Philip Oreopoulos, and Lisa Sanbonmatsu. "The Role of Application Assistance and Information in College Decisions: Results from the H&R Block FAFSA Experiment." *Quarterly Journal of Economics* 127, no. 3 (2012): 1205–42.

Bhargava, Saurabh, and Day Manoli. "Why Are Benefits Left on the Table? Assessing the Role of Information, Complexity, and Stigma on Take-Up with an IRS Field Experiment." *ACR North American Advances* (2012).

Card, David, Carlos Dobkin, and Nicole Maestas. "Does Medicare Save Lives?" *Quarterly Journal of Economics* 124, no. 2 (2009): 597–636.

Dobkin, Carlos, Amy Finkelstein, Raymond Kluender, and Matthew J. Notowidigdo. "The Economic Consequences of Hospital Admissions." *American Economic Review* 108, no. 2 (2018): 308–52.

Dranove, David, and Michael L. Millenson. "Medical Bankruptcy: Myth versus Fact: This Response to a Widely Cited Paper by David Himmelstein and Colleagues Challenges the Basis of Its Conclusions." *Health Affairs* 25, no. Suppl1 (2006): W74–W83.

Dynarski, Susan, C. J. Libassi, Katherine Michelmore, and Stephanie Owen. "Closing the Gap: The Effect of Reducing Complexity and Uncertainty in College Pricing on the Choices of Low-Income Students." *American Economic Review* 111, no. 6 (2021): 1721–56.

Finkelstein, Amy, Neale Mahoney, and Matthew J. Notowidigdo. "What Does (Formal) Health Insurance Do, and for Whom?" *Annual Review of Economics* 10 (2018): 261–86.

Finkelstein, Amy, and Matthew J. Notowidigdo. "Take-Up and Targeting: Experimental Evidence from SNAP." *Quarterly Journal of Economics* 134, no. 3 (2019): 1505–56.

Finkelstein, Amy, Sarah Taubman, Bill Wright, Mira Bernstein, Jonathan Gruber, Joseph P. Newhouse, Heidi Allen, Katherine Baicker, and Oregon Health Study Group. "The Oregon Health Insurance Experiment: Evidence from the First Year." *Quarterly Journal of Economics* 127, no. 3 (2012): 1057–106.

Goldin, Jacob, Ithai Z. Lurie, and Janet McCubbin. "Health Insurance and Mortality: Experimental Evidence from Taxpayer Outreach." *Quarterly Journal of Economics* 136, no. 1 (2021): 1–49.

Gross, Tal, and Matthew J. Notowidigdo. "Health Insurance and the Consumer Bankruptcy Decision: Evidence from Expansions of Medicaid." *Journal of Public Economics* 95, no. 7–8 (2011): 767–78.

Hu, Luojia, Robert Kaestner, Bhashkar Mazumder, Sarah Miller, and Ashley Wong. "The Effect of the Affordable Care Act Medicaid Expansions on Financial Wellbeing." *Journal of Public Economics* 163 (2018): 99–112.

Mazumder, Bhashkar, and Sarah Miller. "The Effects of the Massachusetts Health Reform on Household Financial Distress." *American Economic Journal: Economic Policy* 8, no. 3 (2016): 284–313.

Taubman, Sarah L., Heidi L. Allen, Bill J. Wright, Katherine Baicker, and Amy N. Finkelstein. "Medicaid Increases Emergency-Department Use: Evidence from Oregon's Health Insurance Experiment." *Science* 343, no. 6168 (2014): 263–68.

Health Insurance versus Broccoli

In 2010, after an exhausting, bruising debate, the Affordable Care Act (a.k.a. Obamacare) just barely passed Congress. Obamacare created a seismic shift in American health policy. The most controversial part, the "individual mandate," required the purchase of health insurance, making it effectively against the law to be uninsured. All Americans who did not buy health insurance would face a tax penalty.

And for many freedom-loving Americans, the law seemed like a complete departure from the American way. Sure, dictators around the world have always restricted freedom. Nicolae Ceaușescu of Romania prohibited television newswomen from wearing jewelry. Saparmurat Niyazov of Turkmenistan outlawed beards. But the United States is supposed to be the "land of the free."

Senator Tom Cotton compared the individual mandate to the government requiring Americans to eat three servings of fruits and vegetables a day. Judge Robert Vinson, a Reagan appointee, argued that the individual mandate was like the government mandating that "everybody has to buy a certain quantity of broccoli each week." Supreme Court Justice Antonin Scalia called the individual mandate the "broccoli mandate."

And, sure, there's something to that analogy. Having health insurance is good, healthy behavior (see the previous chapter), and eating broccoli is also good, healthy behavior. In the land of the free, Senator Tom Cotton would argue, people should be free to do precisely what is unhealthy. Surely that means that Americans should be free to be uninsured?

Aaron through Zack

Let's first talk about why policymakers felt it was important for Obamacare to have an individual mandate at all. In order to understand the individual mandate, we first have to understand adverse selection. Unfortunately, adverse selection is a tricky concept. We can't summarize the idea in just a couple sentences. Instead, we need to construct an economic model.

We start with a guy named Aaron. Aaron is in excellent health. He drinks a green smoothie every morning, he lifts weights, he practices tai chi. He's never had a cavity, much less a serious medical problem. And so Aaron's expected annual healthcare costs are only $1,000 a year. That thousand dollars is an average: most years, Aaron's healthcare costs will be close to zero. But there's always the chance that he'll pull a hamstring during tai chi and be rushed to the ER.

Then there's Bob, who is in slightly worse shape. Bob skips the green smoothie every morning, opting instead for eggs with toast. Bob's expected healthcare costs each year are $2,000, just a thousand dollars more than Aaron's, because Bob is in slightly worse health.

Then there's Chad.[1] As you have already guessed, Chad has expected healthcare costs each year of $3,000. (If you're curious: Frosted Flakes.)

We keep on going here: Dave has expected healthcare costs of $4,000 a year; Ethan, $5,000; Frank, $6,000. This goes on, all the way to Zack. Through no fault of his own, Zack consumes a lot of healthcare. He has asthma, which forces him to purchase an expensive inhaler every few months. He is also a type 1 diabetic, and so he needs a glucose monitor, testing strips, insulin, and so on. And those chronic conditions require not just regular, predictable costs—test strips, insulin—they also raise the risk of a serious medical event. For that reason, Zack's expected healthcare costs are $26,000 a year.

That's how we explore the concept of adverse selection: with twenty-six guys, Aaron through Zack, each of whom has a thousand dollars more in expected healthcare costs than the last guy.

If this discussion sounds silly to you, just know that we are following one of our favorite economists, Paul Krugman, who once wrote: "You can't do serious economics unless you are willing to be playful. Economic theory is not a collection of dictums . . . it is a menagerie of thought experiments that are intended to capture the logic of economic processes in a simplified way."[2]

We next need to add an insurance company. Now, insurers often get a bad rap. After all, insurance companies tend to be large, for-profit bureaucracies with poorly maintained websites and lousy phone support. But adverse selection is a fundamental problem with the market for health insurance, one that exists regardless of whether the insurance company is a good or bad actor. So, let's imagine that the insurance company here is not just a nonprofit organization—let's imagine that the insurance company here is profit averse. The company seeks only to provide insurance to Aaron through Zack, not to make money. This nonprofit insurance company we'll call Ann's Insurance, owned by Ann.[3]

Ann opens for business to sell insurance to Aaron through Zack. And being a profit-averse, altruistic insurer, Ann starts out by setting a price of zero dollars. Our twenty-six dudes—lucky ducks—get health insurance for free. They pay a premium of zero dollars every month, and then Ann covers all of their healthcare costs.

Now, this arrangement works well for the guys, but Ann soon realizes that she's made a mistake. She might not want to make money, but she still has to break even. And with these current numbers, Ann is not breaking even.

Let's think about Ann's finances here. On average Aaron costs her $1,000 each year, Bob costs her $2,000, all the way to Zack, who costs her an average of $26,000 a year. We've done the math: add up those costs and divide by 26, and that's an average of $13,500 in expenses per insured customer. So Ann is spending an average of $13,500 for each guy she insures, and getting $0 in premiums from each of them. You don't need an MBA to realize that that's going to be a problem. With no money coming in, Ann is losing money hand over fist. She has to raise prices.

We assume that Ann has to set the same price for everybody because she doesn't know who is who. Aaron knows that he's Aaron, but Ann cannot tell Aaron apart from Zack. So Ann cannot set a special price just for Aaron. If she could do that, the story would end happily. Ann would design an insurance contract for Aaron, another insurance contract for Bob, and so on. But that's not an option, since each man's "type" is hidden from Ann.

So Ann has to charge just one price for everyone she insures. She deliberates: What price is best? As a charitable enterprise, she wants the price to be as low as possible, just barely breaking even. What if she sets a price of precisely the average of Aaron through Zack's expected healthcare costs? She sets a price of $13,500, and then all will be well: Aaron through Zack will be insured, and she'll break even.

Unfortunately, this new price leads to a new problem. At a price of $13,500, Aaron backs out of the whole deal. The guy knows his expected healthcare costs—$1,000—and so he sees $13,500 as just way too steep a price for him to pay for insurance. He's making a rational choice here: he wants to be insured, but $13,500 is simply a raw deal.[4]

Bob makes a similar calculation: his expected healthcare costs are $2,000 a year. Perhaps he's willing to pay up to $2,400 for health insurance, but there's no way he's paying $13,500 for insurance, that's just too high. Same with Chad: the price is too steep for him too.

On the other hand, some of the men are happy to stay insured for $13,500. Zack, for instance, is getting a terrific deal: his expected costs are $26,000 and he only has to pay $13,500 for insurance. It's not obvious precisely which men will choose to become uninsured like Aaron and which will choose to remain insured like Zack. To keep things simple, let's assume that all men whose expected healthcare costs are below $13,500 will choose to become uninsured. In that case, Aaron through Martin (whose expected healthcare costs are $13,000) drop out of the market and choose to become uninsured. That leaves Ned (expected costs $14,000) through Zack insured.

Ann thought the price of $13,500 would solve her problem, but now she has a new problem. With Aaron through Martin out of the picture, she's only covering Ned through Zack: now there are only thirteen guys still paying for insurance. Ned has an average healthcare cost of $14,000 a year; Zack, remember, has $26,000 in average healthcare cost. So Ann is now covering a population with an average per capita healthcare cost of $20,000. Each customer is paying $13,500, but Ann faces average costs of $20,000 per person. She is once again losing money hand over fist.

It should be clear now where the term "adverse selection" comes from. Ann faces a pool of customers that is "adversely selected"—the people who select insurance have higher expected costs than the people who choose to remain uninsured. Ann would much prefer a different selection of customers. If they were all like Aaron or Bob, there'd be no problem. Instead, she tries to make do with the selection she has, and she can't seem to keep them all insured.

Ann tries again to adjust the price. She raises the price from $13,500 to $20,000, since that new price is just equal to her current average costs. But at a price of $20,000, Ned is going to reconsider this whole business of buying health insurance. Ned's expected healthcare costs are $14,000 and so the new price of $20,000 is just too high. Ned wants to be insured, but for a reasonable price. So Ned chooses to be uninsured. Owen, with expected healthcare costs of $15,000 is going to make a similar decision. So is Paul.

The process repeats: the healthiest enrollees choose to become uninsured, and then the insurer has no choice but to raise the price again. But by raising the price, more relatively healthy consumers choose to become uninsured, and so the insurer has to raise prices yet again (fig. 2.1).

This process is sometimes called "unraveling." The key issue is that the insurer cannot tell consumers apart. In the language of our metaphor, Ann can-

At a price of zero dollars a year, all 26 men choose to be insured, and so average costs are $13,500 a year.

At a price of $13,500 a year, only half of the men choose to be insured, and so average costs are $20,000 a year.

At a price of $20,000 a year, even fewer men choose to be insured, and so average costs are $23,500 a year.

FIGURE 2.1. This little diagram summarizes our story of Aaron through Zack, showing how the market for health insurance "unravels."

not tell that Aaron is Aaron, and so she cannot offer him a better deal when he balks at a price of $13,500. That one assumption leads to the entire market falling apart. In the end, only Zack is insured and everyone else is priced out.

What to Do When a Market Unravels?

For these twenty-six men, the health insurance market has failed. All twenty-six men want to buy insurance, and a nonprofit insurer wants to provide that insurance. But there's one central problem: each man's "type" is hidden from the insurer. All of a sudden, the market doesn't work. Transactions should occur: Aaron wants to buy insurance and Ann wants to sell it to him. But those transactions cannot occur because of adverse selection. The tragedy here is that healthy consumers want health insurance, but then they look at the market and only see insurance that is unfairly expensive for them, so they decide not to buy it.

This model might not only apply to health insurance. It might also apply to long-term care insurance, which is insurance that pays for care at the end of life, either nursing home care or at-home care. Adverse selection might also rule out entirely new types of insurance. For instance, consider entrepreneurs who quit their jobs and take on the incredibly risky proposition of starting their own business. They might be interested in "business failure insurance," a policy that pays off if their small business doesn't work out. That insurance does not exist, and one explanation why it does not exist is adverse selection.

Health economists believe that this dynamic is especially relevant to health insurance, and that it is central to the individual market for insurance. Throughout history and across countries, there has never been a robust market for individual health insurance. The business of insurance cannot work when people are left to buy health insurance on their own with risks that insurers cannot observe.

What regulation will solve this problem? Well, what creates the problem in the first place? The problem arises because the healthiest people choose to become uninsured. If we could just get those guys to stay insured, then the market wouldn't unravel. So a solution has to keep Aaron and Bob from dropping out—from choosing to become uninsured.

And this is where the government comes in. Imagine that the government were to persuade consumers to continue buying insurance. Suppose that a law is passed that imposes a tax penalty on anyone who is uninsured. Now, the penalty would have to be pretty serious: Aaron faces a price of $13,500 for his health insurance and his expected healthcare costs are only $1,000. So perhaps the government would need to not only penalize him if he does not buy insurance (the stick) but also subsidize the price of insurance for him (the carrot). Both of those policies together—a subsidy and a penalty, a carrot and a stick—may persuade Aaron to buy health insurance. And then the market for health insurance would no longer unravel. The mandate and the subsidies would, perhaps, keep all twenty-six men insured, and the individual market for health insurance would become sustainable.

Some Evidence on Adverse Selection: The Case of Huntington's Disease

So that's the *theory* of adverse selection: the story of Adam through Zack explains the basic idea. It's natural to ask: Is there any evidence that the theory actually matters in the real world? After all, for the theory to be relevant, ordinary people would have to have more information about their expected healthcare costs than insurance companies do. And yet, insurance companies are large, sophisticated organizations. They employ analysts and physicians, they have access to terabytes of data. Is it really the case that ordinary consumers know more than an insurer? That Aaron knows that he's Aaron and yet the insurer cannot tell him from Zack?

As a first piece of evidence, we turn to an example that is rooted in the tragedy of a terrible disease. Huntington's disease arises from a genetic mutation that runs in families. People with the disease tend to live for thirty, forty, or fifty years with no symptoms whatsoever.[5] Starting in middle age, the symptoms begin. Gradually, over time, people with Huntington's disease lose their ability to control their movements. Often, they lose their memory and their cognitive ability is impaired. As the process continues, they need increasing levels of support. The process of dying of Huntington's disease can last years. And such a death is expensive. Toward the end, the patient requires care around the clock. In a private home, that could easily cost more than $15,000 each month.

When faced with the risk of requiring that kind of long-term care, many Americans choose to buy long-term care insurance. Long-term care insurance is a financial product that people typically buy in their fifties. They pay a premium every month, and then, if they end up requiring long-term care, either at home or in a nursing home, the insurer will pay for that care.

From a long-term care insurer's perspective, a person with Huntington's disease is the worst kind of customer. Such a customer would pay their premiums for some years but then would end up needing very expensive care. In the language of our metaphor, a person with Huntington's disease is Zack. And the key question is whether Zack knows that he's Zack and whether he buys insurance as a result.

Emily Oster wrote a series of fascinating papers about Huntington's disease. Oster, an economist, teamed up with medical researchers—Ira Shoulson, Kimberly Quaid, and Ray Dorsey—who had been studying Huntington's disease for years. The team surveyed about a thousand Americans who had a parent with the disease but had not yet been tested for the disease themselves. That meant that all thousand of them had a 50 percent chance of having the mutation—a 50 percent chance of having the disease. The team followed those patients over about ten years, checking in with them every nine months or so over the phone. The surveys captured whether the patients chose to get tested and how their behavior changed once they were tested (Oster et al. 2010).

Now, it's important to recognize the fraught situation in which these patients found themselves. They all had one parent with the disease, so they had seen what the disease does to people. They knew that they themselves had a 50 percent chance of having the genetic mutation and dying in the same way. The test was definitive: it would tell them whether they had the mutation or not.

Oster wondered whether a positive test would affect patients' decisions to buy long-term care insurance. After all, patients who are told that they have the genetic mutation go from knowing they have a 50 percent chance of needing long-term care due to Huntington's disease to a 100 percent chance of needing long-term care due to Huntington's disease. What would that knowledge do to their choices around long-term care?

Oster and her coauthors analyzed all of the survey data they had collected. Among the people that Oster studied who tested negative, about 25 percent bought long-term care insurance. Among those who tested positive, about 50 percent bought long-term care insurance. In other words, those who found out that they were destined to suffer the onset of symptoms were twice as likely to go out and buy long-term care insurance.

Importantly, insurers were never made aware of the test results. So this is a context in which the tests gave people information: they learned whether or not they had the mutation. But the tests did not provide that information to insurers, and so insurers could not adjust prices accordingly. In other words, this is a real-world example of Zack learning that he is Zack—learning, tragically, that he will die of Huntington's disease—and then buying insurance accordingly. This directly leads to adverse selection in the market for long-term care insurance. This is a real-world example of people holding private information about their healthcare needs that insurers, with all their data and expertise, do not have.[6]

In presenting her research, Oster took pains to express sympathy for the people she was studying. These were ordinary people faced with an extraordinary, wrenching medical situation. And we hope that our description of the research here does not come off as blithe or callous. The healthcare world is filled with tragedies—situations that involve intense human misery. But, occasionally, those situations offer health economists an opportunity to learn. In this case, patients being tested for this genetic mutation face the flip of a coin. And, sure enough, those who are given the bad news are more likely to go out and buy insurance.

Cream Skimming among Insurers: Beth Enters the Market

The concept of adverse selection justifies government intervention in the private market. Many products are bought and sold routinely with minimal government intervention and few problems, but health insurance is not one such product.

Without a mandate and subsidies, the private market for individual health insurance will unravel. And indeed, it is impossible to find examples of a robust and yet unregulated private market for individual health insurance out there.

But wait, there's more. Our story so far leaves out an important feature of markets: competition. What happens when a new insurer enters the market, when Ann faces competition? Once new competitors are free to enter, the problems of adverse selection can reappear in a different form. To see that, we have to go through the related concept of cream skimming.

Imagine that we have somehow fixed the unraveling problem among Aaron through Zack. A combination of subsidies and a mandate induce all twenty-six of our hypothetical customers to stay insured. And so our story, at least temporarily, has a happy ending: Ann insures all twenty-six customers for one, relatively low premium. Aaron and his healthy brethren choose to remain insured because the premium is subsidized and low and he does not want to pay a penalty for being uninsured.

A happy market tends to attract new entrants. Suppose that a second insurer, let's call her Beth, starts eyeing this market. Now, Beth, like Ann, cannot tell the guys apart. But she comes up with an interesting plan. She offers health insurance with a catch. Her insurance plan is just like Ann's *except* that she doesn't cover any healthcare costs related to diabetes. Beth's insurance will happily pay for a broken leg to be set, will happily pay for an annual physical or an MRI, but her plan won't cover a cent of any healthcare service related to diabetes. And because Beth does not cover diabetes, she can afford to charge a slightly lower price than Ann.

Now the highest-risk consumers—William, Xavier, Yohannes, and Zack—are completely uninterested in Beth's plan. They are at high risk for diabetes, and some of them have it already. So they would never leave Ann for Beth. But what about the healthiest consumers: Aaron, Bob, and Chad? They don't have diabetes, and they know that they are at low risk for the disease. So if Beth happens to be a bit cheaper than Ann, why not switch?

But if the healthiest consumers leave Ann for Beth, then Ann's average healthcare costs will rise. Ann might have to raise prices. And such a situation could lead to a kind of unraveling, even after a mandate has been imposed. The healthiest consumers leave Ann, so she has to raise prices, which persuades even more consumers to switch to Beth, and so Ann has to raise prices again, so on and so forth. In order to avoid that unraveling, Ann might be forced to mimic Beth and cease covering diabetes herself.

The term of art for Beth's business strategy is "cream skimming." Beth deliberately designed her health insurance plan to attract only the lowest-risk applicants. She cut out coverage for diabetes not because of some medical insight but because dropping that coverage meant attracting more-profitable enrollees.

Cream skimming can also work in the opposite direction. Imagine that instead of cutting coverage of diabetes, Beth offered free gym memberships and personal training sessions. Only the healthiest consumers—Aaron, Bob,

Chad, and so on—are interested in free gym memberships and personal training sessions. So that additional offering might benefit Beth and cause problems for Ann.

Normally, economists are in favor of competition. It's usually a good thing for two companies to change their products to compete with one another. After all, if Ford makes its cars more spacious so as to attract more customers from General Motors, then we would all nod approvingly and stretch out our legs in our newly elongated Ford Tauruses. But when it comes to the market for insurance, it's more complicated. Beth can make her product worse in order to attract healthy consumers, and then Ann may have no choice but to follow suit. In this way, unregulated competition across plans could lead to health insurance that doesn't cover important types of care.

The business of health insurance is different from most other businesses. A car company does not care *who* buys their cars. At the dawn of the millennium, Ford was selling about 200,000 Ford Tauruses each year. Managers at Ford didn't care who bought those Tauruses, only that 200,000 people did. By contrast, an insurer deeply cares about *who* buys her product. If very sick people enroll in her plan, then she'll earn less profit than if very healthy people enroll in her plan. In that sense, health insurance is a "selection business": its profitability depends on the "selection" of who becomes a customer.[7] And, as a result, selection businesses need to be regulated very differently from other businesses.

There is then a role for the government in regulating what costs insurers have to cover. It might even make sense for the government to prevent insurers from offering extra services like free gym memberships, so long as those extras exist only to attract healthier applicants and not for their own medical value.

In other words, once you see that adverse selection matters in the market for health insurance, then you see a large role for government regulation. First, regulators need to prevent the individual market from unraveling. That first step requires an individual mandate and subsidies, so that healthy consumers remain insured. Second, those regulators also need to dictate what services insurers cover. Without that second step, insurers may try to cream skim the healthiest applicants by offering plans that are cheap but stingy. Cream skimming across plans, left unchecked, would otherwise lead to the disappearance of generous insurance plans.

More Evidence on Adverse Selection: The Famous Harvard Death Spiral

The story of two competing insurers, Ann and Beth, is just a story. It's fair to ask whether that story is actually relevant for the real world. Does the story really matter?

To see whether that's the case, we turn to Harvard. Harvard University was where much of the economic theory of adverse selection was originally hashed out. But, ironically, Harvard University was also the place where the consequences of adverse selection were first carefully documented. Economists call it the "Harvard Death Spiral," and it happened in 1995.

That year, Sarah Reber was a rising senior at Harvard College and she needed a topic for her undergraduate thesis. Sarah took a list of ideas to her adviser, David Cutler. David, who happens to be one of the nation's foremost health economists, sat with Sarah in his office and, together, they talked through her list.

At the top of the list, Sarah had written "managed competition." She was interested in situations in which employers allow multiple insurance plans to compete to cover their employees. At the time, more and more American employers were giving their employees a choice of several insurance plans with different premiums. Sarah was interested in that new style of providing private health insurance to employees.

David pointed out that Harvard itself had recently transformed its own system. In the mid-1990s, accountants at Harvard started to worry that the university was plowing through its budget for employee benefits. The leading cause was health insurance, which was costing the university too much money. So the accountants started looking for ways to cut costs.

At the time, Harvard offered its employees two insurance plans: a generous preferred provider organization (PPO) and a less generous health maintenance organization (HMO).[8] The PPO had a wider network and did not require that beneficiaries see a primary-care physician before visiting a specialist. Normally, a more generous plan would be more expensive for employees—the premium would be higher. But for years, like many employers, Harvard had subsidized the PPO, paying a larger share of the PPO's costs itself, so that the employees paid only slightly more for the PPO even though the total premium was much higher than the HMO's premium.

In 1995, Harvard University stopped contributing more for employees who chose the PPO. Employees could still choose either plan—the PPO or the HMO—but Harvard would pay the same fixed subsidy regardless of which plan an employee chose.[9] As a result, in 1995, the PPO became more expensive for employees.

That day in David's office, Sarah decided to study how Harvard's employees responded to the rise in the price of the PPO. She—and David—thought of the analysis as a straightforward exercise. Harvard's policy change meant that the price of the PPO had increased, so surely that meant fewer Harvard employees would enroll in the PPO. Sarah wanted to measure how much demand had decreased in response to the price change. Economists write such studies all the time, estimating how consumers respond to an increase in the price of, say, cigarettes or lottery tickets or wheat. It's a good topic for an undergraduate thesis.

So Sarah got to work. She made some calls, she sent some e-mails. And in due course, Sarah convinced administrators at Harvard to give her anonymized personnel records. She was given detailed records on which Harvard employees were on which plan and which employees had switched plans.

Sarah loaded the data onto her laptop and analyzed it with Stata, a software tool that economists use to analyze data.[10] She worked in the Harvard library and in her dorm room, staring at her laptop for hours, trying to measure how Harvard employees reacted to the higher price for the PPO. As the price of the PPO increased, the share of employees who chose the PPO went down. Before the policy change, about 20 percent of Harvard employees chose the PPO, and that decreased to about 15 percent in 1995.

Sarah documented those facts in her thesis and then, that spring, she graduated magna cum laude from Harvard. After graduation, she moved to Washington, DC, and took a job as a staff economist at the Council of Economic Advisers, the CEA. But before she left Harvard, she and David agreed to work together on a revised version of her thesis, perhaps extending the analysis to cover another year of Harvard's experience with managed competition. It seemed to them like there was still more to the story.

David secured data on premiums and health plan choices for an additional year, 1996. And so on nights and weekends, Sarah turned away from her full-time job at the CEA, fired up her laptop, and studied Harvard's personnel records. At first, she updated and refined what was originally her undergraduate thesis. But then she uncovered a striking pattern that was much more complicated.

In 1995 the price of the PPO for employees increased from about $500 to about $1,000 per year. That increase in price was to be expected. After all, Harvard did drop its subsidy for the PPO, so more of the cost would fall on employees' shoulders. But then in 1996, the year after the policy change, the PPO's premium *more than doubled*, going from $1,000 to well over $2,000 (Cutler and Zeckhauser 1998). Why did the price go up again, and go up by so much? The first increase in price was like a gunshot for which everyone had

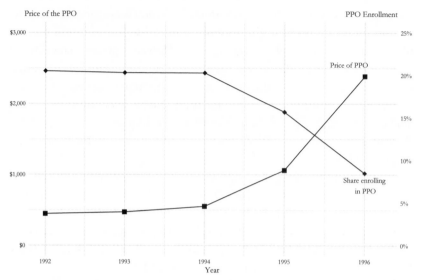

FIGURE 2.2. Prices faced by Harvard employees for a family PPO policy, in 1996 dollars (Cutler and Zeckhauser 1998).

been bracing, but the second increase in price was like a nuclear bomb's blast (fig. 2.2). What was going on?

Slowly, Sarah and David started to grasp what had happened to Harvard's PPO. A key question was: *Who* switched to the HMO? After some digging, Sarah hit on a key insight. It came from just two numbers. Employees who switched to the HMO were, on average, forty-six years old. Those who stayed on the PPO were, on average, fifty years old.

Why were younger employees more likely to leave the PPO? Because the younger employees were, on average, healthier, and so valued the PPO the least. Those healthy employees were the first to leave the PPO. But, if healthier employees left the PPO, then the PPO would have to raise its premium to adjust for the loss of those healthy enrollees. And it was that dynamic that explained the sharp increase in price in 1996.

Sarah and David eventually realized that they were looking at a real-world example of Aaron-through-Zack unraveling. The more they analyzed the data, the more clearly they saw the basic cycle. Harvard's initial policy change raised the price of the PPO. That price increase pushed out the healthiest enrollees. And then the loss of the healthiest enrollees meant that the PPO's administrators had to raise the price further. This was bound to continue. Unless something changed, the PPO would be driven into the ground.

Eventually, Sarah realized how much she enjoyed the research. All those nights and weekends writing Stata code, figuring out how managed competition works. It wasn't a chore, it was thrilling. So she decided to apply for graduate school and eventually ended up back at Harvard as a PhD student. She worked with David to summarize their work in a paper and published it in one of the field's most prestigious journals. Health economists took to referring to the paper as documenting the "Harvard Death Spiral."

Sarah and David only followed the data through 1996, but administrators at Harvard continued to grapple with the pricing of the PPO. In 1997, the PPO's premium went even higher, and it continued losing money and healthy enrollees. Administrators planned to increase the PPO's premiums yet again for 1998. Eventually, though, the accountants realized that that increase in premiums was simply going to be too large and so they disbanded the PPO. Adverse selection, in the end, had destroyed the plan entirely.

As she progressed through graduate school, Sarah's interests started to drift away from health economics. Instead, Sarah wrote much of her PhD thesis on education. But, ironically, many situations in education are similar to the change in Harvard's PPO that originally fascinated her. A school that has more special-education students, or more students for whom English is a second language, will face higher costs than a similar school without such students. Despite leaving health economics, she ended up studying the same phenomenon, just across schools rather than across health plans. Nine years after leaving Harvard, she became a tenured professor at UCLA's Luskin School of Public Affairs.

At the end of the day, the Harvard Death Spiral is a cautionary tale. The story demonstrates that the Aaron-through-Zack model is relevant for the real world—that unregulated competition can lead generous plans to unravel. And it shows that regulating insurance markets is tricky work. In this case, Harvard's PPO disappeared entirely.

What to Do about Adverse Selection: Romneycare

Administrators at Harvard had to shut down their PPO due to adverse selection. But what about everyone outside of Harvard? Adverse selection is a challenge wherever health insurance is sold, and not all Americans are lucky enough to work for large employers that offer a cafeteria of well-regulated health insurance plans from which to choose. So what to do about adverse selection elsewhere?

The most successful American response to adverse selection happened in Massachusetts in 2007. State lawmakers were persuaded by the story of Aaron and Zack. They understood that the individual market for health insurance wasn't working on its own, and it would never operate well without regulation. Indeed, individual health insurance was remarkably expensive in Massachusetts, and over 10 percent of state residents were uninsured.[11]

Now, one solution was single-payer insurance. The state of Massachusetts could have simply started its own insurer and directly provided health insurance for all state residents. If the insurance were free, then healthy residents would no longer choose to be uninsured, and the unraveling problem would be resolved. But transitioning to a single public insurer would create two massive problems. First, a single insurer would be remarkably expensive, and the state would have to raise taxes. Second, Massachusetts already had a lot of private insurance companies, and they wouldn't stand for such a thing. In a democracy, it is difficult to push out powerful special interests. And so Massachusetts healthcare reform had to proceed with the cooperation of all of the major players, insurers included.

State lawmakers looked for a solution to the unraveling problem that would be politically viable. What the lawmakers settled on was an arrangement that became the inspiration for Obamacare three years later. The state legislature passed an individual mandate: all Massachusetts residents would have to buy health insurance or else face a penalty. Low-income Massachusetts residents would be allowed onto publicly provided programs, but many others would be mandated to buy health insurance from a newly created private market.

How might you expect Massachusetts residents to respond to that mandate? The idea of adverse selection suggests a particular dynamic. Before the Massachusetts healthcare reform, the market for individual health insurance had unraveled. In the language of "Aaron through Zack," only Zack was buying individual health insurance—everyone else had been priced out. Once the mandate was imposed, healthier and healthier residents would gradually buy into the market.

A few years after the fact, three Massachusetts economists—Jon Gruber, Amitabh Chandra, and Robin McKnight (2011)—were interested in documenting such a dynamic. They studied Massachusetts residents just before and just after the mandate went into effect. They put together table 2.1. Before the mandate, about 35 percent of Massachusetts residents who were purchasing·individual health insurance had a chronic condition. That's Zack: relatively unhealthy people trying to buy expensive health insurance before the mandate. Then Massachusetts started to phase-in the mandate. Suddenly, new enrollees were less likely to have a chronic condition: about 30 percent. That's men in the middle of the alphabet gradually getting on board and buying health insurance. Finally, once the mandate was fully effective, only 24 percent of new enrollees had a chronic condition. That last number represents

TABLE 2.1. Characteristics of New Enrollees in Commonwealth Care, According to Enrollment Period[*]

	Before mandate	During phase-in of mandate	Once mandate was fully effective
Average Age (yr)	45.1	43.3	41.3
Diagnosis of Chronic Illness[†] (%)	35.5	29.6	23.9
Average Monthly Health Care Spending ($)	518	454	356

[*] Shown are data for Massachusetts residents with incomes between 150 and 300% of the poverty level who were eligible for state insurance subsidies. These enrollees were required to pay insurance premiums that were meaningful but much smaller than those mandated by the federal program.

[†] Chronic illness was defined as a diagnosis of hypertension, high cholesterol level, diabetes, asthma, arthritis, an affective disorder, or gastritis within the first twelve months after enrollment.

Source: Chandra, Gruber, and McKnight (2011).

Aaron, reluctantly buying health insurance once he faces both subsidies and penalties. In other words, as the mandate was implemented, new enrollees became healthier and healthier. And that pattern is consistent with the basic idea of adverse selection.

The Bottom Line

Many left-of-center commentators argue that the government needs to intervene for the sake of social justice. They argue that there is simply something *unjust* about residents of the wealthiest country in the world being afraid to visit the emergency room for lack of insurance. We are certainly not dismissing that argument. After all, the uninsured do not exist in other wealthy countries. And it is important to recognize the misery and suffering that occurs when Americans do not have health insurance.

But, that said, the concept of adverse selection suggests a very different argument for government intervention. It's not about social justice, or fairness, or equity. Rather, the key issue is that an unregulated private market for individual health insurance will fail.

Here's one analogy. There are many Americans who cannot afford a new car. And in many parts of the country, it's hard to live without a car. And yet, if you can't afford a new car, maybe you can afford a used one. Or a motorcycle. Or a moped. The private market for personal transportation is robust. But the same is *not* true for health insurance. There's no moped for health insurance: Aaron quickly gets priced out of the market.

It's not easy to understand adverse selection—the logic of unraveling is counterintuitive. But once you see how adverse selection works, you start to see why, around the world, governments are so heavily involved in health insurance. Without regulation, the individual market for health insurance just doesn't work. (The same can be said for long-term care insurance.) The market needs mandated coverage and subsidies to prevent unraveling. And even that's not enough: the business of insurance has to be regulated to grapple with cream skimming and to prevent the disappearance of generous coverage. In other words, health insurance is different. It can't be left to the free market.

References

Chandra, Amitabh, Jonathan Gruber, and Robin McKnight. "The Importance of the Individual Mandate—Evidence from Massachusetts." *New England Journal of Medicine* 364, no. 4 (2011): 293–95.

Cutler, David M., and Sarah J. Reber. "Paying for Health Insurance: The Trade-Off between Competition and Adverse Selection." *Quarterly Journal of Economics* 113, no. 2 (1998): 433–66. https://doi.org/10.1162/003355398555649.

Cutler, David M., and Richard J. Zeckhauser. "Adverse Selection in Health Insurance." In *Frontiers in Health Policy Research*, Vol. 1, 1–32. Cambridge, MA: MIT Press, 1998. https://www.nber.org/books-and-chapters/frontiers-health-policy-research-volume-1/adverse-selection-health-insurance.

Kolstad, Jonathan T., and Amanda E. Kowalski. "The Impact of Health Care Reform on Hospital and Preventive Care: Evidence from Massachusetts." *Journal of Public Economics* 96, no. 11 (2012): 909–29. https://doi.org/10.1016/j.jpubeco.2012.07.003.

Krugman, Paul. "The Accidental Theorist." *Slate*, January 24, 1997. https://slate.com/business/1997/01/the-accidental-theorist.html.

Miller, Sarah. "The Effect of Insurance on Emergency Room Visits: An Analysis of the 2006 Massachusetts Health Reform." *Journal of Public Economics*, 96, no. 11 (2012): 893–908. https://doi.org/10.1016/j.jpubeco.2012.07.004.

Oster, Emily, Ira Shoulson, Kimberly Quaid, and E. Ray Dorsey. "Genetic Adverse Selection: Evidence from Long-Term Care Insurance and Huntington Disease." *Journal of Public Economics* 94, no. 11 (2010): 1041–50. https://doi.org/10.1016/j.jpubeco.2010.06.009.

Free Care Is Not Free: Who Pays for the Uninsured?

Many medical emergencies are terrifying. A man wakes up in the middle of the night with severe chest pain. He doesn't know if it's a heart attack or just indigestion.

An insured person, when faced with such a crisis, will go to the emergency room. Best case, the doctors will rule out a heart attack, and then the happy patient will face a $100 copay. Worst case, it's a heart attack, and the trip to the ER saves her life.

For the uninsured, things are different. A friend of ours once worked as a social worker in Oregon. She told us about a call she once had. An ambulance crew arrived at the house of a man who thought he might have suffered a heart attack, and so his family called the ambulance. But he was uninsured and refused to get in the ambulance.

Our friend was called in, via speakerphone, to urge the man to come to the ER. Over the phone, he explained why he wanted to stay home. "I'd rather die at home with all my money than die in the hospital and have the hospital get all my money."

Our friend eventually persuaded the man to come to the ER. The hospital treated him—in fact, the hospital, in such a case, is required by law to treat emergent patients. But the hospital is still allowed to bill the man after the visit. And those bills can be expensive.

That's the way healthcare often works for the uninsured in the United States. As George W. Bush put it in 2007, "People have access to healthcare in America. After all, you just go to an emergency room" (Bush 2007). What Bush didn't mention, however, is what happens after the visit.

The Samaritan's Dilemma and Uncompensated Care

In the Gospel of Luke, Jesus tells the story of the Good Samaritan. A Samaritan was traveling along a road in biblical Israel when he saw a fellow traveler lying on the side of the road, stripped of his clothing and bleeding badly. Others had ignored the injured traveler, but the Samaritan stopped and helped him.

That story is why, today, we call someone who helps those in need a "Good Samaritan." Modern medical ethics require doctors to be Good Samaritans. Doctors are taught to treat people in need regardless of whether or not they can pay for treatment (Annas 1986). American public policy, in a similar fashion, requires the same of hospitals. All hospitals are required to provide emergency medical treatment, even if the patient is uninsured, even if the hospital knows that the patient will never pay for the treatment.[1]

As a result, when the uninsured need emergency treatment, hospitals are required to treat them. The hospital can bill the patients after the fact, but many of the bills are left unpaid. In fact, unpaid medical bills are incredibly common: nearly a fifth of all Americans have medical debt (Kluender et al. 2021). Hospitals often send unpaid bills to collection agencies, but the collection agencies only pay hospitals pennies for each dollar of debt that they take on.

The care that hospitals provide the uninsured without compensation is referred to as "hospital uncompensated care." Together with a third coauthor, Craig Garthwaite, we wrote a paper studying uncompensated care. We dug up data that, at the time, no one else had accessed and found that hospitals provide about $50 billion in uncompensated care each year. Even for American healthcare, that's a lot of money. By way of comparison, it's 30 percent of how much care hospitals provide for Medicaid patients and an even larger share—around 70 percent—of all hospital profits (Garthwaite, Gross, and Notowidigdo 2018).

What does this have to do with health insurance? Well, think about the prospect of uncompensated care from the perspective of a young, healthy uninsured person. In fact, let's take Aaron from the previous chapter. Aaron is healthy and faces a very small risk of needing medical care. He could buy health insurance coverage or he could risk being uninsured. Aaron also knows the rules: he knows that if he needs emergency treatment, local hospitals will have to treat him in the ER. Now he also knows that it's better to be insured than uninsured. He knows that uninsured patients in the ER get hit with enormous medical bills and they might not be treated as well as insured patients (Doyle 2005). But, that said, he knows that being uninsured doesn't mean that he'll be totally on his own if there's an emergency.

As a result, Aaron might choose to be uninsured because he anticipates hospitals providing him with uncompensated care.[2] That phenomenon is sometimes called the "Samaritan's Dilemma." The hospital is required to be a Good Samaritan, to treat all emergent, uninsured patients, and that leads some people to choose to be uninsured as a result. Because the uninsured know they will be taken care of in an emergency, they may choose to remain uninsured even if they are offered very generous subsidies to purchase health insurance.

Now, to be clear, not everyone believes in the Samaritan's Dilemma. The concept makes a strong prediction about people's behavior. It suggests that ordinary people are highly strategic: they recognize that hospitals treat the uninsured, and so they choose to be uninsured. There is some evidence supporting that view, but it's definitely not an airtight case (Mahoney 2015).

That said, the Samaritan's Dilemma offers another argument for why the government should require people to have health insurance. The previous chapter focused on adverse selection as one argument for government intervention—the Samaritan's Dilemma is another argument. So long as hospitals cannot turn away uninsured people, there may be a perverse incentive for some people to stay uninsured.

And it was that argument that Mitt Romney made, years ago, as governor of Massachusetts. Romney was a conservative governor in a liberal state. Some Massachusetts economists argued for healthcare reform because of adverse selection, because the individual market for health insurance may unravel as a result of adverse selection. Other Massachusetts residents argued for healthcare reform for the sake of social justice: because no one ought to be uninsured. Romney, by contrast, referred to the Samaritan's Dilemma. As he put it: "Forty percent of the uninsured were earning enough to buy insurance but had chosen not to do so. Why? Because it is expensive and because they know that if they become seriously ill, they will get free or subsidized treatment at the hospital. By law, emergency care cannot be withheld. Why pay for something you can get for free?" (Romney 2006).

Does Everyone Else Pay for the Uninsured?

To hospital executives, there are two types of patients. First, there are patients who are privately insured. Second, there's everyone else: those covered by Medicare, those covered by Medicaid, and those who are uninsured.

Privately insured patients are the most lucrative for the hospital. The hospital charges the highest rates to those private insurers each time one of their beneficiaries is admitted to the hospital. And every few years, hospitals sit down with those insurers and renegotiate those rates. Medicare patients are much less lucrative: Medicare pays hospitals about half of what private insurers pay (Cooper et al. 2019). Then there's Medicaid, which pays hospitals even less. And finally, there are the uninsured, for whom hospitals provide uncompensated care.

So let's take those two groups of patients—privately covered patients and all other patients—and ask a natural question: What happens to the first group when the second group becomes more costly to the hospital? For instance, suppose that there are more uninsured patients, and so hospitals face greater costs from that population—what happens to the other group of patients, the privately insured?

One hypothesis: hospitals pass the added cost of the uninsured on to privately insured patients. Hospital executives have a meeting in which they, sadly, note the increase in free care that they have to provide to uninsured patients. They're not happy about that free care—it kills the hospital's bottom line. And so, this hypothesis goes, they decide to raise the price that they charge private insurers.

That hypothesis is sometimes called the "cost-shifting hypothesis": hospitals "shift" the costs they face from Medicaid and uninsured patients onto privately insured patients. In response to higher costs, they raise the prices that they charge private insurers.

A lot of people believe in the cost-shifting hypothesis. Back when he was governor of Massachusetts, Mitt Romney referred to cost shifting when describing the uninsured visiting emergency rooms: "while it may be free for them, everyone else ends up paying the bill, either in higher insurance premiums or higher taxes." The idea also appears in the text of the Affordable Care Act: "to pay for [uncompensated care], health care providers pass on the cost to private insurers, which pass on the cost to families." In fact, when the debate over the Affordable Care Act reached the Supreme Court, Justice John Roberts mentioned cost shifting in his legal opinion. He wrote: "hospitals pass on the cost [of uncompensated care] to insurers through higher rates, and insurers, in turn, pass on the cost to policy holders in the form of higher premiums" (*New York Times* 2012).

The cost-shifting hypothesis appears intuitive, maybe even obvious. The hospital provides free care to the uninsured and then it makes up for that free care by raising prices on everyone else. But if you really think about the cost-shifting hypothesis, it becomes less and less obvious.

Suppose that a hospital starts to see more and more uninsured patients, and that those patients become more and more costly to treat. The cost-shifting hypothesis predicts that the hospital will then turn to private insurers and negotiate higher rates with them. But why didn't they do that before? After all, hospital executives are always anxious to improve cash flow, so why wait for an increase in the uninsured population before they raise private prices?

In fact, economic theory suggests that hospital executives ought to respond to more uninsured patients by *lowering* prices for privately insured patients. Imagine that a hospital suddenly experiences an increase in the amount of care it has to provide the uninsured. What do hospital executives do next? Well, since their costs are higher, they now want *more* privately insured patients. But how do they get more privately insured patients? There's only one way: they have to offer new insurers lower prices. Insurers are happy to add the hospital to their networks and send more patients there, but they only agree to do so if the hospital charges them favorable rates. To get more private patients, the hospital has to lower prices for those insurers.

This is confusing. On the one hand, the cost-shifting hypothesis is intuitive, leading both politicians and Supreme Court justices to make the argument to the public. On the other hand, economic theory makes the opposite prediction. So what is one supposed to believe?

In our work with Craig Garthwaite, we tried to test the cost-shifting hypothesis. We did so by focusing on an event that happened in Tennessee in 2005. In that year, the state of Tennessee removed 180,000 people from its Medicaid program. This was one of the largest sudden increases in the uninsured population in history: over a couple months, nearly 3 percent of the state's adult nonelderly population lost Medicaid coverage.

So, all of a sudden, there were more uninsured people in Tennessee. What did that do to Tennessee hospitals? Those hospitals suddenly faced higher costs. Figure 3.1 comes from our study. After Tennessee cut 180,000 people from its Medicaid program, hospitals in Tennessee started to provide a lot more uncompensated care than they had before. Each additional uninsured person costs hospitals about $800 to $900 each year in extra uncompensated care.

Now the cost-shifting hypothesis would predict that Tennessee hospitals simply passed those costs onto private payers. But we found no evidence for that! Instead, we found that hospitals' margins fell by about the same amount that we would have predicted if hospitals absorbed the costs entirely. In other words, we found that hospitals ate the costs. They faced more uninsured patients, and so their costs went up accordingly.

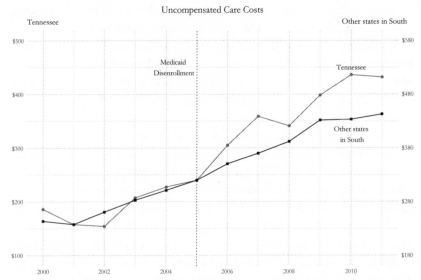

FIGURE 3.1. Evolution of uncompensated care costs in Tennessee compared to other states in the southern United States. The vertical axis plots the uncompensated care costs per capita, dividing total uncompensated care costs across all hospitals by the adult population. Uncompensated care costs trended similarly between Tennessee and other southern states prior to 2005. After the 2005 disenrollment, uncompensated care costs increased faster in Tennessee compared to other southern states (Garthwaite, Gross, and Notowidigdo 2014).

We're not the only researchers to find no evidence for the cost-shifting hypothesis. Austin Frakt (2015) reviewed decades of studies on hospitals and found that few credible studies, if any, demonstrated cost shifting in the real world. If anything, private prices for hospitalizations move in the way described above: hospitals lower prices rather than raise prices (White 2013).

Why Are People (Still) Uninsured?

Before the Affordable Care Act was implemented, about 50 million Americans lacked health insurance coverage. Afterward, about 25 million Americans lacked health insurance coverage. Before the law, many Americans were uninsured due to adverse selection—the Aaron-through-Zack unraveling that we discussed in the last chapter led the individual market for health insurance to unravel. But what of the 25 million Americans that were uninsured years after the law was passed? How come there are still so many Americans without health insurance?

A first reason why people in this country remain uninsured is that the law does not apply to undocumented immigrants. Undocumented immigrants comprise about 16 percent of the uninsured, and no policy exists that might provide them with affordable coverage (Blumberg 2016). When it comes to immigration, Americans are divided. We are both the children of immigrants—immigrants built this country. But many Americans today do not see it that way, and it does not seem as though undocumented immigrants are going to be covered by public health insurance anytime soon.

A second reason that Americans are still uninsured is that many of them fall through the cracks of the system. As of 2023 eleven states have chosen not to expand Medicaid under the Affordable Care Act. That decision has meant that millions of low-income Americans in those states have found themselves too poor to qualify for subsidies for private health insurance and yet ineligible for their state's Medicaid program. In addition, in 2017, the Trump administration lowered the Affordable Care Act's penalty for being uninsured, the individual mandate, to zero.

All of that being said, there's a third reason that Americans are still uninsured. Many Americans *choose* to be uninsured rather than pay a small, token premium. A team of researchers led by Betsy Cliff studied that phenomenon in Michigan (Cliff et al. 2021). When the state of Michigan expanded Medicaid under the Affordable Care Act, it decided to make the program free for all enrollees with incomes below the federal poverty line. But enrollees with incomes above the federal poverty line were required to pay a small monthly premium, about $3 a month.

Now, $3 a month is not nothing, especially for anyone near the poverty line. But for $3 a month, an enrollee just above the poverty line would receive thousands of dollars of value. Betsy Cliff and her coauthors studied how enrollees who faced that $3 premium behaved relative to those with similar incomes, just barely below the federal poverty line, who were not charged a premium. They found that the $3 premium had an enormous effect: it increased the probability that enrollees dropped out of the program by 2.3 percentage points. Those enrollees would have consumed about $166 per month in healthcare from Medicaid, and yet they chose not to join Medicaid for a $3 fee (fig. 3.2). Converted annually, this means there are low-income people unwilling or unable to pay something like $36 a year to get almost $2,000 of (insured) Medicaid spending on average.

Such a phenomenon is not limited to Michigan. Researchers in Massachusetts found that an increase of $40 per month in the price of health insurance caused 25 percent of people to decline Medicaid coverage (Finkelstein et al. 2017). In California, a group of researchers found that the average amount people were willing to pay for insurance on the exchange there was far lower than the expected costs to the insurers (Tebaldi 2021).

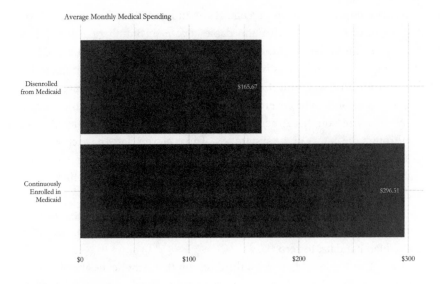

Average Monthly Medical Spending

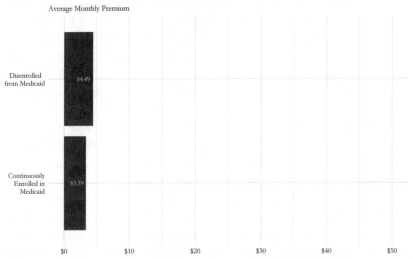

Average Monthly Premium

FIGURE 3.2. Average spending and average monthly premium for individuals who had enrolled in Medicaid. The first panel shows the average spending for individuals who remained enrolled compared to those who did not remain enrolled because they had to pay slightly higher monthly premiums; the second panel shows the average difference in premiums. The fact that those who remain enrolled have higher average spending is consistent with adverse selection, but the large difference between spending and premiums shows that many individuals are not willing to pay even a few dollars a month for health insurance coverage (Cliff et al. 2021).

All of this presents something of a puzzle. Why not pay fifty bucks a year for an average of $2,000 in value? Why is it that even tiny monthly fees cause people to decline health insurance coverage?

One hypothesis is that signing up for health insurance is painful. Perhaps all of the paperwork involved is just too much for ordinary, busy people. Applying for Medicaid, in particular, requires a lengthy application, providing necessary documentation to demonstrate income eligibility. In many states, an in-person interview is required too.

But, beyond the paperwork, it's also possible that many Americans just don't see health insurance as all that valuable. Perhaps some are unsophisticated and so don't quite understand the value of being insured. Perhaps others are so pressed for cash that they cannot afford low monthly fees.

Still, other Americans may turn down cheap health insurance because of the Good Samaritan problem. Those Americans realize that, if they have an emergency, hospitals will treat them. And so, knowing that, they may decide that even five dollars a month is just too much for health insurance.

This is a difficult situation to navigate. On the one hand, some people are turning down $5 health insurance by mistake, and others are turning it down strategically. But regardless, at the end of the day, policymakers have a problem. Even trivially small prices for health insurance will induce some Americans to pass up that insurance.[3]

The Bottom Line

So at the end of the day, who pays for the uninsured? Hospitals bear most of the cost of the uninsured—charity care and unpaid bills are just part of the cost of doing business as a not-for-profit hospital. That's not to say that hospitals' role in all of this is blameless: many hospitals—both for-profit and non-profit hospitals—have been incredibly aggressive in collecting medical debt from patients. But, that being said, the nature of the industry is such that the hospitals are exposed to the cost of the uninsured.

All of this is a uniquely American problem: no other wealthy country has a large population of uninsured residents. And there's no easy solution to the problem of the uninsured. The federal government could strengthen the individual mandate, penalizing all Americans if they are not insured. But such a policy is not politically popular. The government could also simply automatically enroll everyone who is uninsured into some type of insurance plan. "Medicare for All" proposals take that form: providing Medicare for either everyone or everyone who is uninsured. But those proposals have also lacked widespread political support in Washington.

References

Annas, G. J. "Your Money or Your Life: 'Dumping' Uninsured Patients from Hospital Emergency Wards." *American Journal of Public Health* 76, no. 1 (1986): 74–77. https://doi.org/10.2105/AJPH.76.1.74.

Blumberg, Linda J., Michael Karpman, Matthew Buettgens, and Patricia Solleveld. *Who Are the Remaining Uninsured, and What Do Their Characteristics Tell Us about How to Reach Them?* Washington, DC: Urban Institute, 2016.

Bush, George. "President Bush Visits Cleveland, Ohio." White House Archives. July 10, 2007. https://georgewbush-whitehouse.archives.gov/news/releases/2007/07/20070710-6.html.

Cliff, Betsy Q., Sarah Miller, Jeffrey T. Kullgren, John Z. Ayanian, and Richard A. Hirth. "Adverse Selection in Medicaid: Evidence from Discontinuous Program Rules." *American Journal of Health Economics* 8, no.1 (2022): 127–50. https://doi.org/10.1086/716464.

Cooper, Zack, Stuart V. Craig, Martin Gaynor, and John Van Reenen. "The Price Ain't Right? Hospital Prices and Health Spending on the Privately Insured." *Quarterly Journal of Economics* 134, no. 1 (2019): 51–107.

Doyle, Joseph J., Jr. "Health Insurance, Treatment and Outcomes: Using Auto Accidents as Health Shocks." *Review of Economics and Statistics* 87, no. 2 (2005): 256–70.

Finkelstein, Amy, Nathaniel Hendren, and Mark Shepard. "Subsidizing Health Insurance for Low-Income Adults: Evidence from Massachusetts." *American Economic Review* 109, no. 4 (2019): 1530–67.

Frakt, Austin. "Hospitals Are Wrong about Shifting Costs to Private Insurers." *New York Times*, March 23, 2015, sec. The Upshot. https://www.nytimes.com/2015/03/24/upshot/why-hospitals-are-wrong-about-shifting-costs-to-private-insurers.html.

Garthwaite, Craig, Tal Gross, and Matthew J. Notowidigdo. "Public Health Insurance, Labor Supply, and Employment Lock." *Quarterly Journal of Economics* 129, no. 2 (2014): 653–96. https://doi.org/10.1093/qje/qju005.

———. "Hospitals as Insurers of Last Resort." *American Economic Journal: Applied Economics* 10, no. 1 (2018): 1–39. https://doi.org/10.1257/app.20150581.

Kluender, Raymond, Neale Mahoney, Francis Wong, and Wesley Yin. "Medical Debt in the US, 2009–2020." *JAMA* 326, no. 3 (2021): 250–56.

Mahoney, Neale. "Bankruptcy as Implicit Health Insurance." *American Economic Review* 105, no. 2 (2015): 710–46.

New York Times, "Supreme Court Decision on Obama's Health Care Law," June 29, 2012, 193. https://archive.nytimes.com/www.nytimes.com/interactive/2012/06/29/us/29healthcare-scotus-docs.html#document/p7.

Romney, Mitt. "Health Care for Everyone? We Found a Way." *Wall Street Journal*, April 11, 2006, sec. Opinion. https://www.wsj.com/articles/SB114472206077422547.

Tebaldi, Pietro. "Estimating Equilibrium in Health Insurance Exchanges: Price Competition and Subsidy Design under the ACA." Working Paper 29869. National Bureau of Economic Research, 2021.

White, Chapin. "Contrary to Cost-Shift Theory, Lower Medicare Hospital Payment Rates for Inpatient Care Lead to Lower Private Payment Rates." *Health Affairs* 32, no. 5 (2013): 935–43. https://doi.org/10.1377/hlthaff.2012.0332.

4
Moral Hazard

A seventy-year-old woman goes to the pharmacy to pick up medication for her arthritis. How much should that cost her? Maybe $5 for the prescription? Or $20? Or should it all be free?

There's surely a lot going on. The seventy-year-old woman might be grappling with poverty and discrimination and a plethora of challenges beyond arthritis. A pharmaceutical company may have priced the medication very aggressively. The woman might not have access to good medical advice. For now, though, we want to focus on one, narrow question: How much should she have to pay for her medical care?

Health economists have grappled with that question for as long as there have been health economists. The answer is not simple, and the debate continues to this day. The short answer: it depends. The long answer requires a tour of research on the issue, research that goes back nearly half a century.

What Is the Moral Hazard Problem?

High prices are awful. No one likes it when things are expensive. What kind of *monster* would like high prices?

An economist.

High prices do something important: they force people to agonize over whether or not they really want to make the purchase. It can be problematic for people to consume goods without having to grapple with their price.

That's why, whenever an organization wants to reduce the consumption of something, there's a simple solution: just raise the price! If there's too much traffic in a city center, raise the price on driving downtown, through higher toll prices or "congestion charges." If there's too much pollution, raise the price on pollution through a carbon tax. If too many people smoke, raise the price of cigarettes through tobacco taxes.

Why turn to higher prices? Because higher prices lead people to consume less and force them to align their personal decisions with the true cost of production. High prices force people to "internalize" the full cost of production, whether those prices reflect the costs we typically think about or harder-to-measure costs like congestion and pollution. That is the benefit of high prices.

What does this have to do with healthcare? Health insurance fundamentally breaks the relationship between individual decisions and the costs of production. It breaks that relationship because, by definition, generous health insurance shields consumers from the high price of healthcare. A problem with generous health insurance is that it makes healthcare too cheap. And when healthcare is too cheap, people buy too much of it.

Health insurance, in other words, can eliminate the benefit of high prices, the way that they force people to grapple with the costs of production. And that can lead to waste. If a seventy-year-old woman doesn't have to pay anything for her arthritis medication, she might buy the medication even if it's not working. That medication still costs the healthcare system money, money that could be better spent on more effective forms of healthcare.

There are plenty of contexts in medicine in which there's a cheap option and an expensive option. Sometimes, the cheap option is just as good as the expensive one. For instance, an upper respiratory infection can be treated in an emergency room (expensive) or in an ordinary doctor's office (cheap). Some conditions can be treated with generic drugs (cheap) or branded drugs (expensive). If the consumer pays the same price for either option, then why not choose the expensive option? And if all consumers face the same incentives and behave in the same way, then healthcare spending, overall, might rise in ways that don't actually improve health.

There's a technical term for this issue: it's called the "moral hazard problem." In general, moral hazard problems are situations in which there are two parties in a transaction and one party cannot control the actions of another. In the case of health insurance, there's the insurer and the consumer, and the insurer bears the costs of the consumer's healthcare decisions. The consumer can choose the cheap option or the expensive option, and the insurer pays either way.[1]

Now, to be clear, that's not to say that generous health insurance is a bad thing. As we described in the first chapter, generous health insurance also protects consumers from risk. The issue here is that there's a trade-off. On the one hand, we want health insurance to be generous so that people are protected from risk. On the other hand, we *don't* want health insurance to be generous, because of moral hazard. So the generosity of health insurance—how much the consumer has to pay for healthcare—has to balance those two forces.

But all of that is *theory*, words on a page that describe how some people *think* the world works. Theory needs to be tested. So, let's turn to real-world evidence on moral hazard in health insurance.

What Do Copayments Do?

Health economists first examined moral hazard in health insurance with a field experiment. In the late 1970s, a team of health economists sat down at the RAND Corporation, a think tank in Santa Monica, California. Joe Newhouse was a young economist just starting out at RAND. He asked his colleagues a simple question: How do people respond to the price of healthcare? If ordinary people have to pay more for healthcare, do they consume less of it? Newhouse found that lots of economists had opinions on that question, but no one had any good evidence.

Some argued that healthcare was different than other goods, that healthcare is always a matter of "your money or your life." So, they argued, people would pay whatever price they faced for healthcare—the price didn't matter, because healthcare was so important. And, by extension, those people were not concerned with moral hazard: since healthcare is different from other goods, it doesn't matter, they argued, that health insurance makes healthcare cheap.

Economists knew that prices mattered for ordinary goods: coffee, wheat, motorcycles. If the price of coffee goes up, people buy less coffee. That is, as we say in Econ 101, a matter of the demand curve. Is the same true for healthcare? No one knew.

So the researchers, led by Newhouse, decided to run an experiment. They took 2,750 American families and randomized them into two groups.[2] The study included both urban and rural households and spanned a broad range of income levels.[3] One group of families was put on a free-care plan: for several years, all of the healthcare they needed would be free. Every doctor visit, every dentist visit, every medication: they would pay nothing.

Other families were put on a high-deductible healthcare plan. They would be responsible for all of their healthcare costs up to a thousand dollars. After a thousand dollars, their health insurance plan would kick in and cover everything. But until then, they had to foot the bill on their own.

Remember: randomization makes experiments valid—it means that both groups began the experiment with the same health, on average. They have the same average income, the same average levels of education, the same numbers of children, the same number of televisions, and, most importantly, the same average health. As a result, any differences in outcomes in the years following the RAND experiment can be interpreted as the impact of the health insurance plans themselves.

The experiment became known as the RAND Health Insurance Experiment and it lasted from 1976 until 1982. For health economists, the RAND Health Insurance Experiment amounts to a combination of NASA launching a space shuttle, Bill Gates starting Microsoft, and Ayatollah Khomeini's return to Iran. It happened in the late 1970s, and it's a big deal to us. The RAND experiment is one of the most expensive experiments ever performed by social scientists.

For years, the families participating in the RAND Health Insurance Experiment led their ordinary lives; the only thing out of the ordinary was that a team of researchers at RAND was handling their health insurance. Then, after years of being on either the free-care plan or the high-deductible plan, everyone was given a final physical exam and the experiment was over.

Newhouse and his colleagues spent years poring over the data, trying to understand how having to pay for healthcare affected families. The researchers studied the results from every possible angle, slicing and dicing the data every which way. The results of the experiment filled hundreds of academic papers and also a 516-page book (Manning et al. 1987; Keeler et al. 1988; Newhouse et al. 1993). But, decades later, the most relevant discoveries from the experiment boil down to three main conclusions.

First, the researchers compared the amount of healthcare consumed by families that were put on the free-care plan to those of families randomly assigned to the high-deductible plan. That comparison is summarized in figure 4.1. Those put on the free-care plan consumed an average of $1,999.83 dollars (in 2021 dollars) as compared to $1,623.36 dollars in healthcare for those on the high-deductible plan.[4] That's roughly 20 percent, a large difference. And so the first conclusion of the experiment was this: high prices really do cut how much care people choose to consume.

In other words, incentives matter, even for healthcare. People who face a higher price for healthcare consume less healthcare. In the language of Econ 101, demand curves slope down, even for healthcare. Yes, healthcare is important, and people treat it as important, but, at the end of the day, the price still matters.

The second conclusion of the experiment arose as the researchers tried to figure out *which* healthcare the families on the deductible cut out. The re-

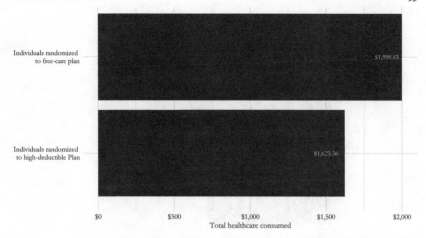

FIGURE 4.1. Average healthcare consumed (in 2021 dollars) among families randomly assigned to the high-deductible health insurance plan and the families randomly assigned to the free-care plan.

searchers assembled a panel of physicians and gave them all of the medical charts associated with the experiment. They asked the physicians to categorize all of the healthcare as "highly effective" care or "rarely effective" care. Going to the ER for a runny nose: that's rarely effective care. Going to the ER for a heart attack: that's highly effective care.

The panel of physicians worked through the stack of charts, methodically categorizing all visits as highly effective or rarely effective. Then they studied how the high-deductible plan affected those two categories.

The bar charts in figure 4.2 summarize the analysis. Families facing a deductible cut back on highly effective care by about 30 percent relative to those on the free-care plan. And then the researchers found roughly the same effect for rarely effective care: a roughly 30 percent drop in utilization. The contrast across those two findings is the second conclusion of the experiment: the deductible led families to cut back on *all* healthcare, regardless of whether it was effective or ineffective.

And that finding alone is kind of disappointing. Health policy would be much simpler if people behaved like shrewd medical experts whenever they faced a deductible. Unfortunately, that's not how it works. Patients are not physicians themselves—they don't know what is effective and what is ineffective. So when faced with a high price, they just cut back on all of it, both care that really matters and also care that is probably wasteful.

Lastly, the researchers at RAND studied what deductibles did to people's health. Remember that families were randomized to different health insurance

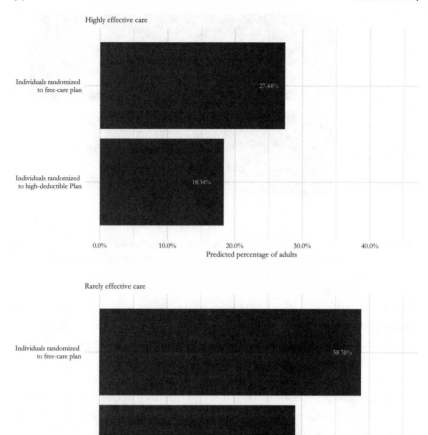

FIGURE 4.2. Percentage reduction in total healthcare consumed for "highly effective care" and "rarely effective care." These categories are defined by physicians based on their expert judgment about the average effectiveness of different types of care.

plans, so any differences in health outcomes during the RAND experiment years were probably a result of the impact of the health insurance plans.

After several years on the health insurance plan that they were assigned to, everyone's health was evaluated. Overall, there was no difference: people who spent three to five years on the high-deductible plan finished the experiment in roughly the same health as people who spent that time on the free-care plan (Newhouse, Group, and Staff 1993).

Things were different, however, for one group of participants. The researchers focused on what they called "elevated-risk participants." That group consisted of people who were in poor health at the start of the experiment. Maybe they already had a chronic condition or maybe they were obese. For that group, the researchers found that the deductible plan harmed their health. A couple years on a high-deductible plan took people from bad shape to worse shape (fig. 4.3).

That finding is, perhaps, intuitive. If you're in good health, then a deductible will induce you to consume less healthcare, and that's going to have a very

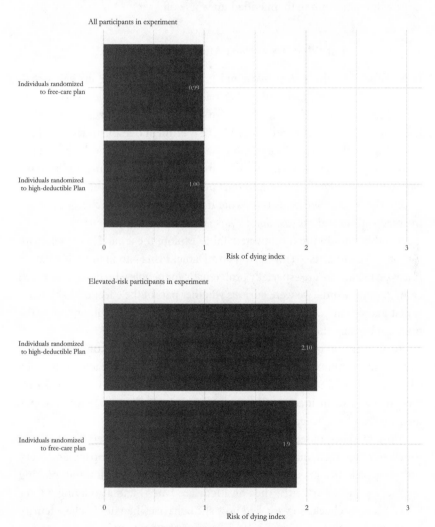

FIGURE 4.3. Average differences in health for families randomized into the high-deductible plan and summary measure of health.

small impact on your health. After all, you're in good health, so a bit more or a bit less healthcare is not going to have a big effect, at least on average. But if you're already at elevated risk, then a deductible leads you to consume less healthcare, and for you, that really matters.

All in all, the three conclusions of the RAND experiment paint a confusing picture of what deductibles do to people. On the one hand, deductibles lead people to cut back on healthcare a lot and they do not hurt people, on average. On the other hand, the participants who were assigned a high-deductible plan cut back on *all* healthcare, not just ineffective care. And the most vulnerable among them ended up worse off.

But What If You Can't Afford the Copayment?

Let's go back to the seventy-year-old grandmother picking up her arthritis medication. She watches the pharmacist tap at the register—how much should she have to pay? Well, what we've discussed so far makes for a confusing debate. On the one hand, the RAND experiment demonstrated that high prices on healthcare save a lot of money and do not, on average, lead to medical problems. On the other hand, there are those other, troubling findings, the way in which deductibles seem to hurt people who are at elevated risk.

But there's another issue, too. What if the grandmother is charged $20 for the medication, and *she just doesn't have the money*? What then?

It is that question that motivated Tal to explore the issue. He worked with two other economists—Tim Layton and Daniel Prinz—to figure out whether prices on healthcare are especially problematic for people who don't have much cash. In other words, we were curious whether part of the effect of deductibles is that people cut back on healthcare not because they're unwilling to pay the price but because they actually cannot afford to pay the price.

To answer that question, we focused on older Americans on Social Security. About 64 million Americans are on Social Security, and each month they all receive a Social Security check. For many, those Social Security checks are their sole source of income. They rely on those checks to buy food, to pay their rent, and also to pay for their prescriptions.

Most of those older Americans are on the Medicare Part D program, which pays for their medications but also charges them a copayment every time they pick up a prescription. That seventy-year-old grandmother picking up a script for her arthritis: she's on Medicare Part D and also living off her Social Security check. So we asked how she behaves when her Social Security check arrives. And we found a clear answer: she postpones picking up her medications until her Social Security check arrives.

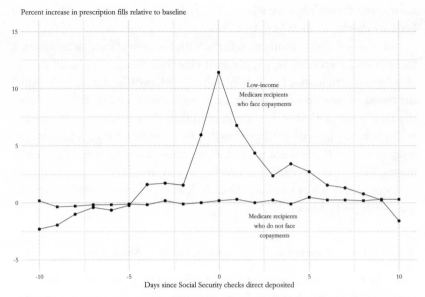

Percent increase in prescription fills relative to baseline

FIGURE 4.4. Percent increase in prescription fills comparing Medicare recipients who face copayments to Medicare recipients who do not face copayments in the days around when they receive their Social Security checks.

Figure 4.4 summarizes our analysis. We studied two groups of people. First is a group of older Americans who qualify for both Medicare and Medicaid, who typically pay no copayments at the pharmacy—all their medications are free of charge. Those people are just as likely to fill a prescription before they receive a Social Security check as after they receive a Social Security check. After all, the medication is free, so they don't need to wait for their checks to pick up their meds.

For other Medicare recipients, the story is very different. Nearly everyone else on Medicare is typically required to pay a fee at the pharmacy. For them, we found enormous increases in the number of prescriptions they pick up when Social Security checks are distributed. The number of prescriptions filled increases by 6 to 14 percent when Social Security checks are deposited in Medicare recipients' bank accounts. Our estimates suggest that 1.3 million prescription fills are delayed each year until Medicare recipients' Social Security checks arrive. People delay picking up their medications until they have the necessary cash on hand.

Those estimates even apply to necessary medications. We asked physicians for examples of common drugs that patients need to take regularly, medications that can lead to health problems if people stop taking them. The physicians told us about blood thinners, antiseizure medications, insulin, and statins. For those drugs, we still found large spikes in purchases after Social Security checks are distributed.

All of this suggests another challenge with copayments and deductibles: if those costs are prohibitive, people don't take their medications until they've saved up enough money to buy them. That is, prices on healthcare can distort the *timing* of when people consume care. Many wait until their Social Security checks arrive. Others might wait until their deductibles reset in January. Still others might wait until they switch to a health insurance plan that is more generous (Cabral 2017). And all of those delays in care might really matter. Most healthcare requires timeliness: you shouldn't just put it off until the price goes down or you have the cash. And yet, it seems, healthcare prices induce people to do exactly that.

When People Face Copayments, Do They Shop Around?

Let's turn our attention back, yet again, to that seventy-year-old woman, who has to pay for her arthritis medication. Suppose that she faces a deductible and so is responsible for all of her healthcare spending up to a couple thousand dollars. While facing that deductible, a doctor suggests that she get an MRI. Now, the deductible means that she has to pay for the MRI herself. And we know from the RAND experiment that the deductible may convince her to forgo the MRI entirely.

Suppose that she, despite the deductible, still decides to get the MRI. She still has a decision to make: *where* to get the MRI. There's an imaging center right down the street, and then there's another one ten minutes away. She could call the two imaging centers and ask them how much they'll charge for her MRI. Does she do that? That is, does the deductible induce her to "price shop," to find the cheapest provider?

A team of researchers—Zarek Brot-Goldberg, Amitabh Chandra, Ben Handel, and Jon Kolstad—set out to answer that question, to measure how deductibles affect price shopping. We know that people price shop for ordinary goods. If you're buying a big-screen television, you might visit a few stores before making the purchase. If you're having the roof replaced on your suburban home, you get estimates from a couple roofers. Do deductibles cause people to do the same thing when it comes to healthcare?

The research team studied a large private employer that shifted tens of thousands of its employees to a high-deductible plan. For years, the employees were on a fairly generous private plan, and then, all of a sudden, the employer shifted them onto a high-deductible plan.

First, the researchers estimated the overall effect of the deductible. The deductible led to a roughly 12 percent drop in healthcare spending (Brot-Goldberg et al. 2017). That drop is somewhat smaller than what we might expect from the RAND experiment, but still, a large drop in healthcare spending. Deductibles cut spending—that's clear.

Second, the authors tested whether the deductible affected price shopping. And, to the authors' surprise, they found *no* evidence that employees responded to the deductible by starting to price shop. People were no more likely to choose low-cost providers after they faced a deductible as compared to before.

In other words, our seventy-year-old friend probably goes to the same imaging center for an MRI, regardless of whether she has to pay for the service via a deductible or whether her insurer pays for it. In general, there's very little price shopping in healthcare.

Now, in fairness, it's often pretty difficult to price shop for healthcare. When you're buying a car, you can call up dealerships and get price quotes very easily. When you're buying surgery, it can be more difficult. Many healthcare providers are not prepared or willing to give you a price (Rosenthal, Lu, and Cram 2013).[5]

In addition, when it comes to healthcare, many people might worry about quality. When you're buying a particular big-screen television, you should find the cheapest price you can. But when you're buying an MRI, there's a concern, perhaps, that cheaper providers are cheaper because they provide lower quality images. For MRIs, and for some other medical treatments, quality might be less of an issue. But for some surgeries, quality is a first-order concern. A dirt-cheap can of Coca-Cola sounds great—a dirt-cheap sushi dinner, less tempting.

Some insurers have experimented with tools designed to facilitate price shopping among consumers (Ackley 2020; Brown 2019; Whaley et al. 2019). There are websites that consumers can check, with prices listed across providers. And some insurers run incentive programs: "choose the cheapest imaging center, and we'll send you a check for $300." Those kinds of tools do have an effect: *some* people will start price shopping when prompted. But, in general, in healthcare the scope for price shopping is small, and there's not much savings to be had.

So How Should We Set Copayments?

At this point, one can be forgiven for being confused. On the one hand, entirely free healthcare is a recipe for moral hazard, that is, for overconsumption. If it costs you nothing, why not visit the ER for the sniffles? If it costs you nothing, why not choose the much more expensive medication? And, indeed, the RAND experiment, along with subsequent work, has found that higher prices on healthcare save a lot of money.

On the other hand, a high price on healthcare leads people to cut back on healthcare that they really need. The RAND experiment and subsequent studies suggest that high prices hurt the vulnerable (Chandra, Flack, and Obermeyer 2021). That's a confusing trade-off: prices prevent waste but also hurt some people. Then there's the added complication that when faced with high healthcare prices, consumers don't price shop very much. What do we do with all of this?

Here's one solution: "value-based insurance design," which some people call "VBID." VBID is the notion that copayments should change based on the value of the underlying medical care. Deductibles are a very blunt instrument: they impose a high price on all care. And yet we know that healthcare is heterogeneous: some healthcare is incredibly valuable, and other healthcare is wasteful. The VBID crowd argues that people should face no deductibles at all but rather a different price depending on their health and the healthcare they are seeking.

For instance, suppose that there are two alternative medications for a given condition: a cheap, generic medication and an expensive, branded medication. If the two medications are similarly effective, then according to the VBID crowd, people should face a much higher copayment for the more expensive option.

Similarly, consider medical procedures whose benefits are dubious. For instance, there exists a simple orthopedic procedure called arthroscopy of the knee, and evidence suggests that it is actually no better than a placebo at treating knee pain (Howard, David, and Hockenberry 2017; Moseley et al. 2002). If a person wants arthroscopy of the knee, despite the evidence that the procedure provides few real benefits, then they should pay a very high price.

On the opposite extreme, there are some procedures that are incredibly valuable. Consider colonoscopies for those older than forty-five. The VBID crowd believes that people should pay a price of zero for a colonoscopy. In fact, some argue for a negative price: colonoscopies are so important that insurers ought to give rewards for going out and getting one.

VBID can also involve a change in the price of healthcare when a person's circumstances change. For instance, consider a middle-aged man who has a heart attack in the middle of the year. Under a high-deductible plan, the man might still face high prices for healthcare for the rest of the year. But under VBID, his insurer ought to eliminate prices for him, because it's important that he take all of the medications that he is prescribed and that he pursue all of the follow-up care recommended after his heart attack.

Given the challenges we have laid out here, VBID makes a lot of sense. It negotiates the tension between the benefits of deductibles (they save a ton of money) and the costs (they deter important care). But, that said, VBID is probably not coming to an insurer near you anytime soon, for a couple reasons. First, it's often not clear what healthcare ought to be priced low and what ought to be priced high. Medicine is often murky, and it's not so easy to single out which care is worthy of either zero cost or a high price.

A second challenge relates to adverse selection (see chap. 2). What happens when a single insurer starts to practice VBID? Let's say that they take VBID very seriously and so eliminate prices for all enrollees with diabetes. After all, diabetes is a serious condition and a lot of medical care is incredibly important for people with the condition. The insurer sets a price of zero for insulin, metformin, appointments with endocrinologists, appointments with podiatrists, and so on. The word gets out, and now all diabetics choose this insurer. And so it is no wonder that an insurer might hesitate before putting VBID in place.

Still, even if individual insurers don't voluntarily sign up, the basic principles of VBID may be catching on. For instance, in 2010, the Affordable Care Act required that certain preventive services be covered by all insurers and be exempt from deductibles and copayments. Specifically, the law incorporated recommendations from the US Preventive Services Task Force, a panel of experts that ranks preventive practices. The Affordable Care Act requires insurers to cover for free all preventive services to which the panel assigns an "A" or "B," such as certain cancer screenings and routine immunizations. One might imagine more such regulations in the future, forcing insurers to exempt from copayments the care that is deemed most important.

The Bottom Line

So, at the end of the day, what's the bottom line on moral hazard? Well, like nearly everything else in healthcare, we end up with a pretty tricky trade-off.

On the one hand, copayments and deductibles save lots of money. That's important: money that we save by cutting low-value healthcare is money that can go into high-value healthcare (or, for that matter, money that can go into schools, and housing, tax cuts, higher wages, bridges, tunnels, etc.). And, on top of that, copayments and deductibles probably don't hurt people at low risk for health problems. On the other hand, copayments and deductibles *do* hurt those at high risk for health problems. And they create a barrier that leads many people to delay important care.

There's no easy solution here. Value-based insurance design might try to balance these trade-offs, but, as we described above, it hasn't gone very far. If you were hoping for this chapter to end with a neat and tidy recommendation, then you're going to be disappointed. What makes health economics so interesting, at least for us, also makes it frustrating. There's often no tidy bottom line.

References

Ackley, Calvin A. "Essays on Insurance Design and the Demand for Medical Care." PhD diss., Boston University, 2020. https://www.proquest.com/docview/2458763991/abstract/E9C1C7813AC44F7EPQ/1.

Arrow, Kenneth. "Uncertainty and the Welfare Economics of Medical Care." *American Economic Review* 53, no. 5 (1963): 941–97.

Brot-Goldberg, Zarek C., Amitabh Chandra, Benjamin R. Handel, and Jonathan T. Kolstad. "What Does a Deductible Do? The Impact of Cost-Sharing on Health Care Prices, Quantities, and Spending Dynamics." *Quarterly Journal of Economics* 132, no. 3 (2017): 1261–318. https://doi.org/10.1093/qje/qjx013.

Brown, Zach Y. "Equilibrium Effects of Health Care Price Information." *Review of Economics and Statistics* 101, no. 4 (2019): 699–712. https://doi.org/10.1162/rest_a_00765.

Cabral, Marika. "Claim Timing and *Ex Post* Adverse Selection." *Review of Economic Studies* 84, no. 1 (2017): 1–44. https://doi.org/10.1093/restud/rdw022.

Chandra, Amitabh, Evan Flack, and Ziad Obermeyer. "The Health Costs of Cost-Sharing." Working Paper 28439. National Bureau of Economic Research, 2021. https://doi.org/10.3386/w28439.

Howard, David H., Guy David, and Jason Hockenberry. "Selective Hearing: Physician-Ownership and Physicians' Response to New Evidence." *Journal of Economics and Management Strategy* 26, no. 1 (2017): 152–68. https://doi.org/10.1111/jems.12178.

Keeler, Emmett B., Joan L. Buchanan, John E. Rolph, Janet M. Hanley, and David Reboussin. "The Demand for Episodes of Medical Treatment in the Health Insurance Experiment." Santa Monica, CA: RAND Corporation, 1988. https://www.rand.org/pubs/reports/R3454.html.

Manning, Willard G., Joseph P. Newhouse, Naihua Duan, Emmett B. Keeler, and Arleen Leibowitz. 1987. "Health Insurance and the Demand for Medical Care: Evidence from a Randomized Experiment." *American Economic Review* 77, no. 3 (1987): 251–77.

Moseley, J. Bruce, Kimberly O'Malley, Nancy J. Petersen, Terri J. Menke, Baruch A. Brody, David H. Kuykendall, John C. Hollingsworth, Carol M. Ashton, and Nelda P. Wray. "A Controlled Trial of Arthroscopic Surgery for Osteoarthritis of the Knee." *New England Journal of Medicine* 347, no. 2 (2002): 81–88. https://doi.org/10.1056/NEJMoa013259.

Newhouse, Joseph P., RAND Corporation Insurance Experiment Group, and Insurance Experiment Group Staff. *Free for All? Lessons from the Rand Health Insurance Experiment.* Cambridge, MA: Harvard University Press, 1993.

Pauly, Mark V. "The Economics of Moral Hazard: Comment." *American Economic Review* 58, no. 3 (1968): 531–37.

Rosenthal, Jaime A., Xin Lu, and Peter Cram. "Availability of Consumer Prices from US Hospitals for a Common Surgical Procedure." *JAMA Internal Medicine* 173, no. 6 (2013): 427–32. https://doi.org/10.1001/jamainternmed.2013.460.

Whaley, Christopher M., Lan Vu, Neeraj Sood, Michael E. Chernew, Leanne Metcalfe, and Ateev Mehrotra. "Paying Patients to Switch: Impact of a Rewards Program on Choice of Providers, Prices, and Utilization." *Health Affairs* 38, no. 3 (2019): 440–47. https://doi.org/10.1377/hlthaff.2018.05068.

5

Behavioral Economics

A gracious host offers a guest a scoop of ice cream: Would she like chocolate or vanilla? This isn't rocket science: she ought to pick whichever flavor she prefers. Guests who prefer chocolate will ask for a scoop of chocolate and those who prefer vanilla will ask for a scoop of vanilla. That is rational behavior: the guest's actions—whichever flavor she picks—are aligned with her preferences—whichever flavor she prefers.

A lot of behavior is rational. At the supermarket, when faced with two identical types of laundry detergent, people pick the cheaper detergent. When faced with two identically priced ice creams, people choose whichever flavor they prefer.

But some behavior is *not* rational. Often, people make choices that are clearly not aligned with their preferences. They smoke cigarettes when they want desperately *not* to smoke cigarettes. They put off saving for retirement, even though, if asked, they'll explain that they do want a comfortable retirement. They join a gym and never work out.

Economists rely on two types of models to explain behavior. First, the rational model: people's actions are aligned with their preferences. If you don't save for retirement, that must be because you want to spend all your money when you are young. A second type of model is what economists sometimes call a "behavioral" model: people's actions are not aligned with their preferences, because their actions are shaped by a variety of "behavioral biases." If you don't save for retirement, that may be due to a kind of bias. Perhaps you cannot control your own spending ("self-control problems"), or you do not think about the future costs of your current spendings ("present biased"). In either case, your behavior—how much you save for retirement—is not aligned with your actual preferences.

Thus far, we have restricted ourselves, for the most part, to the rational model. For instance, in chapter 2, we discussed adverse selection, when high-risk consumers exhibit the greatest demand for generous insurance. Such a model requires rational behavior: those high-risk consumers recognize that they are better off with expensive insurance and so choose accordingly. In the same way, when we discussed moral hazard in chapter 4, we focused on how people buy more healthcare once insurance makes it cheaper. That also assumes rational behavior: people carefully take price into account when choosing their healthcare.

Reality is complex, and so both rational models and behavioral models may be relevant, though for different people in different contexts. Still, over the past few decades, a new wave of "behavioral economists" have demonstrated how often the rational model falls short. Quite a few of those contexts are in healthcare, contexts in which economists have to leave the rational model behind.

Default Bias

Let's start with a decision that many Americans face when they register for a new driver's license. They go to the registry in their state, they wait in line for three minutes short of eternity, they fill out paperwork, they take a driving test, and then they, eventually, are handed a new driver's license. But just before their new license is printed, they are asked one last question: "Would you like to be an organ donor?"

Roughly half of Americans say yes—they become organ donors. The other half choose not to become organ donors (Penn Medicine, 2022). Are those Americans making a rational choice? Is the organ donation question like the "chocolate or vanilla" question—just a matter of choosing whichever option best matches your preferences?

In some countries, no one is ever asked "Would you like to be an organ donor?" Instead, in those countries, everyone is automatically enrolled as an organ donor, and they have to actively choose *not* to be an organ donor. Such a policy is sometimes called "automatic enrollment" or an "opt-out policy." The question is not "Would you like to be an organ donor?"; rather, the question is "Would you like to opt out of being an organ donor?"

Automatic enrollment has an enormous effect on the share of people who choose to become organ donors. Countries with opt-out organ donation programs have organ donation rates that are well over 95 percent, whereas countries in which people have to opt-in to organ donation have organ donation rates well under 30 percent (fig. 5.1).

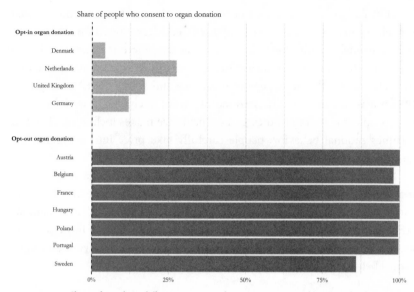

FIGURE 5.1. Share of people in different countries who consent to organ donation. The figure groups countries where people "opt in" to organ donation and countries where people are defaulted into organ donation and must "opt out."

That pattern is difficult to reconcile with the rational model. A rational consumer would weigh the costs and benefits of becoming an organ donor and then choose whichever option they preferred. That rational consumer wouldn't care whether they faced an opt-in program or an opt-out program: they would just choose whichever option aligned with their preferences. It would be simple: chocolate or vanilla? And yet, opt-out programs really do induce more people to become organ donors.

Dick Thaler and Cass Sunstein popularized opt-out programs as "nudges." Automatic enrollment, they say, "nudges" people to become organ donors. Thaler and Sunstein's book, appropriately titled *Nudge*, has led businesses and policymakers around the world to ask how their organizations might employ nudging to shape behavior.

The publication of *Nudge* led to an interest in nudges throughout healthcare. Organ donation is one of several places in healthcare where a nudge could be employed. Many people believe that the United States ought to switch to an opt-out system for organ donation rather than its current opt-in system. There might be many other contexts in which automatic enrollment would improve health-related behaviors. What if patients were automatically enrolled in appointments for a flu vaccine? One study experimented with exactly that and found a big increase in vaccination rates (Patel et al. 2017).

The discussion even extends to school cafeterias (Goto et al. 2013; Hanks et al. 2012; Just and Price 2013; Liu et al. 2014). Typically, there is no default option in a cafeteria. The server behind the counter asks, ". . . and what to drink?" Imagine instead if every cafeteria visitor were automatically given a glass of water. Sure, you could have soda, but you'd have to ask for it—the default option would be a glass of water.

There's something appealing about these kinds of policies. They're not "shoves," they're "nudges." Everyone in line at the cafeteria is free to drink whatever they want, they just have to opt out of the glass of water. The path of least resistance is the healthy option, but everyone is free to choose whichever path they'd like.

And yet, there are limits to nudging in healthcare. There are only so many contexts in which one choice can be singled out as worthy of becoming the default option. Sure, when it comes to the binary decision of becoming an organ donor or not, it makes sense to automatically enroll everyone in organ donation. And when new employees have to decide between enrolling in a retirement plan or not, automatically enroll all new employees in the retirement plan (Madrian and Shea 2001). And, sure, in the cafeteria, have the default option be a glass of water.

But there are many other contexts in which it's hard to nudge. When people have to choose an insurance plan, it's unclear which plan ought to be the default. Some people are lucky to be very healthy, and so a cheap, narrow-network plan is best for them. Other people are very attached to a particular doctor, and so they need a plan that includes that doctor in its network. There's no way to pick out one health insurance plan and argue that it ought to be the default option for everyone. The same is true for many other contexts: choosing a doctor, choosing treatment plans, so on and so forth.

Plan Choice

"OK, let's see. First, we have your I-9 form, then your W-4, then a consent statement, you have to choose an email address, we need an emergency contact . . . and that should finish your onboarding." The HR rep lays out the forms in front of you.

"Oh and one more thing." He forgot one more thing. "You need to pick a health insurance plan."

For health economists, this is where the fun starts. How do you pick a health insurance plan? Well, to start with, you pick a plan that will cover all of the healthcare that you will need. So pick the plan that includes your primary-care physician in its network. And pick a plan that covers that expensive medication you take each morning. And maybe look at which hospitals are in each plan's network: choose the plan that covers your favorite hospital.

Now, suppose that the plans all have the same network and cover the same drugs. There's still work to be done. The plans differ in their premiums—how much you have to pay each month—and in terms of their cost sharing: deductibles, copayment, and coinsurance rates. How do you handle all of those numbers?

It might be tempting to just focus on the premium. Maybe just choose the plan with the lowest premium? Or maybe choose the plan with the middle premium, a Goldilocks strategy? Either way, that would be focusing only on part of the cost of the plan—the premium, not the cost sharing.

The proper way to choose a plan is to consider both the premium and the cost sharing. Figure out the total cost of each plan: the plan's premium *plus* the fees you will have to pay to buy the medications and visits that you'll likely consume.

And yet, people do not do that. Jason Abaluck and Jon Gruber have written a series of papers about the Medicare Part D program. The two economists were interested in Medicare Part D because it involves a complex plan-choice problem. When most Americans turn sixty-five, they enroll in Medicare Part D for their drug coverage. In most states, they have a choice of about forty Part D plans. Each plan has a different premium and also a different formula for mapping drugs to out-of-pocket fees.

How does one choose among forty drug-coverage plans? In theory, there's a lot of work involved. A person has to take every drug that they need and calculate the out-of-pocket payments for that drug for each plan. Then, add those out-of-pocket payments to each plan's premium to calculate the total out-of-pocket cost of the plan. Then, think about the insurance value of each plan: If the person hits a medical emergency in the middle of the year and so is prescribed more drugs, how much protection will each plan provide?

Fortunately, Medicare offers an automated phone system and a website to do all of this work for each recipient. These types of calculations, after all, are hard for people but easy for computers. So all ordinary Medicare recipients have to do is recognize that it's not obvious which plan is best for them, and then turn to the website or the phone system to advise them on the best choice.

And yet, Abaluck and Gruber find that most Medicare recipients don't do that. People tend to fixate on the plans' premiums, ignoring each plan's expected out-of-pocket payments. On average, they could save $300 a year by choosing a better plan (Handel and Schwartzstein 2018).

In other words, choosing an insurance plan is not simply a matter of rational choice. People tend to do a lousy job of choosing a plan—it is not a matter of vanilla versus chocolate. And so economists cannot solely rely on the rational model when it comes to contexts in which people have to choose insurance plans. It's more complicated than that.

Inertia

Not only are people lousy at choosing insurance plans—they are also lousy when it comes to *leaving* those insurance plans. Here's the thing about most plans: the details change from year to year. The plan's premium tends to rise year over year. Also, the care that the plan covers can change over time. And, for that matter, people's health changes over time.

Due to all of those changes year after year, a careful consumer ought to reevaluate whether they are in the right insurance plan every year. "I chose this plan two years ago, and since then, the premium has increased 20 percent and I've been prescribed a statin. Is this still the best plan for me?"

And yet do people actually reevaluate their choices that way? The path of least resistance is to do nothing and just stay in the same plan. Indeed, a variety of studies have found that when it comes to insurance plans, people tend to be remarkably "inertial." They choose insurance plans and then tend to stick to them year after year.

Tal bought a house five years ago, when moving to the Boston area to join Boston University. Houses require homeowners' insurance, and so Tal went online and found an insurance broker in the area. The broker recommended a particular insurer for both Tal's new home and his new Subaru. When it was time to close on the new house, Tal sat down with the realtors and lawyers to sign all of the paperwork. The insurance broker showed up, too. She brought homemade brownies for the occasion. The brownies were delicious, which was fitting, since they cost thousands of dollars. It's now been five years, and Tal is still enrolled in the same insurance plan and the broker has gotten a commission each year. There is surely a plan that is better by now. But things are always hectic and this book is not going to write itself. And so a health economist, who is well versed on "consumer inertia in plan choice," ends up being inertial himself.

Consumer inertia is not just an academic curiosity, it's also a business opportunity. Tal's insurance broker went to the trouble of baking brownies because she knew that this one new customer would be generating revenue for her for quite some time. The same is true in the markets for other plans.

Consider, again, Medicare Part D plans. The managers that operate Part D

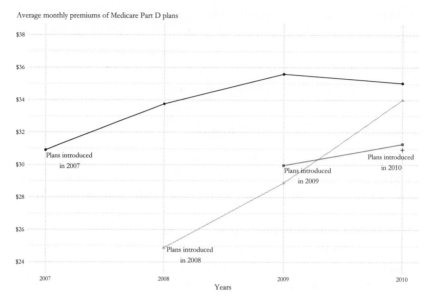

Average monthly premiums of Medicare Part D plans

FIGURE 5.2. Average Medicare Part D prices for plans introduced in different years.

plans understand that people have forty plans to choose from, and that once they make a choice, they tend to stick to that plan for years. And so the managers have developed a particular strategy for how to price those plans. Sometimes the strategy is called "invest-then-harvest" pricing. Sometimes—and this is a much more fun way to describe it—the strategy is called "bargains-then-ripoffs" pricing (Farrell and Klemperer 2007).

To see what those terms mean, consider figure 5.2, which was compiled by Keith Ericson (2014) with data on Medicare Part D plans. When plans are introduced, they tend to charge low monthly premiums. Those low monthly premiums attract Medicare Part D recipients. After all, when people are making an active choice across forty Part D plans, they are very focused on those premiums. That's the "bargain" step: the plans are introduced with especially low premiums.

But then, every year after, managers raise premiums. Ericson finds that, all else equal, a plan that has been around for three years has a premium that is 13 percent more expensive than a plan in its first year. By their fourth year, plans are nearly 20 percent more expensive than new plans. That's the "ripoff" stage of the pricing strategy. That's when the initial "investment" of low premiums pays off, when the harvesting happens.

It doesn't have to be this way. If Medicare recipients weren't inertial—if people were careful to reevaluate their plans each year—then such a strategy wouldn't pay off. And so this pattern in the data leads to concrete advice for both policymakers and for ordinary people.

Policymakers might consider intervening to counteract invest-then-harvest pricing. Some policy experts have proposed requiring some consumers to make an active choice every now and then (Sunstein 2015). That is to say, take people who would otherwise be inertial and force them to reevaluate the plan choice they made years ago.

Meanwhile, the advice for ordinary consumers is simply not to fall into this trap. Sit down every year and reevaluate whether or not your plan is still the best one for you. Then again, neither of us has switched homeowners' insurance plans in quite some time. Do what we say, not what we do.

Commitment Mechanisms

In graduate school, Noto went through a phase where he had a tough time getting up early each morning. Noto had few commitments in the morning—he did not teach that semester and meetings with his thesis advisers were scheduled for the afternoons. This made it difficult to get out of bed each morning. Noto's ambition was to jump out of bed at 6:00 each morning and get an early start on the day. In practice, he kept hitting the snooze button until he limped out of bed at 7:00.

Behavioral economists sometimes describe such a problem as a conflict between two selves. First, there's the present self: Noto lying in bed, warm, relaxed, and hitting snooze. Second, there's the future self: Noto during the day, anxious to get work done and wanting to be able to call himself an early riser. When Noto would decide to hit the snooze button, he would do so to benefit his present self at the expense of his future self.

To understand the conflict between those two selves, consider two questions posed by the behavioral economist Dick Thaler (1981):

1. Which would you rather have, one apple today or two apples tomorrow?
2. Which would you rather have, one apple in one year, or two apples in one year plus one day?

A rational, "time consistent" consumer would view those two choices in the same way. If you can think through the tricky phrasing of the second question, it turns out that in both cases, it's a matter of waiting a day to get an extra apple. But an irrational, "time inconsistent" consumer would view the two questions very differently. The first question is a matter of the present self versus the future self: I can have an apple *now* or else my future self gets two apples tomorrow. By contrast, the second question is all a matter of the future self: my future self in one year and my future self in one year plus one day.

In that sense, irrational consumers might treat the present differently from other time periods, because the present is a matter of the present self, whereas the future involves the future self. Noto hits the snooze button now, even though it might hurt his present self later.

And so behavioral economists suggest one way to grapple with such a problem. The problem amounts to a conflict between the present self and the future self, and so the solution must change the balance of power between those two selves. At 6:00 a.m., Noto's present self has a choice between an hour more of bliss and giving his future self some pride and satisfaction. That choice is easy: bliss. What if the choice were harder? What if there were some way to shift the incentives so that the present self starts to make a different choice?

Back in graduate school, Noto came to Tal with an offer. Every time Noto slept in, he would pay Tal $20. That's it: that was the deal. Tal agreed.

Such an arrangement is sometimes called a "commitment contract." The goal is to shift the calculus performed by the present self. Before the commitment contract, 6:00 a.m. offers the present self a choice between another hour of sleep and giving the future self some satisfaction. Once the commitment contract is in place, 6:00 a.m. offers the present self a choice between another hour of sleep and the future self losing $20. If that's not sufficient, then $20 could be $200 or $2,000. (We were graduate students at the time, and $20 was plenty.)

Some behavioral economists argue that commitment contracts might offer a useful intervention to encourage healthy behaviors. For instance, three behavioral economists—Xavier Giné, Dean Karlan, and Jon Zinman (2010)—designed a commitment contract to encourage people to quit smoking. The research team worked with a bank in the Philippines that wanted to encourage healthier behavior among its customers.

Bank customers who smoked were offered the following deal. The customers would make weekly deposits in a special bank account. After six months, the bank would give the client a urine test. If the test did not detect nicotine or cotinine byproducts, then the customer had probably successfully quit smoking. In that case, the bank would give the client the money back. If the test revealed that the client was still smoking, then the money would be donated to charity.

That's it—that's the deal. Over six months, we'll take your money. If you actually quit smoking, then we'll give it back to you. No rational person would ever sign such a contract. To a rational person, such a contract would be entirely silly—the bank is not actually providing a service: it's not even giving interest. The bank is only offering to do something that, in theory, anyone can do themselves. Anyone could, on their own, save their money over six months and then donate it to charity.

And yet, this silly contract actually got some people to quit smoking. The research team randomly assigned bank customers to be offered the contract. Those who were offered the contract were 3 percentage points more likely to have quit smoking after six months than those who were not offered the contract. Customers who wanted to quit smoking were actually interested in this silly contract and it got them to quit smoking.

Back in graduate school, Noto slept in twice and had to hand over two $20 bills to Tal. But that $40 loss spurred Noto to be more disciplined. Eventually, he became an early riser.

Behavioral Hazard

In chapter 4, we described the moral hazard problem inherent in health insurance: healthcare becomes so cheap that people consume healthcare that they barely value. That phenomenon is real. There exist many types of low-value care, and when it is made free of charge, people don't hesitate. Indeed, we described the RAND Health Insurance Experiment, which demonstrated that people consume much less healthcare on high-deductible plans and, on average, do not seem to be hurt by that reduction in healthcare.

That said, the issue is much more complicated than just moral hazard. There's ample reason to suspect that many people don't make rational decisions when it comes to their healthcare (Baicker, Mullainathan, and Schwartzstein 2015). For instance, people who suffer from diabetes can live longer and avoid amputations and blindness if only they take their medication. And yet most estimates suggest that fewer than 70 percent of diabetics reliably take their medication (DiMatteo 2004). There are also examples of the opposite phenomenon: people demanding medications that are expensive and yet not useful. For instance, patients seek antibiotics for ear infections even though physicians believe such a treatment is a bad idea (Spiro et al. 2006).

As another example, consider ER visits. The emergency room is the appropriate place to treat a gunshot wound or a suspected heart attack, but it's not a good place to treat bronchitis. And yet, many people end up in the ER for all sorts of reasons, from real emergencies to situations that are very much not emergencies.

A group of medical researchers in the 1990s studied the introduction of a $25 to $35 copayment for visiting the ER (Selby, Fireman, and Swain 1996).

Now, from the perspective of moral hazard, such a copayment is a good idea—again, we are referring back to chapter 4 on this. The copayment will raise the price of care, reducing the number of low-value ER visits. The researchers found evidence for such an effect: the copayment lowered nonemergency visits to the ER by 21 percent. *But* it also lowered the number of emergency visits by nearly 10 percent. The $25 fee kept people from coming to the ER for serious conditions that really need to be treated in the ER: coronary arrest, heart attack, appendicitis, and so on.

Kate Baicker, Sendhil Mullainathan, and Josh Schwartzstein argue that such an effect demonstrates what they call "behavioral hazard." In contrast to moral hazard, behavioral hazard is the misuse of care for reasons other than price (Baicker, Mullainathan, and Schwartzstein 2015). Sure, some people exhibit behavior that is consistent with the rational model, responding to copayments by reducing their consumption of low-value care. But others, the researchers argue, are clearly behaving in a manner that cannot be rationalized.

For example, consider people at high risk of coronary heart disease not taking their cholesterol-lowering medications because of a $10 copayment. Baicker, Mullainathan, and Schwartzstein argue that health economists ought to turn to behavioral economists for guidance on how to deal with this. Perhaps copayments and deductibles ought to be much more complicated. Sometimes, maybe copayments should even go negative: some patients should be paid to consume care that they really need. For that matter, behavioral economists believe that more needs to be done beyond simply setting deductibles. Nudges, coaching, reminders, and other interventions are necessary to make sure people receive the healthcare that they need.

The Bottom Line

These days, behavioral economics is one of the most vibrant areas of research. In healthcare, behavioral economists have made two main contributions. First, researchers have developed interventions that can guide people toward healthier options. We've described two of those interventions: nudges and commitment mechanisms.

Second, behavioral economists have documented the ways that people make poor health-related decisions. One is in plan choice: just deciding on an insurance plan is a remarkably difficult task that people handle poorly. We also described behavioral hazard: people forget to take their pills, when they face a true emergency they don't visit the ER, and they ignore their doctor's advice.

And so we know where there is a need for yet more interventions. The first step is to show that people forget to take their meds. The second step, which is where we are now, is to figure out how to nudge them to remember. It's there, in that second step, that research is ongoing.

References

Abaluck, Jason, and Jonathan Gruber. "Choice Inconsistencies among the Elderly: Evidence from Plan Choice in the Medicare Part D Program." *American Economic Review* 101, no. 4 (2011): 1180–210.

———. "Evolving Choice Inconsistencies in Choice of Prescription Drug Insurance." *American Economic Review* 106, no. 8 (2016): 2145–84.

Baicker, Katherine, Sendhil Mullainathan, and Joshua Schwartzstein. "Behavioral Hazard in Health Insurance." *Quarterly Journal of Economics* 130, no. 4 (2015): 1623–67. https://doi.org/10.1093/qje/qjv029.

DiMatteo, M. Robin. "Variations in Patients' Adherence to Medical Recommendations: A Quantitative Review of 50 Years of Research." *Medical Care* 42, no. 3 (2004): 200–209.

Ericson, Keith Marzilli. "Consumer Inertia and Firm Pricing in the Medicare Part D Prescription Drug Insurance Exchange." *American Economic Journal: Economic Policy* 6, no. 2 (2014): 38–64. https://doi.org/10.1257/pol.6.1.38.

Farrell, Joseph, and Paul Klemperer. "Chapter 31 Coordination and Lock-In: Competition with Switching Costs and Network Effects." In *Handbook of Industrial Organization*, edited by M. Armstrong and R. Porter, 3: 1967–2072. Elsevier, 2007. https://doi.org/10.1016/S1573-448X(06)03031-7.

Giné, Xavier, Dean Karlan, and Jonathan Zinman. "Put Your Money Where Your Butt Is: A Commitment Contract for Smoking Cessation." *American Economic Journal: Applied Economics* 2, no. 4 (2010): 213–35. https://doi.org/10.1257/app.2.4.213.

Goto, Keiko, Alexandra Waite, Cindy Wolff, Kenny Chan, and Maria Giovanni. "Do Environmental Interventions Impact Elementary School Students' Lunchtime Milk Selection?" *Applied Economic Perspectives and Policy* 35, no. 2 (2013): 360–76. https://doi.org/10.1093/aepp/ppt004.

Handel, Benjamin, and Joshua Schwartzstein. "Frictions or Mental Gaps: What's Behind the Information We (Don't) Use and When Do We Care?" *Journal of Economic Perspectives* 32, no. 1 (2018): 155–78.

Hanks, Andrew S., David R. Just, Laura E. Smith, and Brian Wansink. "Healthy Convenience: Nudging Students toward Healthier Choices in the Lunchroom." *Journal of Public Health* 34, no. 3 (2012): 370–76. https://doi.org/10.1093/pubmed/fds003.

Johnson, Eric J., and Daniel Goldstein. "Do Defaults Save Lives?" *Science* 302, no. 5649 (2003): 1338–39. https://doi.org/10.1126/science.1091721.

Just, David, and Joseph Price. "Default Options, Incentives and Food Choices: Evidence from Elementary-School Children." *Public Health Nutrition* 16, no. 12 (2013): 2281–88. https://doi.org/10.1017/S1368980013001468.

Liu, Peggy J., Jessica Wisdom, Christina A. Roberto, Linda J. Liu, and Peter A. Ubel. "Using Behavioral Economics to Design More Effective Food Policies to Address Obesity." *Applied Economic Perspectives and Policy* 36, no. 1 (2014): 6–24. https://doi.org/10.1093/aepp/ppt027.

Madrian, Brigitte C., and Dennis F. Shea. "The Power of Suggestion: Inertia in 401(k) Participation and Savings Behavior." *Quarterly Journal of Economics* 116, no. 4 (2001): 1149–87. https://doi.org/10.1162/003355301753265543.

Patel, Mitesh S., Kevin G. Volpp, Dylan S. Small, Craig Wynne, Jingsan Zhu, Lin Yang, Steven Honeywell, and Susan C. Day. "Using Active Choice within the Electronic Health Record to Increase Influenza Vaccination Rates." *Journal of General Internal Medicine* 32, no. 7 (2017): 790–95. https://doi.org/10.1007/s11606-017-4046-6.

Selby, Joe V., Bruce H. Fireman, and Bix E. Swain. "Effect of a Copayment on Use of the Emergency Department in a Health Maintenance Organization." *New England Journal of Medicine* 334, no. 10 (1996): 635–42. https://doi.org/10.1056/NEJM199603073341006.

"Six Quick Facts about Organ Donation—Penn Medicine." *Penn Medicine* (blog). March 26, 2022. https://www.pennmedicine.org/updates/blogs/transplant-update/2022/march/6-quick-facts-about-organ-donation.

Spiro, David M., Khoon-Yen Tay, Donald H. Arnold, James D. Dziura, Mark D. Baker, and Eugene D. Shapiro. "Wait-and-See Prescription for the Treatment of Acute Otitis Media: A Randomized Controlled Trial." *JAMA* 296, no. 10 (2006): 1235–41. https://doi.org/10.1001/jama.296.10.1235.

Sunstein, Cass R. "Active Choosing or Default Rules? The Policymaker's Dilemma." *Behavioral Science and Policy* 1, no. 1 (2015): 29–33. https://doi.org/10.1353/bsp.2015.0009.

Thaler, Richard. "Some Empirical Evidence on Dynamic Inconsistency." *Economics Letters* 8, no. 3 (1981): 201–7. https://doi.org/10.1016/0165-1765(81)90067-7.

PART II

Supply

How Much Should Physicians Be Paid?

You board the plane and sit down, preparing yourself for the long flight. You've got a couple magazines, a book, plus some work on your laptop. You are looking forward to hours of productivity and movie watching and book reading. And then, the man next to you opens his mouth. He starts talking to you, and he does not stop. "Hi. I'm a vegan, I do CrossFit, and I'd like to talk to you about bitcoin."

Decades ago, a sociologist at the University of Chicago discovered a solution.[1] When your neighbor on the flight mentions his work, which will happen sooner or later, turn to him and ask a simple question. "Interesting! How much money do you make?" That, according to the sociologist, will shut him up.

In the United States, the open discussion of salaries is taboo. And so one of the most uncomfortable topics in healthcare is physicians' salaries. Physicians don't enjoy it when researchers point out that their occupation is one of the most common among America's wealthiest 1 percent. Average salaries for physicians are well over four times the average household income.[2]

We emphasize at the outset that physicians do important, difficult work. The two of us sit down to write this chapter in good health. If disaster were to strike, and one of us was rushed to an operating room, we would *not* be worried that the salaries of those treating us were too high. Instead, as a surgeon picked up a scalpel in an effort to save us, we would think to ourselves: "whatever this person is being paid, it's not enough."

Physicians do heroic work. The COVID-19 pandemic made that heroic work more visible, harder, and more dangerous. In addition, *becoming* a physician is incredibly difficult and, in a sense, involves a kind of hazing. It's hard to find occupations that require so many years of training, so many hours up front while paid less than the minimum wage, and, really, so much anguish.

That said, it is important to talk about physician pay. Physicians' salaries comprise nearly 10 percent of healthcare spending. If we care about healthcare spending, which is nearly a fifth of *all* spending, then we have to care about physicians' salaries. So let's have that uncomfortable conversation.

How Much Money Do Physicians Make?

Doctors enjoy high salaries, and remarkably few of them ever experience unemployment. In 2017, the average salary among physicians was about $340,000. A quarter of physicians were in the top 1 percent of the income distribution and half were in the top 2 percent (Gottlieb et al. 2020; Brooks 2021).

That high average salary for all physicians conceals tremendous variation *among* physicians. About 30 percent of physicians provide primary care (Antono et al. 2021). Those physicians make an average of $243,000 a year. Meanwhile, many specialists earn much more. Anesthesiologists, for instance, earn nearly $400,000 a year on average, and surgeons earn an average of half-a-million dollars a year.

What is striking here is not the absolute numbers but rather the relative magnitudes. Anesthesiologists, surgeons, and dermatologists earn roughly twice what primary-care physicians earn each year. These doctors were all classmates in medical school—they all took the same exams and shared the same post-exam pitcher of beer. And yet their earnings dramatically diverged depending on which path they chose out of medical school.

Years ago, Tal was teaching a health economics class and started the session by writing average salaries on the blackboard. A surgical resident was sitting in the front row and immediately became agitated. "Hold on, it's not fair to just list salaries like that!"

Now, Tal was simply jotting down some average salaries to start the discussion—why the sudden outburst? Over time, we've come to understand that any discussion of physicians' salaries makes physicians very uncomfortable. And, in fairness, we need to acknowledge some complications.

First off, the dollar figures above are *salaries*, not hourly wages, and physicians work long hours doing very difficult work. So, to start with, solely looking at annual earnings would be incomplete. If one person makes twice as much money a year, but also works twice as many hours, then focusing on the total salary alone is not the way to go.

It's also important to acknowledge that high salaries alone should not trigger resentment. Physicians are highly trained and provide some of the most important services that any person can provide another. In the most frightening moments of life—a cancer diagnosis, a heart attack—we turn to physicians for help.

In addition, it's important to recognize that these high salaries come after years of training. Take about 98 percent of Americans and offer them a salary of half-a-million dollars a year. Such a salary would sound terrific to nearly all of them. When you add that the hours are long and the work difficult, the job becomes somewhat less attractive. Oh, and then one more thing: that salary comes after, say, fourteen years of working extremely hard and earning very little: college, then medical school, then residency, then fellowship. All of a sudden, the job starts to seem less cushy. How much less cushy? We go through some numbers below.

That said, 9 percent of American healthcare costs are accounted for by physician earnings. By comparison, pharmaceutical costs account for about 15 percent. It is important for us to study physician salaries just as it is important for us to study pharmaceutical spending (which we do in chap. 12). No part of the healthcare system is exempt from analysis.

How Much Should Barbers Be Paid?

Imagine a world in which everyone is paid the same salary. Every adult brings in the same money each year, no matter what they do for a living. Everyone gets the same paycheck each week.

In such a world, we might find a lot to admire. There would be less envy and jealousy. Conspicuous consumption would disappear: fewer mansions, fewer sports cars. And, more importantly, poverty would cease to exist. Everyone would be in the same boat, and all children would be brought up with the same financial resources.

But in such a world, there would be something missing. There is something useful about inequality in pay. Inequality in salaries creates an incentive for people to work hard and so reap the financial reward. Eliminating salary inequality entirely would reduce the incentive to undergo expensive training. To become a dentist, it takes four years of dental school plus another two to three years of residency if you want to specialize. To become an internist, it takes four years of medical school, then three years of residency. And most extreme of all, to become a neurosurgeon: four years of medical school and then seven years of residency. If all salaries were identical, why would anyone undergo those years of training? Yes, there is joy in being a highly trained professional. And so perhaps some might enter these professions irrespective of salary. But for many others, a world with only one salary would mean avoiding professions that require years of training.

That said, it is also possible to have too much of a good thing. Imagine, alternatively, a world in which every hairdresser is paid 10 million dollars a year.[3] Yes—this is a juvenile hypothetical, but bear with us for a moment.[4] Suppose that every student graduating beauty school is given 10 million dollars each year until they retire. They need to work a solid forty hours a week, and in return, they are given 10 million dollars a year for the haircuts they provide their customers. What then?

First, we would all stop tipping our hairdressers. Second, many of us would drop everything and become hairdressers ourselves. What profession can top a guaranteed $10 million a year? And that influx of students would then lead to many more hairdressers. With so many new hairdressers, surely the $10 million salaries would have to decrease.

So in this hypothetical world, in order to address these issues, we would have to add a complication: restrictions on supply. There would be strict limits on the number of cosmetology schools. And, for that matter, very few students would be allowed into beauty school each year. What's more, to preserve the $10 million salaries, there would have to be some type of limit on *who* can provide haircuts. It would be against the law to cut people's hair without a license.[5] Only graduates from accredited beauty schools would be allowed to give haircuts. And foreign hairdressers would be prohibited from immigrating here and competing with American hairdressers.

How ought we to think about such a world with tremendous inequality, a world in which a select few are allowed into the lucrative role of hairdressers? There are benefits to that inequality: there would be a large incentive to take on the difficult work of becoming a hairdresser. Beauty schools, in such a world, would attract the best students. And so bad haircuts would no longer exist. All sideburns would be perfectly pruned, all bangs even.

But, of course, such a world would involve too much inequality. With so few hairdressers, haircuts would be too expensive. And perhaps there would be something *unfair* about such high salaries for hairdressers. Those high salaries would be maintained by restrictions on supply—by artificial limits on who is allowed to become a hairdresser.

Those two scenarios are extremes along a spectrum. On one extreme, we have perfect equality: experts are paid the same salary as nonexperts. In that case, we have a problem: too little incentive to train and so too little inequality. At the other extreme, we have guaranteed $10 million salaries. In that case, experts are paid way too much, and restrictions on supply maintain those salaries. There we have too much inequality.

Both too much and too little inequality can be an issue. Highly trained experts should make more money than nonexperts. But it's also possible that they can make too much more, that they can be overpaid.

Market and Nonmarket Forces

One has to be careful in labeling anyone as "overpaid." What does it even mean to be overpaid? After all, what is a fair salary above which one can be overpaid? We cannot say what anyone "should" be paid. What we can do, however, is point out when salaries are determined by *market forces* and when salaries are determined by *nonmarket forces*.

If any of our hypothetical, highly paid hairdressers happen to be curious as to how their salary is determined, economists would structure the conversation around two pieces. First, there are market forces. There are millions of Americans who are willing to pay good money for a good haircut—we can call that "demand." Then, there are only so many Americans who are able and willing to go through the difficult and tedious training of becoming a hairdresser. In other words, there exists a limited supply of competing hairdressers. The free market balances supply against demand and that determines hairdressers' salary.

Those market forces may adjust over time. If, somehow, there is an influx of new hairdressers, then salaries will go down. If, alternatively, Americans suddenly demand more complicated haircuts, then salaries will go up. The market is often in flux and so salaries can fluctuate.

So that's one piece: market forces are a key determinant of salaries. But there's also a second piece, what we might refer to as "nonmarket forces." In all states, you can only work as a hairdresser if you are licensed. And local hairdressers tend to lobby the state government to keep those licenses limited. Until 2019, Arizona had a license just for blow-dry specialists: you couldn't work a blow dryer in Arizona without spending a thousand hours training to earn your license. Really: a thousand hours of training, and if you practice (again: blow drying) without a license, up to six months in prison as a penalty ("Governor Ducey Signs 'Blow Dry Freedom Bill'" 2019).

Those licensing restrictions limit the supply of practicing hairdressers and so raise salaries. And those licensing restrictions do not organically arise from the market. They come from current hairdressers in each state lobbying the government to impose them.[6] That is why we refer to them as *nonmarket* forces.

Take any professional anywhere—a hairdresser, a doctor, a pilot, a lawyer. We can describe their salary as determined by those two factors: market forces and nonmarket forces. In most occupations, the best professionals make a good living, and they earn that living because there are few competitors who are as talented as they are. In addition, they earn a good living because there are many customers willing to pay top dollar for their talent. That's market forces at work.

But often other forces will further raise those salaries. There are occupational licensing requirements. For lawyers, there's the bar exam—for hairdressers, state-regulated licenses. There are limits on accredited schools to train those professionals. It is very difficult to open a new law school or a new medical school. Some professionals are covered by unions that bargain over the salaries of their members. Public-sector employees are paid salaries that are often determined by law. And so on and so forth.

Physicians and Market Forces

Let's put hairdressers aside and talk about physicians. What market forces determine physicians' salaries? Well, to start with, it takes a long time to become a physician. Much of that training is required by the American Medical Association (AMA) and medical specialty boards, but the job would take a lot of training in any case. And when a profession requires more training, then trainees will only choose to take on that training if there's a payoff at the end of it.

That dynamic is a matter of market forces, of supply and demand. Imagine a profession that requires five years of training and that pays the same salary as professions that require no training. Very few young people would choose such a profession. That would then lead to a decrease in supply: fewer people entering the profession. And so that decrease in supply would then raise salaries. In other words, market forces will lead salaries to adjust so that occupations that require more training also offer higher salaries.

And, in fact, there exists a positive correlation between years of training and salaries. Consider figure 6.1, which comes from a paper by Josh Gottlieb, Maria Polyakova, Kevin Rinz, Hugh Shiplett, and Victoria Udalova. That team of researchers compiled a unique data set with nearly all American physicians' salaries. The figure compares the average training for each type of physician to their average annual income. Among physicians, family practitioners earn the lowest average salaries, a paltry average of $200,000 a year. On the other extreme, neurosurgeons earn an average of over $600,000 a year. Part of that difference can be explained by the difference in training: it takes a three-year residency to become a family practitioner but a seven-year residency to become a neurosurgeon. And so, naturally, market forces will lead neurosurgeons' salaries to be higher.

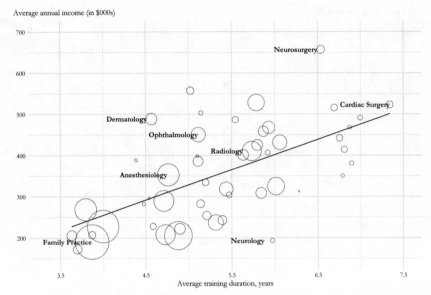

FIGURE 6.1. Correlation between the average annual income and the average years of training for different types of physicians. The solid line is the best-fit regression line.

Another way in which market forces adjust salaries is in response to workload. All else equal, if one profession requires many more hours each week than another, it will command a higher salary. Again, supply and demand might explain such a correlation: if the two salaries were the same, fewer young entrants would enter the more demanding profession, and that reduction in supply would then raise the profession's average salary.

Indeed, that dynamic appears to be in play when comparing physicians' salaries. Figure 6.2 compares average salaries across medical specialties with average weekly hours. Neurosurgeons are paid much more each year as compared to family practitioners, but they also work many more hours each week: an average of over sixty hours a week as compared to under fifty.

Figures 6.1 and 6.2 compare different types of physicians and demonstrate market forces at work. But the same patterns exist if one compares physicians, as a whole, to other professionals. The average salary for physicians vastly surpasses the average salary for all college graduates. Much of that difference can be explained by hours and much of it can be explained by training.

Physicians and Nonmarket Forces: Supply Restrictions

So physician salaries vary in ways that are consistent with market forces: more hours mean higher salaries and more training means higher salaries.

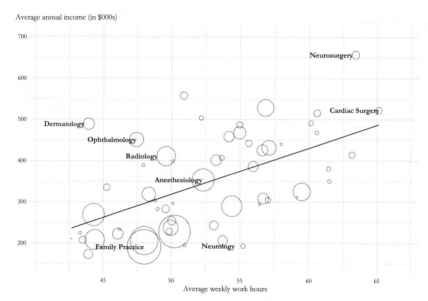

FIGURE 6.2. Correlation between the average annual income and the average weekly hours of work for different types of physicians. The solid line is the best-fit regression line.

That said, physicians' salaries are *not* determined by an entirely free market. Market forces are only part of what shapes the money that physicians earn.

Let's briefly turn to Alaskan dentistry. (Bear with us.) A dentist could move to Angoon, Alaska, which has a population under five hundred. But the non-marine-mammal population in Angoon is small and the locals are not very wealthy. Many people in the area desperately need dental care, but there may not be enough of those people to sustain a traditional dental practice.[7] If a dentist has, say, $300,000 in student loans and has to purchase a million dollars' worth of equipment to start a practice, opening that practice in Angoon may not be a good business idea.[8]

And so, as a result, a new type of profession has arisen: the "dental therapist." Dental therapists are not dentists—they receive three years of training rather than eight (Corr 2019). And so there are many dental procedures that they are not trained to do. When a patient needs one of those procedures, the dental therapist is trained to send them elsewhere. But dental therapists *are* trained to perform basic treatments and preventive services. And rigorous evaluations of dental therapists have found that they provide safe and effective care (Wetterhall et al. 2010).

The profession of dental therapists offers a solution to what would otherwise be a tricky problem. How do low-income people in rural areas gain access to dental care? Many sparsely populated rural areas cannot sustain a dental practice and it can be very expensive to transport a dentist out to rural areas intermittently. For that reason, several states—Alaska, Minnesota, Maine, and Vermont—are experimenting with dental therapists.

But organized dentists, represented by the American Dental Association, the ADA, are adamantly against dental therapists. In most states, dental therapists are *illegal*.[9] The ADA views dental therapists as a threat and has lobbied state governments to shut them down.

Should we view those moves by the ADA through a cynical lens? Fewer dental therapists means, unquestionably, less access to dental care. Without dental therapists, it would be impossible for people in Angoon, Alaska, to have quick access to dental care. But dental therapists also do something else—they threaten dentists' income. If dental therapists were allowed to set up shop everywhere, they would absorb a lot of paid work that is currently done in dentists' offices.

This phenomenon is certainly not limited to dentistry. Consider nurse practitioners, NPs, who are to physicians what dental therapists are to dentists. NPs have five-and-a-half to seven years of training as opposed to the eleven years of training of primary-care physicians (Primary Care Coalition 2010). Like dental therapists, NPs are trained to recognize the limits of their expertise and to refer patients to physicians when their patients need a more highly trained provider.

In 2000, the *Journal of the American Medical Association* published a randomized trial. Over a thousand patients at a walk-in clinic were randomly assigned to either a primary-care physician or a nurse practitioner. The research team, led by Mary Mundinger of the Columbia School of Nursing, studied patient satisfaction along with all of the patients' follow-up care after the visit. Now, if NPs provided significantly poorer care than physicians, you might expect to see more of their patients end up in emergency rooms after treatment. And yet the research team found no evidence for that. Overall, there was no difference in outcomes across patients assigned to nurse practitioners and those assigned to primary-care physicians.

So the evidence we have suggests that nurse practitioners provide comparable care to physicians, at least in ambulatory settings. And yet, just as the ADA is trying to limit dental therapists, the AMA is trying to limit nurse practitioners. About half of states restrict NPs' "scope of practice." Meaning, in some states, NPs can open practices without a physician on staff, and they often do so in areas of the country where patients have few alternatives. But in other states, NPs are not allowed to work independently in this way.

These kinds of restrictions on dental therapists and NPs should make us uneasy. Yes, restrictions increase quality. When all else is equal, an appointment with a dentist or a physician is higher quality than an appointment with a dental therapist or an NP. But, that said, little rigorous evidence exists that that difference in quality actually improves patient outcomes. And so the increase in quality is probably not worth the reduction in access.

Moreover, scope-of-practice laws tend to have an obvious effect on salaries. Morris Kleiner is an economist at the University of Minnesota. He has spent his career studying occupational licensing, laws that restrict who is allowed to do the work of a profession. In a series of papers with other economists, he has found that restrictive scope-of-practice laws tend to lower the salaries of NPs and raise the salaries of physicians (Kleiner et al. 2016; Kleiner and Krueger 2013; Kleiner and Krueger 2008).

A similar debate concerns foreign physicians. Consider the best physician in Europe. Imagine that physician, practicing in France or Italy or Sweden. She's got twenty years of experience and she's fantastic. Can she come to the United States and practice here? No way. To practice medicine in the United States, with some exceptions, requires graduate medical education in the United States. The best physician in Europe would have to secure a residency slot before she could practice here.

Foreigners can't come here and practice medicine, at least not at first. Is that sound policy? Well, it does protect the quality of the physician workforce. Only those who go through America's tightly regulated residency programs can treat Americans. But surely there are other ways to maintain quality. For example, the American healthcare system could recognize trainees from certain foreign programs and allow those physicians to practice here.

These types of supply restrictions limit Americans' access to healthcare and raise its price. With fewer providers out there, we all have to wait longer for an appointment. People who live in rural, underserved areas may not be able to find a nearby appointment at all. And, of course, restrictions on supply increase salaries.

Present Discounted Values

We've established that physician salaries are high for two sets of reasons: market forces and nonmarket forces. And it is that second category that is especially in focus for policymakers. Regulators could make it easier for foreign physicians to move here and practice. They might also remove scope-of-practice restrictions on nurse practitioners in more states. For that matter, dental therapists could be made legal in more states. Certified registered nurse anesthetists could take over more of the work handled by anesthesiologists. Midwives could deliver more babies currently delivered by obstetricians.

In considering those changes to policy, one has to grapple with the actual numbers at play. One benefit of high physician salaries is that the best and the brightest choose to become physicians. Each year, a generation of young people decide whether or not it is worth it to become a physician. So far, the medical system has had no trouble attracting well-qualified students. Medical school is oversubscribed and there are too few residency slots to go around: in 2020, nearly 45,000 registrants competed for just over 37,000 residency positions (Weiner 2021).

So how much might physician salaries be able to change without reducing the quality of incoming medical students? Consider a twenty-two-year-old deciding what to do with the rest of her life. She could go to medical school, complete a residency and then a fellowship, and then practice medicine until her seventies. Alternatively, she could go to law school for three years and then practice law until her seventies. The research team we mentioned above—Josh Gottlieb, Maria Polyakova, Kevin Rinz, Hugh Shiplett, and Victoria Udalova—studied that particular decision.

First, the team calculated the benefits to becoming a lawyer. They used a tool from finance called a "present discounted value." They added up all of the money that a lawyer would earn over a lifetime, using a 3 percent discount rate to account for the fact that a dollar today is not equivalent to a dollar tomorrow. According to their calculation, on average, lawyers will make $6.7 million over their careers. That sum, $6.7 million, includes three years of no earnings during law school, plus tuition, and then decades of earnings afterward.

Second, the team calculated a similar number were that twenty-two-year-old to become a primary-care physician. The present discounted value of her lifetime earnings would be $6.1 million—somewhat *lower* than what she would earn as a lawyer. Primary-care physicians do not enjoy a wage premium relative to their "outside option." If they had chosen law rather than primary-care medicine, their earnings would have ended up slightly higher. Primary-care physicians actually earn slightly higher salaries than lawyers, but lawyers undergo fewer years of training, and that difference tilts the present discounted values in the favor of lawyers.

The story is different, however, for specialists. Remember that specialists earn much higher salaries than primary-care physicians, and, for some specialists, the difference in training is only a year or two. The research team performed the same calculation for all physicians, not just primary-care physicians. The present discounted value of lifetime income among all physicians is $9.6 million, way above the $6.7 million that lawyers earn.[10]

In other words, if the goal is to bring healthcare costs down, and salaries are an obvious part of that puzzle, there is much more scope for specialists' salaries to be cut than for primary-care physicians' salaries to be cut. Primary-care physicians are already earning less money than lawyers, once we account for their training. And so if regulators were to change healthcare in a manner that would especially penalize primary-care physicians, then we would expect even fewer medical students to be interested in primary care. But the same is not true for specialists. Even once we account for specialists' extra years in training, we find that their lifetime earnings vastly exceed what other professionals earn.

Perhaps the easiest way to see that difference is to consider a few simple averages. Anesthesiologists, for instance, spend only one more year in residency than primary-care physicians and earn, on average, twice what a primary-care physician earns each year ever after. Similarly, cardiac surgeons spend three more years in residency than family-practice physicians, and earn, on average, over $300,000 more each year ever after.

The Bottom Line

There is no easier way to offend physicians than to discuss these kinds of numbers. And yet, if we are to think critically about healthcare, then the topic should not be off limits.

When one thinks critically about physician salaries, two key patterns emerge. First, given their years of training, primary-care physicians' salaries are very low. That is to say, in primary care, salaries barely dominate those physicians' "outside option." This is widely known in the medical world and why the medical students who are most focused on salary avoid primary care.

A second pattern is more controversial: specialists' lifetime earnings are far above what they would earn in other fields. Even when one accounts for the years of training required to become a specialist by calculating a present discounted value, the earnings are still remarkably high. Now, that pattern is driven by many factors. The jobs are difficult, most specialists work long hours for their entire careers, and so on. But one key cause of high salaries is restrictions on supply: limits on new medical schools, few residency slots, few foreign physicians allowed to immigrate, so on and so forth. Most professions organize to protect their salaries, and physicians are no exception. As examples we need only look to dentists fighting to eliminate dental therapists.

All in all, the topic of physicians' salaries does not lead us to an obvious policy implication. Perhaps the numbers above suggest that specialists' salaries could be cut without unintended consequences. But such a change would not have an enormous effect on overall healthcare spending. All physicians' salaries amount to less than 10 percent of healthcare spending, and so a cut to some of those salaries would have a limited effect on overall healthcare spending.

More importantly, any policy that would substantially affect physicians' salaries would be politically impossible. To see that, consider the Medicare Sustainable Growth Rate, the SGR. In the mid-1990s, Congress grew concerned about the growth in Medicare spending for physicians' services. Throughout the 1980s, Medicare spending on physician services grew at an average annual rate of 13.4 percent (Steinwald 2004). That growth rate was seen in Washington as simply unsustainable. And so a bipartisan group of lawmakers became determined to force the growth in spending on physicians to become sustainable.

They settled on a simple policy: the new law would create a target for overall Medicare spending on physician services each year. If actual spending exceeded that target, then the law would automatically decrease Medicare payment rates for physician services. The underlying calculations were complex to account for other changing factors: overall inflation, changes in the number of people on Medicare, changes to GDP, and so on. The key goal was to prevent Medicare spending on physicians from growing faster than the overall economy, since that was not sustainable.

That policy seemed like a prudent and reasonable approach to wild growth in Medicare spending. So what happened? In 2002, the law triggered a cut in Medicare's base payment rate by 4.8 percent. In 2003, it looked like there was going to be a similar cut, but physicians lobbied in opposition. And so Congress voted to temporarily postpone any more cuts. That temporary postponement was called the "doc fix," that is "fixing" a policy change opposed by docs.

That 2003 "doc fix" was the first of many. For the next *eleven* years, Congress postponed further cuts each year. It became clear that legislators had no appetite to cut physician payment rates. In 2015, President Obama signed the Medicare Access and CHIP Reauthorization Act, which ended the entire policy.

The saga of the "doc fix" demonstrates that physicians' salaries, like so much else in healthcare, is a matter of political maneuvering. In this case, the political maneuvering of organized physicians was entirely successful. Congress grew concerned that physicians were paid too much—so it tried to cut payments. Then those cuts became politically infeasible.

Physicians need to recognize that their salaries are determined not just by economic forces but also by these types of organized campaigns. The AMA fights to protect physicians from cuts to Medicare rates, from foreign medical graduates, from nurse practitioners, and from other threats to physicians' incomes. Now, the AMA would argue that they are fighting not just for the prosperity of physicians but also for Americans' quality of care. It's not that simple. The goals of organized physicians do not perfectly align with what is best for the American public.

References

Antono, Brian, Andrew Bazemore, Irene Dankwa-Mullan, Judy George, Anuradha Jetty, Stephen Petterson, Amol Rajmane, Kyu Rhee, Bedda L. Rosario, Elisabeth Scheufele, and Joel Willis. *Primary Care in the United States: A Chartbook of Facts and Statistics.* Washington, DC: Robert Graham Center, 2021.

Brooks, David. "Opinion: How to Get Really Rich!" *New York Times*, February 26, 2021, sec. Opinion. https://www.nytimes.com/2021/02/25/opinion/inequality-medicine-law.html.

Corr, Allison. "What Are Dental Therapists?" PEW Research Center, October 9, 2019. https://pew.org/2OzD9w6.

Department of the Treasury, Office of Economic Policy, Council of Economic Advisers, and Department of Labor. "Occupational Licensing: A Framework for Policymakers." Washington, DC: White House, 2015.

Gottlieb, Joshua D., Maria Polyakova, Kevin Rinz, Hugh Shiplett, and Victoria Udalova. "Who Values Human Capitalists' Human Capital? Healthcare Spending and Physician Earnings." *US Census Bureau, Center for Economic Studies* (July 2020): 67.

"Governor Ducey Signs 'Blow Dry Freedom Bill.'" Office of the Arizona Governor. September 13, 2019. https://azgovernor.gov/governor/news/2019/09/governor-ducey-signs-blow-dry -freedom-bill.

"Issue Brief: Collaboration between Physicians and Nurses Works." Primary Care Coalition, 2010.

Kleiner, Morris M., and Alan B. Krueger. "The Prevalence and Effects of Occupational Licensing." *British Journal of Industrial Relations* 48, no. 4 (2010): 676–87.

———. "Analyzing the Extent and Influence of Occupational Licensing on the Labor Market." *Journal of Labor Economics* 31, S1 (2013): S173–202. https://doi.org/10.1086/669060.

Kleiner, Morris M., Allison Marier, Kyoung Won Park, and Coady Wing. "Relaxing Occupational Licensing Requirements: Analyzing Wages and Prices for a Medical Service." *Journal of Law and Economics* 59, no. 2 (2016): 261–91.

Krugman, Paul. "In Praise of Cheap Labor." *Slate Magazine* (March 21, 1997). https://slate.com/ business/1997/03/in-praise-of-cheap-labor.html.

Mizzi Angelone, Kristen, and Allison Corr. "National Coalition Publishes Model Dental Therapy Rules." PEW Research Center, February 2, 2022. https://pew.org/3ghgMrQ.

Mundinger, M. O., R. L. Kane, E. R. Lenz, A. M. Totten, W. Y. Tsai, P. D. Cleary, W. T. Friedewald, A. L. Siu, and M. L. Shelanski. "Primary Care Outcomes in Patients Treated by Nurse Practitioners or Physicians: A Randomized Trial." *JAMA* 283, no. 1 (2000): 59–68. https:// doi.org/10.1001/jama.283.1.59.

Otto, Mary. "Dental Care Where There Is No Dentist." *YES! Magazine*, 2019. https://www .yesmagazine.org/democracy/2019/07/23/dental-alaska-low-cost-program.

Steinwald, Bruce. "Medicare Physician Payments: Information on Spending Trends and Targets." Washington, DC: US General Accounting Office, 2004.

Weiner, Stacy. "Why This Year's Match Will Be Strikingly Different." Washington, DC: Association of American Medical Colleges, 2021. https://www.aamc.org/news-insights/why-years-match-will-be-strikingly-different.

Wetterhall, Scott, James D. Bader, Barri Burrus, Jessica Lee, and Daniel Shugars. "Evaluation of the Dental Health Aide Therapist Workforce Model in Alaska." W. K. Kellogg Foundation, October 2010.

Doctors and Hospitals Respond to Financial Incentives (Just Like Everybody Else)

Imagine you visit a butcher shop.[1] You take a number and wait in line. When the butcher calls your number, you meet him at his counter and look down at all of the meat you can buy. But you're not sure how much meat will be enough. So you turn to the butcher and ask. "Listen, I'm not sure what I need. How many pounds of meat should I buy?"

Is the butcher going to give you good advice? Is the butcher a neutral arbiter in this decision? Is he an impartial judge? No way! The butcher is just trying to keep the lights on. Walmart has opened a superstore down the street, and people are going there for shrink-wrapped strip steaks packed in Styrofoam. The man is struggling to keep his business open, and the more meat you buy, the more of a chance he has to do so.

Despite being an ignorant customer who doesn't know how much meat you need, you recognize the fraught nature of this interaction. The butcher wants to sell you as much meat as possible—the more meat, the more profit— and you will never know whether the amount he recommends is too much or just enough. There's a technical term for such a situation. The meat is a "credence good": a good for which the consumer does not know how much he or she needs.

In this day and age, few people lay awake at night worrying about whether or not their butcher sold them too much meat. But credence goods are still an issue. Tal recently took his car in for repairs. The mechanic informed him that the car had a "faulty shutter valve and solenoid" and that they needed to "clean the throttle body." Tal has no idea what any of that means. But the thousands of dollars the mechanic wanted to charge seemed a bit steep. "Is this really necessary?" The mechanic stared and said, "it's a drivability issue."

Credence goods are not problematic on their own. Suppose that you ask for advice not from the butcher but from the butcher's assistant. The butcher's assistant is just paid by the hour and doesn't care how much money the shop makes. In that case, perhaps there's less of a concern. Credence goods only become problematic when those selling the credence goods face financial incentives that cause them to sell you too much or, for that matter, too little.

What does all of this have to do with healthcare? Well, healthcare is also a credence good. Most patients have no idea what treatments they need. After all, that's why they're consulting the doctor in the first place. Moreover, many doctors are paid "fee for service," meaning that they are only paid for the medical care that they provide. Doctors who are paid via fee-for-service payments bill insurance companies for every service they provide: they collect a fee for every office visit and every procedure. And the trouble with fee-for-service payments is that they put the doctor in the position of the butcher: how much doctors get paid depends on how much medicine they provide.

So imagine that you're not at a butcher's shop—instead, you're consulting an orthopedic surgeon. You've been experiencing some pain while walking, and you ask the doctor whether a hip replacement would help. The surgeon gets paid for every hip replacement performed. Is there a cause for concern here? What if we told you that some studies suggest that over a fifth of joint replacements are inappropriate?[2]

The Case of Obstetricians

We are starting here with a fairly upsetting possibility: What if medical decisions are distorted by how the physician is paid? That possibility is upsetting because we like to think of physicians as immune from the economic forces that shape other areas of life. Sure, your butcher might upsell you on steak. A used car salesman may not be an objective adviser. But a *doctor*?

So let's investigate the possibility that medical decisions might be shaped by issues other than medical need. A useful example comes from hospital maternity wards. Babies are born at hospitals in two ways: a vaginal birth or a cesarean section, a C-section. Often, the mother will start off laboring in a hospital delivery room in anticipation of a vaginal birth. Then a complication might develop. Perhaps the mother's blood pressure spikes, or perhaps her baby's heart rate decelerates. Sometimes, the problem is that the mother's labor is not progressing very quickly, and the baby does not seem in a hurry to come out. The mother's obstetrician then has a difficult decision to make. Should the obstetrician keep trying for a vaginal birth, or are the problems sufficiently severe that they should move the mother to an operating room for a C-section? That's the medical decision faced by the obstetrician: stay in the delivery room or choose a C-section.

For many women with complications in labor, a C-section is the only way to save the mother's life or the life of her baby. But then there are also cases where it's not quite clear which option is best. A C-section is usually harder on the mother—the procedure is a form of abdominal surgery, and women who give birth via C-section require more weeks of recovery than those who give birth vaginally.

But there's also another issue with this particular medical decision: the C-section is much easier on the physician. Think of the two options from the perspective of the obstetrician. One option is to wait and try for a vaginal birth. That requires the obstetrician to carefully monitor the mother for hours longer. The obstetrician may have already been at work for hours. The prospect of waiting longer is not appealing. There's also uncertainty in continuing to try for a vaginal birth. It might not work, in which case the obstetrician will have to provide the C-section later anyway. The alternative is a quick, surgical procedure—the obstetrician would typically be done in well under an hour.

So it's possible that there might be a conflict of interest here. What is best for the physician may not be best for the patient. And what's more, the patient is in the hands of the obstetrician. If the obstetrician were to recommend a C-section too readily, many patients would never know. The patient, after all, is usually not a physician, and so she doesn't know whether the C-section is necessary or not.

It's unclear how to tell if an obstetrician is recommending a C-section because it really is best for the patient (and her baby), or whether the obstetrician is making that recommendation because she is exhausted and wants to go home. After all, many of these cases are close calls. How can we tell if the medical decision is really driven by a conflict of interest and not, simply, by the medical needs of the patient?

Here's one way to assess the potential for a conflict of interest. Imagine that you're a mother in labor and your obstetrician tells you that you need a C-section. If the situation is dire, then the obstetrician will make that clear. But in many cases, the obstetrician will argue for a C-section because "you're at risk for infection" or "you're not progressing." You don't know what to make of that—it really sounds like a gray area. And so you ask the obstetrician: "If you were in my position right now, would you want a C-section?"

What would the doctor do if she were the patient? A couple of health economists—Erin Johnson and Marit Rehavi—set out to answer that question. They collected data on births in California and Texas and studied the share of women giving birth via C-section when the patient happened to be a physician herself. When Texas *physicians* give birth, 31.6 percent of them end up giving birth via C-section. When other highly educated Texans give birth, 32.7 percent of them end up giving birth via C-section. That's a 1.1 percentage-point difference, or a 3.4 percent difference. When the baby's father is also a physician, the C-section rate is even lower, at 28.8 percent.

Now, one explanation for such a difference is that physicians are different from nonphysicians: they are more educated and wealthier, and so perhaps they are simply less at risk for a C-section because they are healthier. For that reason, Johnson and Rehavi present a variety of comparisons, all of which suggest that it's not simply a matter of physicians being healthier. For instance, there are two types of C-sections: scheduled C-sections and unscheduled C-sections. Scheduled C-sections are typically a matter of clear, preexisting medical need. For instance, when the baby's head is pointing in the wrong direction (a "breech baby"), a C-section is typically scheduled in advance. Physicians are just as likely to undergo scheduled C-sections as nonphysicians: there's no difference there. The difference only appears when it comes to unscheduled C-sections, which are more likely to be judgment calls that involve a discussion between the doctor and the patient.

Why do we care if physicians give birth differently than everyone else? We should care because all of this suggests that medical decisions are not entirely functions of medical need. It matters if the patient has some expertise. If the patient knows that she can push back and demand more time to try for a vaginal birth, then she's more likely to get that time. We are rejecting here a naive understanding of how medical decisions are made. It's not simply a mechanical matter of symptoms leading to treatment. Other factors—in this case, whether the patient is an informed patient—play a role in the medical decisions that are made.

It's also worth noting that hospitals usually get paid several thousand dollars more when a patient has a C-section as compared to when a patient has a vaginal birth. Occasionally, payment reforms reduce that gap, narrowing the difference in money hospitals receive for C-sections and vaginal births. When that happens, patients end up less likely to receive a C-section (Oster 2019).

The comparison between physicians and butchers at the start of this chapter might strike you as unfair. After all, physicians take an oath, butchers do not. In the business world, financial incentives certainly matter, but isn't medicine supposed to be different? The World Health Organization recommends countries not exceed C-section rates of 10–15 percent (World Health Organization 2015). In the United States, the C-section rate is above 30 percent, and many health economists believe that financial incentives play a major role in the "excessive" use of the surgical procedure.

You might say, well, this is just one example; when else do financial incentives affect medical decisions? Let's move from maternity wards to cancer clinics.

The Case of Oncologists

When patients are diagnosed with lung cancer, they are often referred to an oncologist at a private clinic. The oncologist recommends a treatment plan, and often that requires the patient to visit the clinic every couple of weeks for an injection of chemo drugs. If the patient is on Medicare, then the Medicare program does not pay for the drugs directly. Instead, the oncologist purchases the chemo drugs from a drug distributor, and then Medicare reimburses the oncologist, paying a fixed fee for every dose of the drug administered.

In the early 2000s, Medicare's analysts noticed a problem. They found that oncologists were buying some drugs at much lower prices than the regulators had expected. One drug, in particular, was especially problematic, a drug called Paclitaxel. A government report in 2004 found that oncologists were being reimbursed for Paclitaxel at six times the rate of what drug distributors had been charging them.

Partially as a result of that report, the system for reimbursing oncologists was reformed. In January of 2005, Medicare's reimbursement rate for Paclitaxel plummeted from about $2,000 per dose to about $250. This was a big change in only one thing: the money that oncologists would get from the Medicare program for administering this drug. The medical needs of cancer patients did not change around this time; the clinical evidence on the drug did not change. All that changed was the financial incentive to prescribe this one drug.

A team of health economists—Mireille Jacobson, Craig Earle, Mary Price, and Joe Newhouse—studied the effects of this change in reimbursement rates. Figure 7.1 comes from their study and plots the sudden change in the reimbursement rate to oncologists for administering a dose of Paclitaxel.

How did the drop in the reimbursement rate for Paclitaxel affect how oncologists handled the drug? The researchers analyzed Medicare records on the share of patients treated with Paclitaxel. The results were clear: after January 2005, oncologists shifted their patients away from Paclitaxel. The second graph plots the change in the number of patients given Paclitaxel. The change in reimbursements was announced well in advance of its implementation—

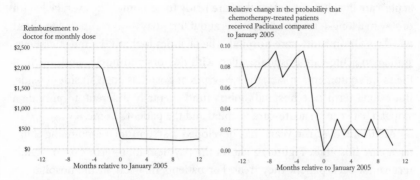

FIGURE 7.1. The first panel plots the sharp change in Medicare's reimbursement rate for Paclitaxel that occurred in January 2005. The second panel plots the change in the probability that oncologists treated patients with Paclitaxel.

oncologists knew of the change months in advance. And, lo and behold, they responded to that change in incentives by shifting patients off Paclitaxel.

This kind of evidence demonstrates how medical decisions can be distorted. Ask any doctor how they choose a treatment plan, and they'll describe to you how they rely on clinical evidence, clinical guidelines, and their own experience. Few doctors will ever mention finances. But this evidence reminds us of the wisdom of James Baldwin: "I can't believe what you say, because I see what you do." Just like in any other business, financial incentives matter in healthcare, too.

The Case of Long-Term Care Hospitals

So some oncologists change the drugs they prescribe depending on how profitable they are to administer. Do healthcare *organizations* behave similarly? What happens when there's a team of healthcare professionals involved in a medical decision: doctors, nurses, and administrators? Is that team also swayed by finances?

Consider older patients who have been admitted to an ordinary hospital, often called an "acute-care hospital." They might have a severe case of pneumonia or a fractured hip. They stay in the hospital for two weeks, and the acute-care hospital saves their lives. But these patients need more around-the-clock care than that, and acute-care hospitals are not designed to care for patients beyond a couple weeks.

This is where "long-term care hospitals" come in. Long-term care hospitals are designed to care for patients after they have been discharged from an acute-care hospital but before they are ready to go home. The average length of stay in a long-term care hospital is about forty days—as compared to about five days for an acute-care hospital. The facilities look, to the untrained eye, similar to acute-care hospitals: filled with doctors and nurses and much of the same equipment. In fact, the two types of hospitals often sit side-by-side. But a long-term care hospital's job is fundamentally different: to provide a stopgap between an acute-care hospital and the patient's home.

Medicare, over the years, has developed a system for reimbursing long-term care hospitals. Figure 7.2 shows the payment long-term care hospitals receive for each patient they treat. For patients that stay in the hospital for only a couple weeks, the hospitals receive very small payments. But once a patient's length of stay reaches a critical threshold, around thirty days in, the hospital receives a large lump-sum payment.

Medicare didn't just settle on that payment scheme at random. It pays long-term care hospitals this way because it wants to avoid two problems. First, it doesn't want long-term care hospitals to hold onto patients forever. The hospitals are designed to care for patients for a long time, but not for *that* long—the facilities are not nursing homes. And so, appropriately, under this system, long-term care hospitals face no incentive to hold patients forever, because their total payment per patient tops out after about thirty days. The

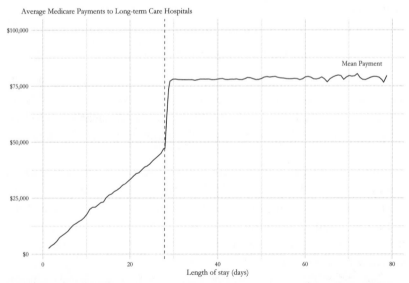

FIGURE 7.2. Average payments to long-term care hospitals from Medicare for different lengths of stay, measured in days. Medicare pays a lump sum for any patient that stays at the long-term care hospital for more than twenty-eight days (Eliason et al. 2018).

hospitals are, of course, free to keep patients for sixty days or eighty days. Some patients may need that much care. But the hospitals cannot make more money by deliberately keeping patients that long.

Second, Medicare wants to prevent long-term care hospitals from churning through short stays, patients who only stay for a week or two. The hospitals are not designed for those types of stays either—they are not acute-care hospitals. And so, appropriately, this system pays long-term care hospitals very little if they keep a patient only for a few days.

This payment scheme solves those two problems: having patients stay for too little time or too much time. But the scheme might create a third problem. That possibility was investigated by a team of health economists: Paul Eliason, Paul Grieco, Ryan McDevitt, and James Roberts. The research team was intrigued by one particular response to the way that long-term care hospitals are paid: the hospitals might delay discharging patients until they receive that lump-sum payment.

The researchers were inspired by the work of Alex Berenson, a journalist working for the *New York Times*, who reported on one long-term care hospital in Kansas. "A case manager at a Select hospital in Kansas had refused to discharge a patient despite the wishes of her physician and family. The hospital calculated it would lose $3,853.52 if it discharged the patient when the family wanted" (Berenson 2010).

For every given patient admitted to a long-term care hospital, there exists a "magic day," the day the hospital receives its lump-sum payment. Administrators then have an easy way to boost their revenue. They can strategically delay discharging patients until it is most profitable to do so, until the magic day.

Eliason, Grieco, McDevitt, and Roberts tested for that possibility. Figure 7.3 is their histogram plotting of patients' length of stay relative to their magic day. Only about 1.4 percent of patients are discharged the day before their magic day, but 10.2 percent are discharged precisely on their magic day, precisely when hospitals receive their lump-sum payment for treating them. Staff at long-term care hospitals, it seems, act strategically in deciding when patients are discharged.

Tragically, not everyone is equally exposed to this kind of behavior. Across all patients, the likelihood of being discharged on their magic day is about ten times higher than the likelihood of being discharged the day before. Among African Americans, that gap is 30 percent larger. In other words, minorities are more likely to have their hospital stays manipulated in this way. The researchers didn't have the data to dig in further on this. They couldn't explore the precise mechanisms involved. But such a result is consistent with a sad

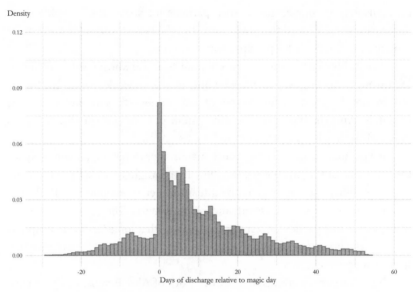

Density

FIGURE 7.3. Distribution of the days when patients are discharged from long-term care hospitals relative to the "magic day" when hospitals receive lump-sum fees.

theme in the American healthcare system: the worst aspects of the healthcare system fall on those who are more vulnerable.

Interestingly, the researchers found evidence for this strategic behavior among both for-profit long-term care hospitals and also nonprofit long-term care hospitals. For-profit entities do seem *more* strategic: more of their patients end up discharged on precisely their magic day, but the histogram for nonprofit long-term care hospitals also has a big spike on the magic day. It's not the case that only being a for-profit business leads to this kind of strategic behavior—instead, it appears to be common across the industry.

In the same vein, the researchers studied what happened when long-term care hospitals were acquired by larger, for-profit firms. Over the years, two firms in particular, Kindred Healthcare and Select Medical, have acquired over one-third of the country's long-term care hospitals.

The two histograms in figure 7.4 show what happens after Kindred or Select acquires a long-term care hospital. The first histogram describes the length of stay of patients who were admitted and discharged before their hospital was acquired by Kindred or Select. The figure clearly shows a spike on patients' magic day: the hospitals were strategically delaying patients' discharge. The second histogram describes the length of stay of patients who were discharged after Kindred or Select acquired the facility. The spike only got bigger. A reasonable interpretation of these results is that the new owners

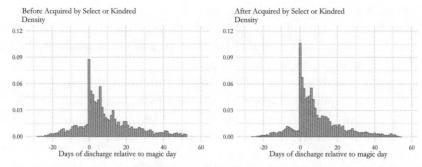

FIGURE 7.4. Distribution of the days when patients are discharged from long-term care hospitals relative to the "magic day" when hospitals receive lump-sum payments. The first histogram shows the distribution before the hospitals are acquired by Select or Kindred, and the second histogram shows the distribution after acquisition.

made the acquired hospitals even more strategic, holding more patients even longer, until it was most profitable to discharge them.

It's tempting to simply view these kinds of numbers dispassionately, but it's important to remember the human stories behind these hospital stays. Behind these histograms are thousands of phone calls from daughters to doctors at long-term care hospitals: "Why haven't you discharged my father yet?" Grandchildren are asking, "Why is Grandma still in the hospital?" And then those grandkids send crayon-and-construction-paper get-well cards, cards that are pasted on the walls of their grandparent's long-term care hospital room, rooms the patients could have safely departed days ago.

Acute-Care Hospitals

The studies we describe above are good examples taken from a large academic literature.[3] Over and over again, health economists have found that financial incentives shape healthcare decisions, determining what drugs doctors prescribe, when patients are discharged from the hospital, and what procedures are performed.

So if the financial incentives facing providers end up shaping healthcare, it is natural to ask whether providers face the right financial incentives. Perhaps the way to improve healthcare is to pay for it differently. And, indeed, there's a long history in America of healthcare reform being really a matter of payment reform.

One of the largest payment reforms occurred in 1983. Before that year, Medicare reimbursed hospitals "retrospectively." When a Medicare beneficiary was admitted to a hospital, the hospital treated the patient in whatever way the doctors felt was appropriate, and then Medicare would pay for every procedure provided and every night in the hospital after the fact. So if the hospital cared for a patient for ten days, Medicare paid the hospital more than if the patient were kept for five days.

Now, on one level, retrospective payment makes perfect sense. After all, it costs the hospital more money to care for a patient over ten days rather than five days. But we've already established that financial incentives can affect medical decisions. What are the incentive effects of retrospective payments?

Over the 1970s, policymakers became concerned that retrospective payment imposed precisely the wrong incentive on hospitals. The longer that patients stayed in the hospital, the more procedures that were done to them, the more money the hospital received. Retrospective payment is sometimes called "fee-for-service payment": hospitals received a fee for every service they provided patients over the course of their hospitalization. And fee-for-service payments create an incentive to provide care, possibly too much care. You get what you pay for. If you pay for services, that's what you get.

In 1983, Congress passed a law that required Medicare to pay hospitals in a very different way. Rather than pay hospitals retrospectively, hospitals would suddenly be paid "prospectively." Prospective payment meant that hospitals were paid a lump-sum fee, up front, for each patient. If the patient required fewer resources than the lump-sum fee, then the hospital made a handsome profit on the patient. If the patient ended up being very expensive to treat, then the hospital lost money on the patient. But, critically, the hospital no longer faced an incentive to provide more care. Senator Bob Dole said that, under the new system, "hospitals are afforded real incentives to become efficient and cost-effective providers of care" (*Adjustments in Medicare's Prospective Payment System*, 1984).

The system worked in the following way. Each patient was assigned a "diagnosis-related group," a DRG. There were about five hundred DRGs at first.[4] All patients with a certain kind of pneumonia were in one DRG, for example.

So what does the switch from retrospective payment to prospective payment do? Suddenly, hospitals have no incentive to treat patients longer than they need to. Each hospital is paid a lump-sum fee for each patient that is admitted, based on that patient's DRG. So the goal is to have many admissions but to treat the patient for relatively little time.

Indeed, the shift to DRGs led to a remarkable, sudden drop in the number of days that Medicare beneficiaries spent in the hospital. Figure 7.5 was compiled by David Cutler and Dan Ly: it plots the number of inpatient hospital

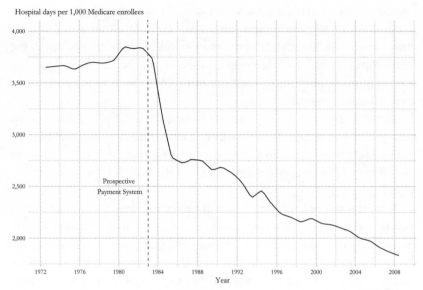

Hospital days per 1,000 Medicare enrollees

FIGURE 7.5. Average number of hospital days per 1,000 Medicare enrollees before and after the implementation of the Prospective Payment System in 1983.

days for every thousand Medicare enrollees. Medicare switched to the DRG system in 1983, and the effect is apparent in the graph: a sharp, sudden drop in hospital stays.

The Downside of Throughput

Most health economists view the prospective payment system as a great success (Coulam and Gaumer 1992). Over the decades, policymakers fine-tuned the list of DRGs but otherwise left the system intact. And the private sector followed the public sector: many private insurers piggybacked off the federal change (Mayes and Berenson 2006). Before 1983, private insurers nearly always paid hospitals retrospectively. After Medicare switched, many private insurers followed Medicare's lead and adopted the DRG system for their own beneficiaries.

Meanwhile, hospitals' accountants watched as DRGs radically transformed the business of running a hospital. Before DRGs, hospital revenue meant both bringing in more patients and also providing more medicine for those patients. The longer a patient was in the hospital, the more money the hospital was paid.

After DRGs, the hospital only received a lump-sum payment for each patient as they came in. The length of time that the patient stayed with the hospital didn't matter: the money only came in per patient, not per service or per night. So revenue became solely a function of the number of patients going *through* the hospital. Hospital accountants began to refer to this as the "throughput model." By "throughput," they meant the number of patients flowing through the hospital. The more admissions, the more lump-sum payments, the more revenue.

The goal, then, was to keep patients flowing through the hospital, to keep the beds full and occupied only briefly by each patient. Hospital profits came from patient throughput: lots of admissions and short lengths of stay. The most profitable hospitals were those that kept the beds full and length of stay short.[5]

Now, the throughput model was great for accountants. It's difficult to manage a complex organization, and so being able to focus on a single metric, throughput, makes the job much easier. But that focus on throughput was not so great for patients. Patients don't care about throughput: they care about quality. And yet, the DRG system did not pay hospitals more if they provided higher quality care, it only paid hospitals more if they provided more hospitalizations.

Over time, American policymakers recognized that aspect of the DRG system as a major flaw. The hospital accountants staring at their spreadsheets faced an enormous incentive to get the hospital to treat more patients. But the accountants saw little return to improving quality of care.

The most disturbing part of this is that, sometimes, medical *errors* were profitable. Think of a patient who is admitted to the hospital for major surgery. The patient is nervous and scared and, as she is anesthetized, she thinks of her children. The surgeons operate on her for hours. A few days later she is sent home to recuperate, but something's not quite right. She is feverish and in pain and definitely not recovering. It takes time, but eventually the problem becomes clear: a retained instrument. The surgeons left an instrument *inside* her. Usually, it's a surgical sponge, but sometimes it can be a stainless-steel surgical tool. Now the patient has to come back to the hospital and the surgeon has to operate again. Again she is nervous and scared and thinking of her children as she is anesthetized. And this time, the surgery is just to remove the instrument, to address the medical error.

Before the early 2000s, Medicare would just pay the hospital for the second surgery the same way it paid for the first surgery. Medicare just paid for the DRGs, ignoring that much of the cost, in this case, was driven by error.

Experts in health policy always saw this arrangement as perverse. And so starting in 2009, Medicare would no longer pay for what it called "never events" (Centers for Medicare and Medicaid Services 2008). Hospital never events are situations that should never occur. Leaving an instrument inside the patient—that's one type of never event. Others include the following.

- Surgery on the wrong patient
- A line designated for oxygen has the wrong gas
- Infant discharged to the wrong person
- Patient suicide
- Wrong blood type transfused
- Certain types of pressure ulcers acquired in the hospital
- Amputation of the wrong body part[6]

Over the years, Medicare extended this list, adding other medical situations that should never occur and for which it would no longer pay. Then policymakers explored other ways to link hospital payment to quality. Doing so was one of the goals of Obamacare, which included several new programs that changed how Medicare pays hospitals.

For instance, there was the Hospital Readmissions Reduction Program, abbreviated HRRP. HRRP was meant to resolve an aspect of the DRG system that, over the years, was singled out as especially egregious. Suppose that a hospital treated a Medicare patient poorly and discharged them very quickly, perhaps for the sake of throughput. Only a day or two later, that patient might be readmitted to a different hospital. That first hospital would be paid its lump-sum payment, even though it did a lousy job, even though the patient ended up right back in another hospital.

Under HRRP, hospitals would be penalized if too many of their Medicare patients were readmitted to a hospital within thirty days. The details of the program were complex. Only patients with certain medical conditions counted toward a penalty. And a mathematical formula determined the magnitude of the penalty. About 79 percent of hospitals ended up penalized under HRRP, with an average penalty of 0.75 percent of those hospitals' Medicare revenue (Boccuti and Casillas 2017).

Even though the penalties were small, HRRP had a big effect. Hospitals started to worry about readmissions and started to track them. Some hospitals instituted "discharge checklists." Has paperwork been sent to the patient's primary-care physician? Does the patient have a follow-up appointment with outpatient care? Does the patient have any questions about necessary follow-up care? Good doctors always cared about this kind of stuff, but now hospital administrators were making these kinds of checks part of a protocol. If those hospital administrators could lower readmission rates, then the hospital wouldn't be penalized. And the best evidence available suggests that HRRP lowered readmission rates and even saved lives (Gupta 2021).

HRRP was one of several experiments in linking hospital reimbursement to quality. There was also HACRP: a program that penalized hospitals if their patients acquired infections in the hospital. And there was HVBPP: a program that modified Medicare payments to hospitals based on measures of mortality and patient safety.

All of these programs—never events, HRRP, HACRP, HVBPP—are departures from prospective payment. Hospitals no longer simply receive a lump-sum payment for each patient they treat. Now that payment is subject to penalties based on the quality of care that they provided.

It's worth pointing out the implicit assumption in all of this. Policymakers chose to link hospital payments to quality of care, and therefore acknowledged that payment affects care. And on that, health economists would agree.

The Bottom Line

At the end of the day, we have one important point here: *financial incentives matter, even for healthcare.* We've seen that financial incentives shape whether births are vaginal or C-section, which drugs oncologists prescribe, when long-term care hospitals discharge patients, and also how long acute-care hospitals treat patients. As Sweden's minister for Health and Social Affairs put it in 2009, "if you want to send a message to a doctor, write it on a cheque" (*Dagens Nyheter* 2009).

That leaves us to grapple with a basic question: How should doctors and hospitals be paid? That question has been answered over and over again by the American healthcare system. The first model was to pay hospitals retrospectively. The second model was to pay hospitals prospectively via DRGs. The third model was to link those prospective payments to quality.

But all of those models are variations on the same theme: paying hospitals for each hospitalization they provide. Hospitals, in all of this, do make money when someone visits the hospital and don't make money when that person does not visit the hospital.

And yet, making people healthier means *preventing* hospitalizations. None of these methods of payment encourage a hospital to keep people away. Whether the hospital is paid retrospectively or prospectively, the goal is still to fill the hospital bed.

Over the years, many policymakers have proposed an entirely new way to pay for care in order to flip the incentives, to induce private organizations to prevent hospitalizations. We turn to that approach next.

References

Asher, Elad, Shay Dvir, Daniel S. Seidman, Sari Greenberg-Dotan, Alon Kedem, Boaz Sheizaf, and Haim Reuveni. "Defensive Medicine among Obstetricians and Gynecologists in Tertiary Hospitals." *PLoS One* 8, no. 3 (2013): e57108.

Berenson, Alex. "Long-Term Care Hospitals Face Little Scrutiny." *New York Times*, February 10, 2010, sec. Health. https://www.nytimes.com/2010/02/10/health/policy/10care.html.

Boccuti, Cristina, and Giselle Casillas. "Fewer Hospital U-Turns: The Medicare Hospital Readmission Reduction Program." Policy brief. Kaiser Family Foundation, March 10, 2017.

Centers for Medicare and Medicaid Services. "Design and Development of the Diagnosis Related Group (DRG)." Washington, DC: Centers for Medicare and Medicaid Services, 2019.

Clemens, Jeffrey, and Joshua D. Gottlieb. "Do Physicians' Financial Incentives Affect Medical Treatment and Patient Health?" *American Economic Review* 104, no. 4 (2014): 1320–49.

Coulam, Robert F., and Gary L. Gaumer. "Medicare's Prospective Payment System: A Critical Appraisal." *Health Care Financing Review* 1991, suppl. (1992): 45–77.

Cutler, David M., and Dan P. Ly. "The (Paper)Work of Medicine: Understanding International Medical Costs." *Journal of Economic Perspectives* 25, no. 2 (2011): 3–25. https://doi.org/10.1257/jep.25.2.3.

Dagens Nyheter. "Göran Hägglund vill straffa läkare som överförskriver antibiotika." May 30, 2009, sec. Vetenskap. https://www.dn.se/nyheter/vetenskap/goran-hagglund-vill-straffa-lakare-som-overforskriver-antibiotika/.

Eliason, Paul J., Paul L. E. Grieco, Ryan C. McDevitt, and James W. Roberts. "Strategic Patient Discharge: The Case of Long-Term Care Hospitals." *American Economic Review* 108, no. 11 (2018): 3232–65. https://doi.org/10.1257/aer.20170092.

Gupta, Atul. "Impacts of Performance Pay for Hospitals: The Readmissions Reduction Program." *American Economic Review* 111, no. 4 (2021): 1241–83. https://doi.org/10.1257/aer.20171825.

Ho, Kate, and Ariel Pakes. "Hospital Choices, Hospital Prices, and Financial Incentives to Physicians." *American Economic Review* 104, no. 12 (2014): 3841–84.

Jacobson, Mireille, Craig C. Earle, Mary Price, and Joseph P. Newhouse. "How Medicare's Payment Cuts for Cancer Chemotherapy Drugs Changed Patterns of Treatment." *Health Affairs* 29, no. 7 (2010): 1391–99. https://doi.org/10.1377/hlthaff.2009.0563.

Johnson, Erin M., and M. Marit Rehavi. "Physicians treating physicians: Information and incentives in childbirth." *American Economic Journal: Economic Policy* 8, no. 1 (2016): 115–41. https://doi.org/10.1257/pol.20140160.

Lam, Vanessa, Steven Teutsch, and Jonathan Fielding. "Hip and Knee Replacements: A Neglected Potential Savings Opportunity." *JAMA* 319, no. 10 (2018): 977–78. https://doi.org/10.1001/jama.2018.2310.

Mayes, Rick, and Robert A. Berenson. *Medicare Prospective Payment and the Shaping of U.S. Health Care.* Baltimore: Johns Hopkins University Press, 2006.

Oster, Emily, and Spencer McClelland. "Why the C-Section Rate Is So High." *Atlantic* (October 17, 2019). https://www.theatlantic.com/ideas/archive/2019/10/c-section-rate-high/600172/.

United States Senate, Subcommittee on Health and Committee on Finance. *Adjustments in Medicare's Prospective Payment System.* Washington, DC: 98th Congress, 2nd session, 1984.

World Health Organization. "WHO Statement on Caesarean Section Rates." *World Health Organization*, no. WHO/RHR/15.02 (2015).

Payment Reform

Years ago, Canadian policymakers were agonizing over how to pay Canadian general practitioners. They had always paid the physicians via fee for service—meaning, they paid a fee for each primary-care visit the physicians handled. But some policymakers grew concerned that Canadian general practitioners were making too much money, that they could be paid much less and still happily handle the same number of patients.

And so the policymakers changed how they paid the doctors—they imposed a cap on how much primary-care physicians could be paid by the government each year. Once doctors' earnings hit the cap, they were expected to still see patients, but they would not be paid as much for those visits. Specifically, once earnings hit the cap, reimbursement rates were reduced to 25 percent of the original fee schedule, effectively a 75 percent pay cut for each visit.

The policy change had a dramatic effect: thousands of Canadian doctors got a tan. By early December, they had spent weeks on Miami beaches. Researchers found a nearly 70 percent increase in vacations in the years following the policy change (Boutin 1980).

That story is a cautionary tale about unintended consequences. When policymakers change how they pay for care, providers often respond in ways that counteract what policymakers originally had in mind. In this case, Canadian policymakers wanted to lower general practitioners' salaries while changing nothing else, but the doctors responded by seeing fewer patients.

Providers can respond to policy changes in all sorts of ways. And their potential responses limit the range of policies that are worth pursuing.

Sergio, the Jelly-Doughnut Man

Before we launch into the specifics of payment reform, allow us to indulge in a somewhat juvenile analogy.

Sergio makes jelly doughnuts. That's all Sergio does, day in and day out: jelly doughnuts. (Down the line, we will reveal that Sergio is actually a surgeon providing joint replacements, but let us masquerade a bit longer.)

Sergio is hired by Mary (Mary is really Medicare) to provide jelly doughnuts at parties that she hosts in her fabulous downtown loft. Mary handles everything else about the party—the music, the drinks—but she needs Sergio to show up and serve jelly doughnuts to any guest who wants one. The jelly doughnut bar is a wonderful addition to the party, like a punch bowl, but more satisfying.

At first, Mary asks Sergio to operate a cash doughnut bar. Guests at the party pay $2 for each doughnut. They put the cash in a little cup next to Sergio and then he hands them a jelly doughnut. Sergio loves this arrangement: it's simple and straightforward, and the $2 per doughnut covers his costs and then some. Sergio considers buying a boat and a house in Montauk.

But, eventually, Mary changes the rules. She starts offering Sergio a flat fee, $200, for each party he handles. Sergio's not happy about this arrangement—he preferred the old model. At a fixed $200 a party, Sergio now bears risk. If guests at a particular party want fewer than 100 doughnuts, then he makes more money than he would under the old model. Say guests at a party only want 50 doughnuts: the old model would have him selling those doughnuts at $2 each, and so he'd earn $100 in revenue; but under the new model, he would earn $200. But the opposite can occur, too. If guests want 150 doughnuts, the old model would mean $300 in revenue and the new model means only that flat $200.

As a result, some parties are profitable for Sergio and some are unprofitable. Still, Sergio's not a complainer, and he realized that this kind of policy was bound to happen at some point. The old model was too good to be permanent. So he tries to adapt to the new payment model.

And he adapts in two ways. First, Sergio's demeanor at the jelly doughnut bar changes. Before, he really sold the doughnuts. He would dress up and smile and make little jokes to nudge guests to buy a doughnut for $2. Now, he changes his body language to discourage guests from asking for a doughnut. *Do you know how fattening these are?*

Economists call that behavior "stinting."[1] The word is not often used in American English, but you can find it in the dictionary. The definition: "to supply an ungenerous or inadequate amount of something." And that's

TABLE 8.1. The Downsides of Paying for Care

Fee-for-service payments	Lump-sum payments
Induced demand: too much care provided	**Stinting**: too little care provided
	Cream skimming: carefully choosing the patient

exactly what Sergio starts to do once he's only paid a fixed fee per party—he tries to provide fewer doughnuts.

Second, the new payment model leads Sergio to try and avoid some parties. Before the change, Sergio was happy to operate a jelly doughnut bar at *any* party Mary threw. After all, nearly all parties were profitable, since each doughnut brought in $2. Now, ahead of time, Sergio starts asking Mary how many guests will be invited. How long will the party last? Will that especially hungry friend of yours be in attendance? *Oh, you know what—I'm actually tied up that night. I'm so sorry: I can't run the jelly doughnut bar at that party. You'll have to find someone else.*

Economists call that behavior "cream skimming," a topic we discussed in chapter 2. Sergio now faces an incentive to work only at the parties that are going to be profitable. So he tries to pick and choose as best he can. He can never be sure ahead of time, but he tries to work only the parties that seem like they'll be profitable.

The story of Sergio and Mary describes the way that payment can shape behavior. When Sergio is paid via fee-for-service payments ($2 per doughnut), he faces an incentive to provide "too many" doughnuts. Every doughnut provided is profitable, so he's in the business of pushing doughnuts. Sometimes that is called the "induced demand" problem. Under fee-for-service payments, healthcare providers make more money by providing more care. When Sergio is paid lump-sum payments ($200 per party), he faces an incentive to serve only the most profitable parties and to provide as few doughnuts as possible.

This is the economic theory of payment reform: you get what you pay for. Fee-for-service payments lead to too much care, and lump-sum payments can lead to two problematic responses: stinting and cream skimming. That's the theory, but is it actually relevant in the real world?

A Real-World Example of Cream Skimming

One example of a lump-sum payment in healthcare is the Medicare Advantage program. Under Medicare Advantage, Medicare recipients can sign up with a private Medicare Advantage plan instead of going on traditional Medicare. Why would a consumer choose Medicare Advantage over traditional Medicare? In some cases, Medicare Advantage plans cover more generous consumer cost sharing, so that the consumer does not have to pay as much out of pocket for healthcare. Also, some plans offer enrollees benefits that are not available to traditional Medicare enrollees, such as eye exams, dental benefits, fitness benefits, and even meal benefits and transportation benefits. All in all, Medicare Advantage is popular and chosen by an increasingly large share of Medicare beneficiaries.

Here's how the financing works: Medicare pays the private Medicaid Advantage plan a fee, call it $10,000 for the year, and then the private plan is in charge of all of the Medicare recipient's needs that year. The private plans lose money on Medicare recipients who require more than $10,000 in healthcare costs that year, and they make money on Medicare recipients who require less than $10,000 in healthcare costs that year.

Such a system works well, so long as the lump-sum payment of $10,000 is roughly similar to the average needs of the Medicare Advantage population. If private plans can somehow attract very healthy enrollees, then a problem emerges. In that case, traditional Medicare would be overpaying for privatization.

And so a key question is whether Medicare Advantage plans are able to cream skim: whether they're able to attract healthier enrollees relative to the lump-sum payments that they receive. And, indeed, over the years, as the Medicare Advantage program has become more popular, experts have become more and more concerned that the system may allow a great deal of cream skimming.

How would these plans cream skim? Consider free gym memberships.

In the early 2000s, eleven Medicare Advantage plans started offering that new perk to their members. Why would an insurer offer free gym memberships? One answer: going to the gym is healthy, and it's the job of an insurer to pay for services that improve their beneficiaries' health. After all, Medicare Advantage plans pay for stents and cataract surgery, because those procedures improve people's health. So does forty minutes on an elliptical.

But there's actually evidence that free gym memberships *don't* improve health. A team of economists in Illinois—Damon Jones, David Molitor, and Julian Reif—ran a field experiment to study how a "workplace wellness program" affected employees at the University of Illinois. They randomly selected about 3,000 university employees and offered them financial incentives to go to the gym and to take part in free classes on tai chi, smoking cessation, or nutrition. This was an enormous, expensive intervention and it did . . . nothing. Compared to a control group, those who were enrolled exhibited the same medical spending, survey responses, and productivity (Jones, Molitor, and Reif 2019).

The authors did, however, find one large, statistically significant relationship: employees who chose to enroll in the wellness program were much healthier than those who were not interested. In other words, the wellness program attracted the healthiest employees. After all, a free gym membership and some tai chi classes: What kind of person is attracted to such an offer? On average, a pretty healthy person.

And that last finding provides some guidance on how to think about Medicare Advantage programs that offer free gym memberships. The Illinois study suggests that offering free gym memberships does not actually improve anyone's health, but it does attract healthier people. And, in fact, there's evidence for such an effect in Medicare. A couple of researchers, Alicia Cooper and Amal Trivedi, published an article in 2012 in the *New England Journal of Medicine*, which studied enrollment in Advantage plans that offered free gym memberships. The authors found a clear effect: Advantage plans that started offering free gym memberships started to see healthier Medicare recipients signing up (Cooper and Trivedi 2012).

That phenomenon is evidence of cream skimming. If you are paid $10,000 for every Medicare recipient that you cover, then there's suddenly an incentive to try to cover very healthy people. A free gym membership will help in that regard: that perk attracts healthier enrollees with, on average, lower medical costs. You then enjoy a profit on those enrollees: earning $10,000 for each one, but paying much less, on average, in healthcare costs. The gym memberships still cost you, but that expense pays for itself.

This kind of cream-skimming behavior then poses a problem for policymakers. The Medicare program gives Advantage plans a lump-sum $10,000 fee for each Medicare recipient they take on. This kind of evidence suggests that Advantage plans then attract especially healthy recipients. And that means that Medicare overpays Advantage plans, given who the plans end up attracting. A free gym membership seems like a victimless crime: the gym itself is getting paid, the Medicare recipient is voluntarily choosing to sign up for an Advantage plan, and the Advantage plan is operating at a profit. The victim here is the American taxpayer, who pays too much for their care.

Bundled Payments

So lump-sum payments can lead to cream skimming. Unfortunately, there's another potential problem: stinting.

Let's turn to dialysis centers. The Medicare program pays for dialysis for

Americans whose kidneys are failing, that is, who suffer from end-stage renal disease. For decades, Medicare paid dialysis centers on a fee-for-service basis. Dialysis centers received $128 for each dialysis session they provided to Medicare beneficiaries, *plus* a separate fee for each additional service. If the dialysis center administered an injectable drug to a patient or if it performed a medical procedure, the center would receive an additional fee for those services.

Over time, Medicare administrators became concerned that this led to an induced-demand problem. Injectable drugs were profitable for dialysis centers, and there was a concern that they prescribed too many drugs. One of the most common and most expensive drugs for dialysis patients was Epogen, an injectable drug that treats anemia. Epogen was extremely expensive and so extremely profitable for dialysis centers. In addition, Epogen is a "Goldilocks drug" that needs to be "just right": a dialysis patient can have too much or too little Epogen prescribed. Physicians are supposed to prescribe Epogen in a limited fashion, administering doses to target certain hemoglobin levels.

After years of worry about the high cost of dialysis and the excessive prescribing of Epogen, Medicare changed how it paid for dialysis. After January of 2011, dialysis centers received a single, lump-sum payment for each dialysis session they provided: $230, regardless of what drugs were administered to the patient.

When Mary changed her payment structure for Sergio from $2 per doughnut to $200 per party, Sergio reacted by discouraging guests from eating doughnuts. Did dialysis centers react in the same way?

A team of health economists decided to find out. Paul J. Eliason, Benjamin Heebsh, Riley League, Ryan McDevitt, and James Roberts studied the behavior of dialysis centers before and after the January 2011 shift to a bundled payment. Figure 8.1 summarizes their findings, plotting the average number of Epogen doses per month over time. For years, Medicare patients were given roughly 60,000 units per month, on average. Starting in late 2010, that average started to decline, and it fell through 2011 and 2012, down to a new average of roughly 40,000 units per month.

So what does such a pattern suggest about dialysis centers? The researchers argued that the decline in Epogen doses in 2010 was a matter of anticipation. Dialysis centers saw the bundled payment coming—the policy change was announced in July of 2010, months before it was implemented. And so dialysis centers started to react. In 2010, prescribing Epogen was very profitable, but in 2011 it would become unprofitable. And the dialysis centers changed clinical practice accordingly.

That figure is only the first step of the research team's analysis. The team wrote an eighty-four-page working paper that dug into the basic pattern.

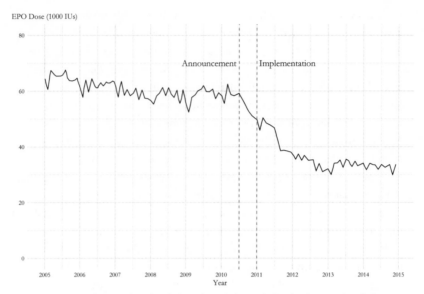

FIGURE 8.1. Use of Epogen (EPO) in dialysis clinics before and after the change to bundled payments in 2011 (Eliason et al. 2022).

They found a natural experiment that allowed them to isolate a treatment-control comparison. And they ran a variety of robustness tests. All of the work pointed in the same direction: the bundled payment reduced provision of Epogen. In some sense, that shouldn't be a surprise—the story of Sergio and Mary suggests that lump-sum payments reduce the incentive to provide care. But, somehow, it's always surprising to see the provision of healthcare change in response to money. Healthcare is like everything else—incentives matter.

Reference Pricing

Noto works at the Booth School of Business at the University of Chicago. Years ago, a few faculty members there organized some seminar dinners and ran up outrageous tabs at very expensive restaurants.[2] The school's dean took one look at the receipts and crafted a policy to keep faculty from spending that much of the school's money ever again. His new policy: a per person cap on reimbursable meal expenses.

But, the thing is, the dean set a fairly generous cap. As a result, the new policy saved much less money than he had expected. Many faculty found the cap surprisingly high and so started arranging more expensive dinners. In other words, for many, the cap didn't function as a hard limit—instead, it became a target.

That story offers a lesson for academic administrators but also for policy-makers in healthcare. Among health insurers, the practice is called "reference pricing." Reference pricing occurs when an insurance company attempts to cap the prices it's willing to cover for a given service.

The best example of reference pricing comes from California in 2011. In that year, the California Public Employees Retirement System, CalPERS, experimented with a new system for covering total hip and total knee replacements. The new policy involved a reference price of $30,000: CalPERS paid all inpatient costs up to that amount. Enrollees could visit any hospital that accepted that price cap, and they would only have to pay their regular deductible and coinsurance rate. If the facility did not accept the cap, then enrollees could still get treatment there, but then they would have to pay all of the costs beyond the cap. Meaning, if an enrollee wanted to visit an especially expensive hospital for hip replacement, and if the hospital were to charge $40,000, then the retiree would have to pay the $10,000 difference between the price and the cap.

Such a policy pushes enrollees to visit hospitals that price below the cap. Enrollees are still free to visit whichever facility they'd like, but they face a strong incentive to choose cheaper facilities. This seems, at first, like a decent approach to payment reform. Everyone is free to do whatever they wish, but now the system imposes some speed bumps on the most expensive options.

Moreover, such a system might cause facilities to charge lower prices. A hospital that prices total hip replacement at well over $30,000 would suddenly see fewer patients coming from CalPERS. Perhaps they'd respond by lowering prices, so that CalPERS patients would return.

So what actually happened? A team of research scientists at CalPERS—Hui Zhang, David Cowling, and Matthew Facer (2017)—published a study of the policy. Sure enough, they found that the policy had the intended effect: CalPERS enrollees shifted their joint replacements to facilities with prices below the cap. Figure 8.2 summarizes that finding: a drop in joint replacements in facilities that did not accept the cap and a corresponding rise in joint replacements in facilities that did accept the price cap.

What's more, the authors found evidence that this policy of reference pricing caused some facilities to lower their prices. Figure 8.3 shows that effect. The average price for facilities that previously were above the cap fell from over $40,000 to just under the cap of $30,000. That is a second, intended effect of the policy, and one that surely delighted executives at CalPERS.

But then the researchers found evidence for an effect of reference pricing that was certainly not intended. Some facilities had been charging $20,000 for joint replacements, and those facilities *raised* their prices in response to

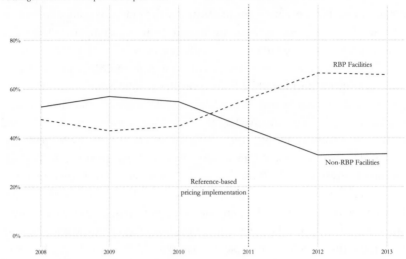

FIGURE 8.2. Trends over time in the percentage of total hip and knee replacements carried out at different facilities (Zhang, Cowling, and Facer 2017). The dashed line shows the increase in the percentage of total hip and knee replacements done at reference-based price (RBP) facilities. These facilities charged prices that were at or below the reference prices set by CalPERS. The solid line shows the decrease in percentage done at the other facilities that did not set prices low enough to be designated as RBP facilities.

Average prices for total hip and knee replacements by type of facility

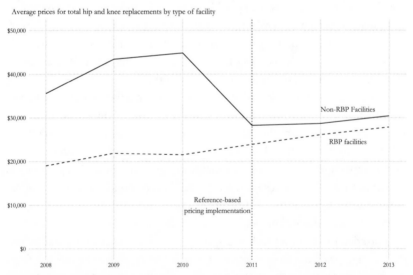

FIGURE 8.3. Trends over time in the average prices of total hip and knee replacements carried out at different facilities (Zhang, Cowling, and Facer 2017). The dashed line shows the slight increase in average prices for reference-based price (RBP) facilities. These facilities charged prices that were at or below the reference prices set by CalPERS. The solid line shows the decrease in average prices at the other facilities that did not set prices low enough to be designated as RBP facilities. However, these facilities still reduced prices following the implementation of the reference-based pricing reform.

the $30,000 cap. In other words, some providers behaved like the Booth faculty choosing a restaurant for a seminar dinner—why choose a price so far below the cap?

On net, reference pricing still saved CalPERS money. On the one hand, enrollees chose cheaper facilities and expensive facilities lowered their prices. On the other hand, some cheap facilities raised their prices. But the first two effects outweighed the third. As a result, the researchers concluded that the program led to considerable savings, reducing average spending on joint replacements by roughly 27 percent.

Now, we should emphasize that this study on the CalPERS reference-pricing policy amounts to a narrow case study. The experience of other organizations may be different. As they say, "your mileage may vary."

One way in which this context is limited: joint replacements are "shoppable." When someone needs a total knee or total hip replacement, they usually have months to choose a provider. And so for months, they talk to different surgeons and perhaps check in with their insurer to get a sense of the bill. Roughly a third of healthcare spending is shoppable in that way (Bloschichak, Milewski, and Martin 2020). And reference pricing only can help when it comes to shoppable services—when patients have a chance to look around and choose some facilities rather than others.

A second complication with reference pricing is that one might worry about quality. After all, joint replacements are serious, complex medical procedures, and some providers are much better than others (Katz et al. 2004). What if the most expensive facilities are also the facilities that provide the best care? In that case, reference pricing would amount to shifting business away from the best providers. The researchers found little evidence for that at CalPERS, but the problem could materialize in other contexts.

A final complication is that it is not obvious what cap to set. CalPERS chose $30,000 for its reference price, which was the 67th percentile. Why not choose an even lower value? A reference price that is too low might lead to a drop in quality. And a reference price that is too low might lead enrollees to complain that it's difficult to find good care that is below the cap. Then again, if the cap is too high, then it won't really do very much. And the higher the cap, the more problematic it is that some facilities will raise their prices to match it.

All in all, the lesson from the CalPERS experience is that reference pricing might hold some promise as a way to manage rising healthcare prices. But there are important caveats, such as that this kind of intervention is only useful for shoppable, elective medical procedures, and that such approaches may end up harming quality of care.

Gaming Bonuses

These new ways to pay for care beyond old-fashioned, fee-for-service payments are called payment schemes. We've just described two types of payment schemes: bundled payments and reference pricing. There are many more alternative payment schemes out there. The entire Medicare Advantage system counts as an alternative payment scheme—it is an alternative to traditional Medicare. Other alternatives abound. Whenever a healthcare provider signs a complex contract with an insurer, one that goes beyond a fee for each service provided, the two parties have established an alternative payment scheme.

Many of those alternative schemes involve "pay for performance." A pay-for-performance scheme exists when an insurer pays a provider based on measures of the quality of the care it provides. For instance, an insurer might set a threshold just for enrollees with diabetes. For each physician, the insurer calculates the percentage of patients with diabetes whose last blood pressure measurement was 145/85 mm Hg or less. If that percentage is above a certain threshold, then the physician is awarded a bonus.

Now, in theory, pay-for-performance schemes allow the insurer to pay for what we actually care about: effective care. Under fee-for-service payments, if primary-care doctors provide more visits, they are paid more. But the number of visits they provide is only a part of what matters. We also care about the effectiveness of those visits. So we want to pay doctors more if they are getting all of their patients vaccinated, if they are getting their patients to follow clinical guidelines, if they are preventing hospitalizations, so on and so forth. And pay-for-performance schemes allow us to pay for that, too: not just a flat fee for each visit, but a bonus if that visit is effective.

In 2004, England's National Health Service began experimenting with a pay-for-performance scheme for family practitioners. The new program provided family practitioners with bonuses that could increase their total salary by up to 25 percent. The physicians' bonuses were based on 146 quality indicators. We mentioned one of those quality indicators above: if a certain share of the physician's diabetes patients had blood pressure below a threshold, then the physician would be awarded points. And the more points, the larger the doctor's bonus.

Now, on its face, these kinds of bonuses for physicians seem like a win-win. The doctors only gain money through their bonuses—no one is made worse off. And the scheme nudges doctors, *perhaps*, to improve the care that they provide.

But there are quite a few reasons to be concerned about physician bonuses. Some experts involved in the program were worried about what they called "measure fixation." They worried that the system would push doctors to focus too much on checking boxes. For instance, one of the 146 metrics related to end-of-life care. The system gave doctors points if they recorded patients' preferred place to receive end-of-life care.

On the one hand, end-of-life care is important and underdiscussed. Many patients would be much better off if they had a plan for the kind of care they would want as they passed away. On the other hand, end-of-life care is a sensitive topic, and it's not obvious that family practitioners ought to raise the issue with every single patient.

Three researchers at the University of Manchester—Helen Lester, Kerin Hannon, and Stephen Campbell (2011)—interviewed physicians a few years into the new program. Many argued that the bonuses were pushing doctors to discuss end-of-life care too aggressively. Doctors "felt that addressing this single indicator risked actual patient harm owing to the lack of sensitivity of asking about this issue in isolation and timing issues in relation to when the question should be raised." In an extreme case, one doctor broached the subject of end-of-life care with a patient but couldn't get the patient to describe where she wanted to receive end-of-life care. Doctors only received points if they recorded the patient's preferred location for end-of-life care—not if they just discussed the topic. So, in this case, the doctor raised the issue *three more times*, all so that she could eventually get an answer and "tick the box."

Another concern with physician bonuses involves multitasking. Multitasking is a big topic among economists and is relevant in many contexts. For instance, suppose that you work as a principal at a large school with many teachers. You, as the principal, are worried that some of your teachers might not be doing a great job. And so you decide to create a bonus scheme with strong incentives for doing good work.

Now to keep this hypothetical simple, imagine that each teacher teaches only two things: art and math. The students take math exams, but there are no exams for art. So if you, as the principal, insist on basing your bonus on quantitative metrics, then you'll have to determine bonuses based on students' math scores. The higher a teacher's students' average math score, the higher her bonus. But what happens to art?

Such a scenario was first described by economists Bengt Holmström and Paul Milgrom in a famous 1991 paper (Holmström and Milgrom 1991). Holmström went on to win the Nobel Prize in 2016, and Milgrom won it in 2020. Their 1991 joint paper was one of the papers cited by the Royal Swedish Academy when Holmström's prize was awarded.[3] (Holmström was chair of the department of economics at MIT while we were graduate students there.) What Holmström and Milgrom pointed out is that teachers in this scenario can focus on two things: teaching art and teaching math. But their bonus is only awarded based on one of those things, math. So there's an unintended consequence of the bonus: teachers may dedicate less time and effort to art and more to math. There'll be more subtraction and division, but less pottery and papier-mâché.

Family practitioners in England are not middle-school teachers, and yet the theory of multitasking may apply to them, too. The British system awarded a bonus based on 146 measures of quality, but family practitioners do many other things. As one family practitioner put it, "I think because there is a limited time with each patient, and if you have to focus on something in order to get the money, obviously if you don't have to focus on it and you don't have the time, then it's going to be ignored automatically" (Lester, Hannon, and Campbell 2011).

Another issue raised by pay-for-performance schemes is cream skimming, a topic we first discussed in chapter 2. Some patients are harder to treat than others, and so physicians who are especially focused on their bonuses may attempt to attract certain patients to their practices and deter others from joining. The British system of physician bonuses did not seem to lead to such behavior on the part of doctors, but other pay-for-performance schemes could certainly induce physicians to nudge some patients out of their practices. After all, a bonus suddenly changes the basic dynamic of how a doctor is paid. Suddenly, *who* the patient is matters deeply—some patients can cost the doctor that bonus.

A final concern with pay-for-performance schemes is the scope for gaming. Doctors may find loopholes in the system that allow them to improve their bonus without actually improving the quality of their care. One potential loophole in the UK system involved what was called "exception reporting." The system allowed family practitioners to exempt some of their patients from the calculations that determined their bonuses. For instance, the doctor could identify some patients as exempt because they had only recently joined the doctor's practice. Doctors could exempt other patients if they refused the treatment that the doctor had recommended. Still other patients could be exempt if they were terminally ill or extremely frail.

Now, at first blush, exception reporting is entirely fair. If a patient just signed up with the practice, then why should they count toward the doctor's bonus? After all, the doctor has had no time to actually provide treatment. And, likewise, if the patient is terminally ill with cancer, then screening for other cancers makes no sense. So why penalize the doctor's bonus for that patient?

A more cynical observer, however, might anticipate a problem here. If a physician has an especially troublesome patient—one whom she knows is going to lower her bonus—then she may find it very tempting to make the patient an exception. We might call that behavior "gaming," though the term is imprecise. The doctor is stretching the exception reporting system beyond its intended purpose solely to protect her bonus. There is some evidence for such a practice after the British bonus system went into effect (Doran et al. 2006).

The Bottom Line

We've described two ways for an insurer to pay for healthcare: fee-for-service payments and alternatives to fee-for-service payments. The insurer either pays a physician a straightforward fee for each procedure the doctor provides, or else the insurer pays the physician through some alternative contract. That alternative payment scheme might be a bundled payment, or a base rate plus a performance bonus, or some other shift toward lump-sum payments.

A natural question then arises: Which payment method is best? And the answer: They're all terrible! Under fee-for-service payments, the insurer worries about induced demand, that is, too much care provided. And under alternatives to fee-for-service payments, the insurer worries about cream skimming, stinting, and gaming. There are serious downsides either way.

Perhaps it's disappointing that there is no straightforward, unique solution to the problem of paying for care. It would be nice were we able to smile and say, *health economists have solved this!* We would then load up a PowerPoint slide with a tidy diagram: here's how insurers should pay providers. We have no such PowerPoint slide—there is no solution.

The challenges inherent in paying providers mean that health policymakers will always be worried about induced demand or cream skimming or stinting or gaming. Since no method of paying for healthcare is perfect, there will always be interesting work to be done.

References

Bloschichak, Aaron, Anna Milewski, and Katie Martin. "CMS-Specified Shoppable Services Accounted for 12% of 2017 Health Care Spending among Individuals with Employer-Sponsored Insurance." Health Care Cost Institute, January 2020. https://healthcostinstitute.org/hcci-research/cms-specified-shoppable-services-made-up-12-of-2017-health-care-spending-among-people-with-employer-sponsored-insurance-1.

Boutin, Jean-Guy. "The Effects of Some Provisions of the Second Agreement with General Practitioners on Their Health Insurance Practices." *L'Actualité économique* 56, no. 2 (1980). https://doi.org/10.7202/600916ar.

Cooper, Alicia L., and Amal N. Trivedi. "Fitness Memberships and Favorable Selection in Medicare Advantage Plans." *New England Journal of Medicine* 366, no. 2 (2012): 150–57. https://doi.org/10.1056/NEJMsa1104273.

Doran, Tim, Catherine Fullwood, Hugh Gravelle, David Reeves, Evangelos Kontopantelis, Urara Hiroeh, and Martin Roland. "Pay-for-Performance Programs in Family Practices in the United Kingdom." *New England Journal of Medicine* 355, no. 4 (2006): 375–84. https://doi.org/10.1056/NEJMsa055505.

Eliason, Paul, Benjamin Heebsh, Riley League, Ryan McDevitt, and James Roberts. "The Effect of Bundled Payments on Provider Behavior and Patient Outcomes: Evidence from the Dialysis Industry." Working paper. 2022. https://sites.google.com/view/pauljeliason/research.

Holmström, Bengt, and Paul Milgrom. "Multitask Principal-Agent Analyses: Incentive Contracts, Asset Ownership, and Job Design." *Journal of Law, Economics and Organization* 7 (1991): 24–52.

Jones, Damon, David Molitor, and Julian Reif. "What Do Workplace Wellness Programs Do? Evidence from the Illinois Workplace Wellness Study." *Quarterly Journal of Economics* 134, no. 4 (2019): 1747–91. https://doi.org/10.1093/qje/qjz023.

Katz, Jeffrey N., Jane Barrett, Nizar N. Mahomed, John A. Baron, R. John Wright, and Elena Losina. "Association between Hospital and Surgeon Procedure Volume and the Outcomes of Total Knee Replacement." *JBJS* 86, no. 9 (2004): 1909–16.

Lester, Helen E., Kerin L. Hannon, and Stephen M. Campbell. "Identifying Unintended Consequences of Quality Indicators: A Qualitative Study." *BMJ Quality and Safety* 20, no. 12 (2011): 1057–61. https://doi.org/10.1136/bmjqs.2010.048371.

Zhang, Hui, David W. Cowling, and Matthew Facer. "Comparing the Effects of Reference Pricing and Centers-of-Excellence Approaches to Value-Based Benefit Design." *Health Affairs* 36, no. 12 (2017): 2094–101. https://doi.org/10.1377/hlthaff.2017.0563.

9

Horizontal Mergers

Imagine a hospital CEO in the 1970s. Every three years, the hospital CEO negotiated with insurance executives to determine how much his hospital would be paid for visits. That was just part of the job.

Then the meetings changed. Insurance executives started to use new terms. They told the CEO that their insurance company was becoming a "managed-care organization." The people they insured could no longer visit any hospital they wanted. Instead, they could only visit hospitals that were "in network."

The insurance executives explained to the CEO what that meant for his hospital: "We want your hospital to be in our network, we really do. But if we can't work something out, then we'll have to move you out of our network, and our beneficiaries will just have to visit other hospitals."

This was an enormous change—hospital-insurer negotiations had never worked like this. The very notion of a hospital being "out of network" was an insurance company's innovation, one that spread across the country from the west to the east. For the hospital CEO, it was devastating. What choice did he have? He agreed to lower rates.

Every time they met, it went from bad to worse. After each negotiation, the insurers paid less for a hospitalization than they had before. After a few years, two dominant insurance companies merged. The executives at the merged insurance company told the hospital CEO, with relish, "We need lower rates—after all, we cover 80 percent of the privately insured patients in this market."

They may as well have taken out an ice pick and pinned the hospital CEO's hand to his desk. With this one managed-care organization covering 80 percent of privately insured patients, he couldn't afford to be out of network—he would be left with too few patients to treat. The hospital would have to shut down.

And so the hospital CEO agreed to pathetic payment rates. It was infuriating. But what could he do?

Well, there was one thing: hospitals could also play the consolidation game.

One of the most important changes in the American hospital sector over the years is its consolidation. Since the 1990s, hospitals have been acquiring other hospitals at an incredible clip. Many American markets these days are dominated by only one major hospital system: MGB in Boston, Sutter Health in Northern California, HCA in Houston. Patients used to have a choice between dozens of small hospitals—that's no longer the case.

Hospital Mergers and Prices

Once the beleaguered hospital CEO merges his hospital with another hospital, then it's *his* turn to casually drop threats in meetings with insurance executives. Sure, you cover 80 percent of the privately insured patients in this town, but now we own 80 percent of the hospital beds. You need us in your network—if you drop us, your beneficiaries will flip out and choose other insurers.

And, indeed, this CEO's story describes how the American hospital industry has changed over the years. Preferred Provider Organizations and other types of managed care arose and became common in the 1990s. All of a sudden, hospitals were either in-network or out-of-network. That meant that hospitals had to accept lower rates or else go out of business. And, in fact, many hospitals *did* close in the 1980s and 1990s. Hospital closures peaked in 1991 (Rehnquist 2003). Since then, though, hospitals have figured out how to play the game.

Over the years, economists have tried to understand what happens when hospitals merge. There's now wide agreement about one critical conclusion: hospital mergers raise prices. To understand why that is, think back to the make-believe story above. The hospital CEO is forced to agree to lower and lower rates as insurers start selective contracting. Then the hospital CEO is forced to agree to still lower rates as insurers merge. If the hospital CEO were to insist on high prices for each hospitalization, then the insurer would put the hospital out of its network, and, over time, that would be devastating to the bottom line. The hospital's merger reverses that trend: all of a sudden it is the insurer that is forced to agree to higher prices. "We control 80 percent of the hospital beds in this market. If you put us out of network, your beneficiaries will have nowhere to go."

That's the theory, and the theory is borne out in the data. As just one example, we refer to a paper by Martin Gaynor, Zack Cooper, and Stuart Craig (2019). Those authors study the commercial prices that hospitals receive from insurers. Those prices are normally kept secret, but the researchers managed to get three insurers to provide their prices under a confidential data-sharing agreement that allowed the researchers to use the data for academic research. The team then studied how hospital prices varied with the local hospital market structure. Figure 9.1 shows the relationship between market structure and prices. For hospital markets with four or more hospitals, the average price of an inpatient hospital admission is about $12,300.[1] We can then compare that baseline to markets with fewer hospitals: triopoly (a hospital market with three hospitals), duopoly (two hospitals), and monopoly (one hospital). The figure shows that as a hospital market gets more concentrated, the average price of an inpatient hospitalization increases. Altogether, if you are treated in a hospital that is a local monopolist, it's going to cost an extra $1,600, about 13 percent, more than if you had gone to a hospital with four or more competitors.

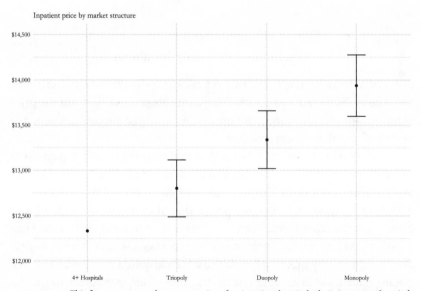

FIGURE 9.1. This figure compares the average price of an inpatient hospital admission across hospitals in different markets that have different levels of market concentration. The error bars represent 95 percent confidence intervals that compare each of the most concentrated markets (triopoly, duopoly, monopoly) to the baseline average for hospitals in the least concentrated markets that have at least four hospitals.

At this point, we should give the standard refrain that "correlation is not causation." Many economists would view the correlation in that figure with skepticism. Are these differences in average prices really driven by market concentration, or is there some other explanation? Perhaps markets with fewer hospitals just have older and sicker patients. Perhaps markets with fewer hospitals involve higher labor costs.

The most convincing evidence addresses those concerns by studying changes in market structure. Suppose two hospitals merge, transforming the market from a triopoly to a duopoly. What happens to prices? Researchers who have studied such events find that each merger increases prices by around 5 percent. That effect isn't all that different from the correlations in figure 9.1, suggesting that the correlations are not misleading.

The bottom line is that the more concentrated a market, the higher its prices. More highly concentrated hospital markets mean that the hospitals have more market power, and businesses use their market power to raise prices and increase profits. A large research literature supports that conclusion. In 2006, William Vogt and Bob Town wrote a metastudy. They reviewed thirteen studies of hospital mergers: ten out of thirteen found evidence that mergers increased prices. Nearly all of the most convincing studies—the ones that were best executed according to the researchers—found increases in price.

Acquisitions in the Dialysis Industry

So hospital mergers tend to increase prices, which should make us concerned about consolidation in healthcare. But we care about more than just the price of healthcare—we also care about quality. What does consolidation do to the quality of care that patients receive?

A priori, it's not obvious how mergers and acquisitions affect quality. On the one hand, quality is kind of like price: when a product gets worse for consumers, that means that either its price went up, or its quality went down, or both. So if mergers lead to higher prices, then they might also lead to lower quality. On the other hand, businesses might need to be big before they can afford to invest in quality. Perhaps a small business just can't manage to produce a high-quality product, but once it's been acquired by a larger firm, the resources are there to improve quality. It's not obvious, without looking at the data, whether mergers would raise or lower quality.

So, to resolve that ambiguity, let's look at the data. To do so, we turn to a different kind of healthcare provider—not hospitals but dialysis clinics. Americans who suffer from end-stage renal disease have to visit a dialysis clinic three times a week. There the patients are connected to dialysis machines and sit for four hours as the machines do the work that the patients' kidneys can no longer do.

There are dialysis clinics wherever there are people, about 7,500 clinics spread out across the country. Over half of the clinics are operated by two publicly traded, for-profit corporations: DaVita and Fresenius. And over time the industry has consolidated in the same way that many other parts of the healthcare sector have consolidated: DaVita and Fresenius have each acquired many dialysis clinics over the years.

A team of economists—Paul Eliason, Benjamin Heebsh, Ryan McDevitt, and James Robers (2020)—studied those acquisitions. Dialysis is a neat area for health economists to study, because we can clearly identify treatment patterns that are profitable. Dialysis patients often suffer from anemia. When they become anemic, they are often prescribed an expensive biologic drug, Epogen (EPO). Before a 2014 rule change, Epogen was a very profitable drug to administer: dialysis clinics would purchase the drug on the private market and Medicare would reimburse the clinic much more than it had paid to purchase the drug. As a result, there was broad concern that Epogen was prescribed too often. And, for that matter, Epogen prescribed inappropriately can be medically dangerous, increasing the risk of stroke and cancer. As much as 25 percent of DaVita's revenue came from the prescription of Epogen.[2]

The research team compiled data on treatment patterns at independent dialysis clinics before and after they were acquired by national chains. They found a stark pattern in how clinics treated Epogen once they were acquired. Figure 9.2 plots the change in Epogen prescriptions before and after a clinic is acquired: the average dose of Epogen per patient increased by over 100 percent within six months of the acquisition.

But that's not all! On top of Epogen, doctors at dialysis clinics choose between two iron-deficiency drugs: Venofer and Ferrlecit. The two drugs are very similar, but for many years, Venofer was much more profitable to dispense. Once clinics were acquired, they tended to shift away from Ferrlecit and toward Venofer (fig. 9.3). That is, they shifted away from the unprofitable drug and toward the profitable one.

So doctors at acquired clinics start to choose more-profitable drugs after the acquisition. Is that such a big deal? After all, so long as there are going to be for-profit healthcare providers, surely we should not be surprised when they make a profit.

But the researchers uncovered some other results here that raised some more uncomfortable questions. Figure 9.4 shows how acquisitions changed the way that clinics handled payments, staffing, and patient health outcomes.

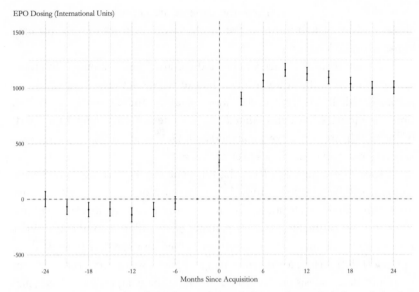

EPO Dosing (International Units)

FIGURE 9.2. Average number of EPO doses in dialysis facilities in the months before and after they are acquired by larger dialysis chains. Each data point is the average number of EPO doses relative to the month right before the acquisition, so that data point is normalized to zero.

Overall, the authors found that acquisitions led to an increase in the revenue that the clinics generated for each session. That effect is consistent with the change in the drugs prescribed: more Epogen and a shift from Ferrlecit to Venofer. In this case, Epogen was a profitable drug to administer, but it was only appropriate for some patients some of the time. And yet it seems that for-profit dialysis chains overprovide that one drug. Even beyond that, the authors found that clinics shifted to employing fewer staff after an acquisition— the patient-per-employee ratio increased by over 10 percent. In other words, the clinics became "leaner," doing more with fewer staff members.

Again, perhaps we shouldn't be surprised that when a profitable, public company acquires a clinic, it makes the clinic more profitable. But the researchers' final result ought to give us pause. The team studied how a clinic's patients fared after an acquisition. They found a clear cost to patients. After an acquisition, patients became more likely to be hospitalized. And, most worrisome of all, following acquisitions, patients' risk of death increased.[3] It looks like the leaner, more-profitable operation led to lower quality healthcare.

All in all, these results suggest a stark change when a for-profit chain acquires an independent clinic. The acquired clinic suddenly starts generating more profits than it had before, but this comes at the expense of the patients. And, for that matter, the profits come at the expense of all of us—most of a

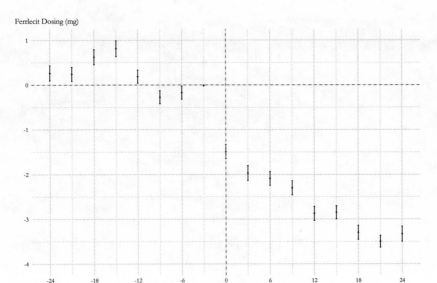

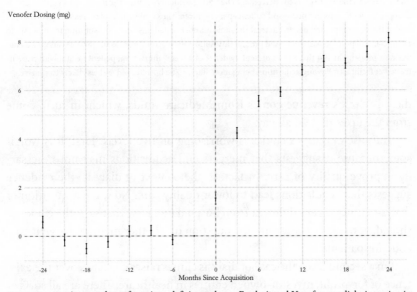

FIGURE 9.3. Average dose of two iron-deficiency drugs, Ferrlecit and Venofer, per dialysis session in the months before and after facilities are acquired by larger dialysis chains. Each data point is the average dose relative to the month right before the acquisition, so that data point is normalized to zero. Venofer is the more profitable drug.

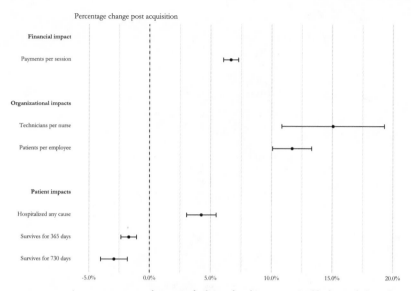

FIGURE 9.4. Average percentage changes in facilities after they are acquired by larger dialysis chains. The first row in the figure plots the percentage change in payments per visit; the next two rows plot percent changes in technicians per nurse and patients per employee. The combination of increased payments per visit, reduction in the staff needed to treat the same number of patients, and a substitution from nurses to technicians all point toward increased profitability following an acquisition, as the facilities adopt a leaner business model. The last three rows present evidence of adverse impacts on patient health, with patients treated at facilities following acquisition being more likely to be hospitalized and less likely to survive.

dialysis clinic's revenue comes from Medicare funds, which, in turn, come from the taxes that we all pay.

The case of dialysis clinics is worrisome on two levels. First, it is worrisome because it suggests that mergers and acquisitions may not necessarily improve quality of care. In fact, in the context of dialysis, the evidence suggests that acquisitions lead to lower quality care. Now, the acquisition of dialysis clinics is very different from hospital mergers. That said, the evidence should, at the very least, raise the question of whether mergers are generally good for patients.

On a second level, the case of dialysis clinics raises concerns over the existence of for-profit, investor-owned entities in healthcare. There are all sorts of contexts throughout healthcare in which what is profitable is not necessarily good for patients.

Insurance Company Mergers

These days, most of the concern over consolidation in healthcare is focused on hospitals. And for good reason: hospitals have become remarkably consolidated in many regions. In many cities, only a couple hospital networks dominate the industry. As a result, those hospital networks manage to negotiate high prices with commercial insurers, leading to high healthcare costs overall.

But there's consolidation on the other side of the market, too. Over the years, many commercial insurers have merged. As of the early 2000s, a majority of geographic areas in the United States have insurance markets that can be classified as "highly concentrated" (American Medical Association, 2008).

It's not obvious how to think about the consolidation of insurers. When insurers merge, they become more adept at negotiating with hospitals. That's the effect suggested by our parable at the beginning of this chapter: the new, consolidated insurer covers 80 percent of the patients in the city, so the hospital has to agree to lower prices. That dynamic, in isolation, is not so concerning: increased pressure on hospitals means lower prices for healthcare.

On one side of the market, commercial insurers negotiate with hospitals, but there's another side to the market. And on that other side, insurers price plans for employers. All else being equal, more powerful insurers mean higher prices for employers. Before a merger, employers in a given city might have five large insurers from which to choose. After a merger, those five insurers become four. With fewer competitors, that means higher prices for the employers.

On net, then, it's not obvious how the merger of insurers might affect the healthcare market. On the one hand, consolidated insurers can extract lower prices from hospitals and physicians. On the other hand, consolidated insurers can also extract higher prices from employers. Sometimes this is called "countervailing market power"—one side raises healthcare spending and the other lowers healthcare spending.

For that reason, Leemore Dafny, Mark Duggan, and Subramaniam Ramanarayanan (2012) studied mergers among insurers. They focused on the 1999 merger of two giant insurers, Aetna and Prudential Healthcare. That one merger amounted to a natural experiment: it made the market for commercial insurance more consolidated in some markets than others.

For instance, before the merger, in Jacksonville, Florida, Aetna covered 19 percent of the market and Prudential covered 24 percent. By contrast, in Las Vegas, Nevada, Aetna covered only 11 percent and Prudential covered only 1 percent of the market. As a result, the merger made Jacksonville a much more consolidated marketplace for commercial insurance than Las Vegas. The authors compare those two markets before and after the merger to isolate a kind of treatment-control comparison: Jacksonville was deeply affected by the merger and Las Vegas was relatively unaffected.

The authors found a clear effect of the Aetna and Prudential merger: it led to higher insurance premiums and lower prices for physicians. The new, larger insurer extracted lower prices from providers, on the one hand, but also raised premiums on employers, on the other. Such a finding suggests that health policymakers ought to be concerned not only about hospital mergers but also about mergers on the other side of the market, among insurers.

What about overall healthcare costs? According to this one study, growing consolidation among insurers leads to higher healthcare costs: "on the order of $34 billion per year, or about $200 per person with employer-sponsored health insurance."

All-Payer Insurance Schemes

We've described a sad state of affairs. On one side of the market, insurance companies have merged, and, on the other, hospitals have merged. And so the market is now dominated by giants: enormous commercial insurers and sprawling hospital networks. Moreover, in many cities across the United States, it is now the hospitals that have the upper hand, and so the price of hospitalizations is sky-high. That leads, in turn, to high healthcare spending, overall.

When an industry is dominated by giant incumbents, it becomes very difficult for new, innovative ventures to enter. Imagine a smart entrepreneur who wants to open up a new kind of insurer. Could a new insurer compete with giant incumbents? As a small player in the market, it would have to pay high reimbursement rates to hospitals, while its giant competitors would have already negotiated much lower rates. And with that disadvantage, why would any employer sign up for such a plan?

Similarly, it is difficult to open up a small, innovative, new hospital. When you start from zero, it can be difficult, if not impossible, to extract reasonable reimbursement rates from incumbent insurers. Sure, you can argue that your new hospital is different, that it'll provide better care. But, at the end of the day, if the dominant commercial insurers are going to grant the new hospital in-network status, it will have to agree to very low reimbursement rates.

There *are* new insurers and providers in healthcare—they just enter via other parts of the market, parts in which prices are not set by bilateral bargaining. For instance, Medicare Advantage plans pay hospitals a fixed fee not much higher than Medicare rates when their beneficiaries visit out-of-network providers. As a result, it's much easier for a small insurance company to enter the Medicare Advantage market. And, in fact, we've seen a variety of new, small entrants in that space.[4]

When it comes to the private market, the key issue is that commercial prices for medical care are determined by bilateral bargaining. And, as a result, what ends up mattering more than anything else is the bargaining power of hospitals and insurers. The bigger the hospital network, the more prestigious the hospital, the higher the prices that can be negotiated. The bigger the commercial insurer, the lower the prices that can be negotiated. So it should be no surprise that we have seen so many mergers. Those mergers are a logical consequence of the way that prices are set in the commercial market.

So it should also be no surprise that many experts have called for a change in how commercial prices are determined: many advocate for "all-payer rate regulations." The proposals vary, but they all share one basic idea: to change the way that hospital prices are set. Some advocate for a simple arrangement in which all hospitals are paid the same fee for treating a patient, a multiple of the reimbursement they already receive from traditional Medicare. Others advocate for a system in which the government somehow determines a fair reimbursement rate for each hospital, and then all insurers have to pay the hospital that rate. Still others suggest that hospitals should be forced to post their prices and charge all insurers the same price.

Those all-payer rate regulations would solve some of the problems we have with the current system. First, we might see less consolidation. There would be less of an incentive for either insurers or hospitals to merge, since the size of their networks would play a much smaller role in determining prices.

Second, such a system might lead to new, innovative ventures. Under all-payer rate regulation, you can thrive as a small, new entrant. A new insurer now pays the same price for a hospitalization as larger, incumbent insurers. A new hospital receives the same reimbursement as the larger, established hospital down the street.

And, in fact, all-payer rate regulation is not entirely new to the American healthcare sector. Maryland is the one state in the country in which prices for hospitalizations are not set via bilateral bargaining. Instead, Maryland has always had a form of all-payer rate regulation. An independent state body sets prices for hospitalizations, and all payers—commercial insurers, Medicare, Medicaid—are charged the same rate.

All of that being said, all-payer rate regulations are not a panacea for the American healthcare system. Many rate-regulation plans would equalize rates across hospitals, even though hospitals do not provide equal care. In many cities, famous, high-quality medical centers enjoy higher bargaining power and so higher commercial prices (Doyle et al. 2015). Those higher prices are earned: the hospitals really do provide higher quality care, and so insurers are willing to pay a premium to keep the hospitals in their networks. Some all-payer rate-regulation proposals would set the rates for those academic medical centers to be the same as the rates given to lower quality hospitals down the street. That kind of change could lead to devastating unintended consequences: it's possible that the drop in rates would, eventually, lead to a drop in quality of care. If high-price-but-high-quality hospitals are forced to face lower prices, it's possible that they may no longer provide the same quality of care.

Another major concern is what economists call "tacit collusion." Suppose that a new all-payer rate-regulation policy requires that all hospitals publicly post their prices and charge all insurers the same prices. Normally, we think of that kind of transparency as a good thing. But with a few hospitals competing, transparency can actually be problematic. Imagine one hospital viewing another's posted prices: "We could lower our prices to compete with them—but why not hold off? If they lower their prices, then we'll lower our prices. Until they lower their prices, let's enjoy high prices." That amounts to a kind of collusion—the two hospitals are effectively conspiring to keep prices high. But it is tacit collusion: the hospital managers are not actually communicating.

All of this is to say that creating the right all-payer rate regulation is a tricky business. We do not want to change reimbursement rates in a way that penalizes high-quality care. We also want to avoid tacit collusion. That said, the status quo is problematic. Without a policy change, there is no end in sight to insurer and hospital consolidation, and never-ending growth in concentration is good neither for consumers nor for innovation.

Antitrust Scrutiny Matters in Healthcare, Too

In addition to all-payer rate regulation, another policy tool at the government's disposal is antitrust scrutiny. The federal government can investigate and prevent proposed mergers from taking place.

Before businesses merge, they have to notify the US government of their plans in what is called a "premerger notification." Following the notification, the government determines whether or not the merger is in the public's interest. The government may decide to prevent the merger from taking place entirely. If that is the case, the Federal Trade Commission (FTC) steps in and files papers to block the merger.[5] The FTC seeks to prevent mergers when it believes that they will raise prices for consumers. Then, in court, federal judges have to figure out whether the mergers are worth blocking or not. This happens across the entire healthcare sector—hospitals, insurers, and pharmaceutical companies have all been prevented from merging.

Some argue that this scrutiny doesn't go far enough. It's a blunt instrument, to be sure. And if the government were more aggressive in preventing mergers, then perhaps healthcare prices would rise more slowly.

The antitrust regulation of today comes from laws that are over a hundred years old. When the Sherman Antitrust Act was passed in 1890, the concern was monopolies in the oil industry, not in healthcare. Back in 1890, healthcare accounted for 2 percent of GDP; today it's nearly 20 percent (Getzen 2017). All of this is to say that it's not obvious that current antitrust enforcement works very well in healthcare.

One example of this issue comes from recent research by Thomas Wollmann (2020). Like the work on acquisitions that we described above, Wollmann focuses on the dialysis industry. He describes how many mergers between dialysis businesses escape antitrust scrutiny entirely—no premerger notification occurs at all. The reason is that only large mergers are required to be reported to the government via a premerger notification. The precise threshold has changed with inflation—as of 2020, only mergers involving more than $92 million in assets required a premerger notification. Wollmann calls mergers and acquisitions under that threshold "stealth consolidations," because regulators never learn of them.

In healthcare, stealth consolidations can still matter a great deal. After all, many healthcare providers can often be bought for less than $92 million. Imagine a small market served by only two dialysis clinics. The two businesses might merge or be acquired, and the transactions might remain under the reporting threshold. And, in such a fashion, a local monopoly could arise, all without antitrust authorities being notified. Consider the title of Wollmann's study: "How to Get Away with Merger: Stealth Consolidation and Its Effects on US Healthcare."

Wollmann shows that much of the consolidation in the dialysis industry has been under the reporting threshold, meaning most dialysis industry mergers consist of stealth consolidations. That consolidation appears to harm patients: dialysis patients experience higher hospitalization rates and mortality rates after the clinic they visit is acquired. Wollmann argues that expanding premerger notifications to cover more healthcare mergers would lead to less consolidation and better outcomes for patients.

The Bottom Line

In every sector of the economy, businesses constantly merge and acquire each other. Mergers deserve scrutiny because competitive markets serve consumers better than markets dominated by monopolists. This is as true for healthcare as any other market. Hospital mergers raise prices and the merger of large insurance companies raises premiums. What's more, the evidence on the acquisition of dialysis clinics suggests that consolidation can also lower quality of care.

All of that is to say that, at the very least, we should be concerned about consolidation in healthcare. What to do about that consolidation is up for debate. Strong antitrust enforcement would certainly help. And more radical changes, such as all-payer rate regulation, are worth exploring.

References

American Medical Association. "Competition in Health Insurance: A Comprehensive Study of US Markets." American Medical Association, 2008.

Autor, David H., and David Dorn. "The Growth of Low-Skill Service Jobs and the Polarization of the US Labor Market." *American Economic Review* 103, no. 5 (2013): 1553–97. https://doi .org/10.1257/aer.103.5.1553.

Cooper, Zack, Stuart V. Craig, Martin Gaynor, and John Van Reenen. "The Price Ain't Right? Hospital Prices and Health Spending on the Privately Insured." *Quarterly Journal of Economics* 134, no. 1 (2019): 51–107. https://doi.org/10.1093/qje/qjy020.

Dafny, Leemore, Mark Duggan, and Subramaniam Ramanarayanan. "Paying a Premium on Your Premium? Consolidation in the US Health Insurance Industry." *American Economic Review* 102, no. 2 (2012): 1161–85. https://doi.org/10.1257/aer.102.2.1161.

Doyle, Joseph J., John A. Graves, Jonathan Gruber, and Samuel A. Kleiner. "Measuring Returns to Hospital Care: Evidence from Ambulance Referral Patterns." *Journal of Political Economy* 123, no. 1 (2015): 170–214. https://doi.org/10.1086/677756.

Eliason, Paul J., Benjamin Heebsh, Ryan C. McDevitt, and James W. Roberts. "How Acquisitions Affect Firm Behavior and Performance: Evidence from the Dialysis Industry." *Quarterly Journal of Economics* 135, no. 1 (2020): 221–67. https://doi.org/10.1093/qje/qjz034.

Garthwaite, Craig, Tal Gross, and Matthew J. Notowidigdo. "Hospitals as Insurers of Last Resort." *American Economic Journal: Applied Economics* 10, no. 1 (2018): 1–39. https://doi.org/ 10.1257/app.20150581.

Getzen, Thomas E. "The Growth of Health Spending in the USA: 1776 to 2026." Rochester, NY: SSRN Scholarly Paper, 2017. https://doi.org/10.2139/ssrn.3034031.

Rehnquist, J. "Trends in Rural Hospital Closure 1990–2000." Washington, DC: Office of Inspector General, Department of Health and Human Services, 2003.

Tolbert, Charles M., and Molly Sizer, eds. "U.S. Commuting Zones and Labor Market Areas: A 1990 Update." Washington, DC: US Department of Agriculture, 1996. https://doi.org/10 .22004/ag.econ.278812.

Vogt, William B., and Robert Town. "How Has Hospital Consolidation Affected the Price and Quality of Hospital Care?" Princeton, NJ: Robert Wood Johnson Foundation, February 2006. https://www.rwjf.org/en/library/research/2006/02/how-has-hospital-consolidation -affected-the-price-and-quality-of.html.

Wollmann, Thomas G. "How to Get Away with Merger: Stealth Consolidation and Its Effects on US Healthcare." Working Paper 27274. National Bureau of Economic Research, 2020. https://doi.org/10.3386/w27274.

Vertical Integration

Type "bad predictions of the future" into Google and enjoy fun examples of history proving people horribly wrong. In 1800: "Rail travel at high speed is not possible, because passengers, unable to breathe, would die of asphyxia." Or 1903: "The horse is here to stay, but the automobile is only a novelty, a fad." Or H. M. Warner, a cofounder of the Warner Brothers movie studio, in 1927: "Who the hell wants to hear actors talk?"

The healthcare sector is not immune to lousy predictions. Here's a great one: "By 2020, the American health insurance industry will be extinct." That's Zeke Emanuel and Jeffrey Liebman in the *New York Times* in 2012, only eight years before the predicted extinction of the American health insurance industry. Why did Emanuel and Liebman believe that insurers were going to disappear in the intervening eight years? Because they believed that "insurance companies will be replaced by accountable care organizations—groups of doctors, hospitals and other health care providers who come together to provide the full range of medical care for patients."

Accountable Care Organizations, "ACOs," were once the future of healthcare. The organizations were created by the Medicare Shared Savings program, part of Obamacare. The law was meant to create a new organizational structure, a new way of providing care—an *integrated* model of care.

The old way of delivering healthcare—nonintegrated care—had providers forming an archipelago, with patients paddling from one island to another. The patient goes to the hospital and then afterward checks in with her primary-care physician. Then she visits a variety of specialists. And all of those providers are separate businesses, with separate electronic medical systems, and with little, if any, communication between the different offices and the hospital. Occasionally, one doctor faxes notes to another, but that's it.

The new way of delivering healthcare is all about integration. All the physicians are logged into the same electronic medical records system. The physicians coordinate with one another—not faxes but actual, real-time phone calls. Or even—*clutch your pearls*—meeting in person.

And this new way of delivering healthcare requires a new financial model. The old way involved every provider receiving his or her own fee-for-service payment—all providers would just bill the insurer on their own. The new way has the providers working together as a team and splitting a single payment from a shared-savings contract.

Harold Miller, an advocate for payment reform, makes an analogy to the production of televisions. No one actually wants to buy individual circuit boards. So, behind the scenes, Sony and Samsung and other TV manufacturers will contract with many suppliers for parts, and then the consumer can just buy a single, assembled TV. ACOs, the argument goes, work in the same way. Instead of going out and getting your primary care in one place and your acute hospitalization in another, patients can just go to one ACO and it'll provide all the healthcare they need (Gold 2011).

In other words, what matters is organizational structure. If we can somehow force healthcare organizations to shift from the old, fragmented model to a new, integrated model, everyone will be better off. That, at least, is what many health policy experts were arguing circa 2010. And those experts convinced the Obama administration to add ACOs into Obamacare.

However, this new system was a theoretical construct. Were ACOs actually the future of healthcare? And, more generally, if we change the structure of healthcare organizations, will that be an improvement? Let's go through the evidence.

Giving ACOs a Reality Check

Circa 2010, there was a whole lot of hype about ACOs. *ACOs will replace insurers. ACOs are the future. ACOs are going to cure cancer, bad breath, and burnt toast.* Those are not direct quotes, but you get the idea.

What actually happened?

The Medicare shared-savings provisions in Obamacare created ACOs. Technically, an ACO is a combination of one or more hospitals with a network of outpatient facilities. The hospitals and outpatient centers form an ACO voluntarily—no one is forced to do anything. But when the organizations team up and create an ACO, they write a shared-savings contract with Medicare. If patients who end up attached to the ACO use less healthcare than predicted, then the ACO gets a share of the forgone costs.

The shared-savings contracts come in different shapes and sizes. In some cases, the ACO faces downside risk: if the patients end up being more expensive than predicted, the ACO faces a penalty. In other contracts, the ACO enjoys a bonus only if healthcare costs go down but faces no penalty otherwise. In either case, the key feature of an ACO is (1) a combination of hospitals and physicians' offices and (2) a financial incentive for that team to lower costs for Medicare recipients.

Here's the theory behind the concept of ACOs. Tal, years ago, attended an interdisciplinary seminar just outside a hospital. In the middle of the seminar, an ambulance drove by the seminar room on its way to the emergency room. The ambulance's siren was on, and the seminar room was so close that the siren became deafening. The seminar had to be stopped until the ambulance had passed by. And then, just when the noise passed, an older man in the seminar, who had once served as a hospital CEO, stood up. "That's a *good* sound," he shouted. "That's the sound of revenue!"

That former hospital CEO was right: for hospitals, an insured ER visit is usually a good thing: the hospital makes money. Many of those ER visits are preventable: a majority of ER visits could actually be handled more efficiently and cheaply outside the ER (Udalova et al. 2022; Grumbach, Keane, and Bindman 1993). But the hospital usually doesn't care: it enjoys the revenue.

An ACO changes that. All of a sudden, the hospital, if it's part of an ACO, faces the opposite incentive. If it *prevents* an ER visit, which lowers spending, then Medicare will reward the ACO. So is that enough? Will those contracts cut costs without hurting anyone?

A skeptic can find plenty of reasons to question the 2010 hype on ACOs. First of all, a hospital sees tons of patients. If it becomes part of an ACO, it will face very different incentives for *some* of those patients. ACOs only involve some Medicare patients and not any patients on private insurance. It's not so easy for a big organization to navigate that complexity. For the Medicare patients enrolled in the ACO, the hospital suddenly wants to prevent hospitalizations. For other Medicare patients, and all patients not on Medicare, the hospital makes money on each hospitalization. How do you prevent visits for some patients, but then continue with business as usual for everyone else?

In addition, complex organizations are difficult to change. The managers at the top of the hierarchy meet in a boardroom and sign paperwork to become an ACO. Then they have to get a diverse group of physicians, nurses, and staff to coordinate based on the new game plan. That's difficult in every industry, but it is an especially big challenge in healthcare. At a hospital, medical ethics, regulations, and bureaucracy make managers' jobs especially difficult. In Facebook's early days, software engineers famously worked under the motto "move fast and break things"—no hospital could ever, in a million years, adopt that motto.

Since 2010, there have been quite a few studies written about ACOs. We quote two economists here, Sherry Glied and Adam Sacarny, who summarized the literature in a 2018 paper. "Initial evidence in favor of ACOs came from Massachusetts, where an early private insurance ACO contract yielded reductions in cost and improvements in quality (Song et al. 2014). Since then, ACOs have expanded, particularly in Medicare and Medicaid. Evaluations of these programs typically find statistically significant improvements in efficiency, *though these effects tend to be modest in magnitude* (Colla and Fisher 2017)." (We added the italics.)

The bottom line from most of the research on ACOs: some ACOs seem to work, but their effects are "modest." Many ACOs have been clear failures and have shut down. The ACOs that have survived tend to lower costs, but not by much. We're talking about a 1 percent drop in healthcare costs. Since healthcare is so expensive, that's nothing to sneeze at. But it's not a game changer. The 2010 hype on ACOs did not pan out.

There is still some disagreement on ACOs. A 2021 op-ed essay by a couple researchers in the field opined, "Accountable care organizations don't cut costs. It's time to stop the managed care experiment" (Sullivan and Kahn 2021). Other review articles argue that the whole ACO saga is a dead end (Lewis, Fisher, and Colla 2017; Burns and Pauly 2012; Barnes et al. 2014; Schulman and Richman 2016).

Even though ACOs didn't pan out, their central premise still matters. Tremendous interest continues in the idea of getting the providers outside of the hospital to cooperate with those inside the hospital.

Other Flavors of Vertical Integration in Healthcare

ACOs are only one part of a broader trend: more integration between hospital and nonhospital care. Economists often call this "vertical integration." The hospital is a "downstream" business: it collects patients from physicians' offices, and those physicians' offices are the "upstream" providers. If two hospitals merge, that's *horizontal* integration. If a hospital merges with a physicians' office, that's *vertical* integration.

Is vertical integration good or bad? Well, like everything else in healthcare, it's complicated.

Many experts in healthcare believe that vertical integration is a force for good. Their belief rests on a few theories. First of all, many believe that physicians do better work when they collect a fixed salary from a hospital rather than when they are running their own practices. The argument stems from the discussion we had in chapter 7: when physicians are running their own practices, and they collect only fee-for-service payments, they may end up providing too much care. *Perhaps*, when physicians are paid a fixed salary by a hospital, that is less of a concern.

Second, advocates of vertical integration point to famous healthcare providers that are vertically integrated and that are seen as providing excellent care. For instance, Kaiser Permanente runs a chain of hospitals in California, Colorado, and a few other states. The hospitals are not stand-alone facilities—they are integrated networks of physicians' practices and hospitals. All the doctors share the same electronic medical record system, work exclusively for Kaiser, and, generally, are paid via fixed salaries. Kaiser Permanente provides excellent care. So if vertical integration in other hospitals means that those hospitals will start to resemble Kaiser, then surely that means that care will improve. At least, that's the theory.

Third, advocates of vertical integration refer to the nuts and bolts of how medical decisions are made. Vertical integration, *perhaps*, means that care is more "coordinated." When different types of physicians all share the same employer, perhaps it is easier for them to discuss patients' needs in real time. Coordinated care, the physicians tell us, is better care.[1]

So that's a long list of reasons to be in favor of vertical integration: the salaried physicians, the coordinated care, the single system for digital records, and so on and so forth. Does that mean that every time a hospital acquires a physicians' office, we should cheer it on?

Two major issues should give us pause. First, the arguments in favor of vertical integration are based more on theory than evidence. It's not necessarily the case that vertical integration leads to better coordinated care or, for that matter, to better care. There are no guarantees.

And there's a second issue. When a hospital buys a physician's practice and integrates it into a larger organization, *prices* are likely to adjust. Before the acquisition, the practice bargained with insurers until they settled on a particular price. Once the practice is part of the hospital, it may be able to charge insurers a higher price. Perhaps the hospital will now get involved in negotiations with insurers and help the practice negotiate higher prices.

For that matter, Medicare *automatically* increases the price it pays to a practice once it has been acquired by a hospital. Medicare payments for outpatient visits include what is called a "facility fee." It's expensive to run a hospital: the giant buildings require lots of janitors, lots of electricity, lots of resources. So Medicare pays practices a higher rate if they are part of a large facility. Many private insurers follow Medicare's lead on this, and, regard-

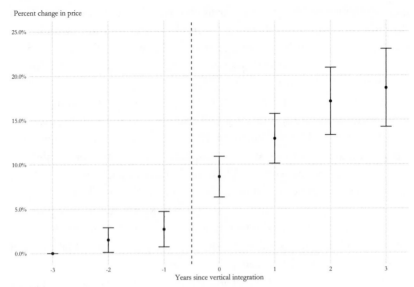

FIGURE 10.1. Percentage change in prices after physicians' practices are acquired by a hospital.

less of bargaining power, the newly acquired practice can thus enjoy a higher price solely due to the facility fees it is now entitled to charge.

A team of researchers at Northwestern University—Cory Capps, David Dranove, and Chris Ody (2018)—wrote a paper that compared prices at physicians' practices before and after they were acquired by a hospital. Figure 10.1 presents their main finding: after a hospital acquires a practice, prices at the practice increase by 14 percent. About half of that increase in prices is due to facility fees and half is due to the practices enjoying better bargaining power.

What's more, that average increase in price hides substantial variation. In some cities, the hospital market is highly competitive: there are many hospitals and no one hospital dominates the city. In those cities, the authors observe a small increase in prices after a practice is acquired by a hospital. But in other cities, the hospital market is monopolistic: one hospital dominates the market. In those cities, the researchers measured much larger increases in prices after an acquisition.

So those kinds of estimates suggest that, when it comes to vertical acquisitions, there's a real trade-off. *Maybe* the vertical acquisition improves quality of care. We are not aware of any good, empirical evidence for such an effect, but it is possible. The paper by Capps, Dranove, and Ody—along with several other studies—suggests that any improvement in quality of care comes at the cost of higher prices (Dafny, Ho, and Lee 2016; Neprash et al. 2015; O'Malley, Bond, and Berenson 2011).

The bottom line is that it's difficult, given the system we have now, to be a reservations-free cheerleader for vertical integration. Yes, there's reason to believe that physicians should be salaried, that everyone should be logged into the same electronic medical system, that the physicians outside the hospital should be communicating with physicians inside the hospital.

But there's that other issue: *prices*. Vertical integration raises prices, and it's hard to imagine improvements in quality of care that are so magical as to outweigh the increase in prices.

We might even think of vertical integration, given our current system, as a matter, once again, of dolphins and tuna: situations in which it is difficult to cut out the bad and keep the good. In the case of vertical integration, it seems as though higher prices arise alongside possible medical benefits. And that makes vertical integration a tough call.

Vertical Spillovers between Providers

If vertical integration does have benefits, though, then a question naturally arises. Why don't providers vertically integrate on their own?

Consider blood thinners. Millions of patients are on them. When they take their pills regularly, they stay in good shape. But some patients forget to pick up their prescriptions at the pharmacy or they forget to take their pills at home. Those patients can end up in trouble. In bad cases, a blood clot might send them to the emergency room. In the worst cases, they end up admitted to the hospital.

When those patients go to the pharmacy to pick up their blood thinners, what kind of copayment should they face? Should they face a $5 copayment or should the blood thinners be free? The $5 copayments lead to fewer patients picking up blood thinners (see chap. 4). But then some of those patients will end up getting a blood clot and having an expensive emergency room visit.

Managers at the insurance company discuss this when they decide what copayment they should set for blood thinners. The managers sit around a board table and decide whether blood thinners should be free or cheap or expensive for patients. The managers are sophisticated and they understand that higher copayments for blood thinners may lead to more hospital visits. But do they care?

Vertical integration can actually play a substantial role in that meeting. First, imagine that the managers deciding on a copayment for blood thinners are running a Medicare Part D "stand-alone drug plan." The managers are in charge of patient drug benefits—all costs associated with the pharmaceuticals that patients pick up—and they are not involved in the patients' other healthcare costs. Stand-alone drug plans only cover the costs of the patients' drugs, not the costs of the patients' doctor visits, ER visits, or hospitalizations.

So the managers of a stand-alone drug plan might not care that getting patients to take their blood thinners will prevent a hospitalization. After all, that hospitalization is someone else's problem. Yes, the managers are human, and they care about the people affected by their decisions. But the managers face no financial incentive to work to prevent hospitalizations. Preventing a hospitalization doesn't save their stand-alone plan any money.

Alternatively, imagine that the managers are running an "integrated" insurance plan. The managers operate a plan that is exposed to both the cost of drugs and to the cost of all other care. If patients end up in the hospital, the same managers have to worry about that bill, too.

Hopefully, the contrast between the two types of plans is clear. If the managers are worried about both the cost of the blood thinners *and* the costs of ER visits, then they face an incentive to make sure that patients take their blood thinners. And lo and behold, researchers have found this to be the case: stand-alone drug plans impose higher copayments on medications that might prevent a hospitalization as compared to integrated insurance plans (Starc and Town 2020).

We call this a "vertical spillover," since the pharmacy is "upstream" and the hospital is "downstream." Whether or not people take their pills determines, for some patients, whether or not they go to the hospital. In other words, upstream decisions determine downstream costs. And so managers make different decisions depending on whether or not their upstream firm is exposed to downstream costs.

This dynamic then suggests a way for integrated insurers to be more profitable: if they are exposed to downstream costs, then consider looking upstream. Maybe the copayments on prescriptions should change. Blood thinners, asthma medication, antiseizure drugs, and many other types of drugs can prevent ER visits and hospitalizations. So lower copayments on those drugs might actually be cost-saving for some patients.

And there are other, similar upstream actions that might lead to downstream profits. Many of the patients sitting in ER waiting rooms would happily trade their seat for an appointment with a primary-care physician (Grumbach, Keane, and Bindman 1993). So perhaps better ways for patients to quickly arrange to meet with a doctor upstream might lower costs downstream.

There's also an obvious business play here: insurers that are exposed to downstream costs should contract with upstream providers. For instance, a health insurer worried about the high cost of ER visits and hospitalizations could contract with a network of pharmacies and urgent care centers.

Such contracts, however, can be tricky to negotiate. A particular problem can arise: the holdup problem.

To understand the holdup problem, let's take a concrete hypothetical. Betna is an imaginary health insurer. Part of Betna's business is a large Medicare Advantage plan that covers a million Medicare recipients. Betna is exposed to the full cost of care for those enrollees: if the company can prevent hospitalizations, it makes more money. So executives at Betna look for a way to prevent hospitalizations.

Executives at Betna turn to RapidClinic, an imaginary network of urgent care centers. Executives at Betna approach RapidClinic and offer them a deal. Here's Betna's proposal.

> A lot of our patients have chronic conditions: asthma, diabetes, epilepsy. If we can get them quick appointments with nurse practitioners in your clinics, they'll be less likely to end up in the hospital. So let's create a joint operation for those enrollees. And for every hospitalization prevented, we'll give you $500.

This sounds like a win-win: Betna has to pay for fewer hospitalizations and so makes more money while RapidClinic turns a profit as well. But the holdup problem can sink the deal. Suppose that Betna and RapidClinic sign a contract and then invest in a joint venture. That joint venture requires a lot of investments on the part of RapidClinic. RapidClinic has to build a new IT infrastructure that is integrated with Betna's computer systems. The two companies invest in a marketing campaign: fancy billboards that advertise the Betna-RapidClinic arrangement.

All of this is well and good. But there exists a certain vulnerability in the arrangement. RapidClinic has sunk tons of money into the joint venture, and that sunk cost only leads to profit if the joint venture persists. Betna can play off that vulnerability. Imagine the e-mail that the CEO of Betna sends to the CEO of RapidClinic, after many of the investments have been made.

> I hope that this finds you well and that you are ready to hit the links again soon; I've got a new set of golf clubs, and I'm ready to win my money back! Quick question about our joint venture. We did an internal study and have decided that the $500 price we initially agreed upon is too high. We will pay $300 for each hospitalization prevented, not $500. We ran this change by legal, and they determined that we do have the right to change that price. Let's play another round ASAP!

That e-mail is a stab in the heart of RapidClinic's CEO. She's spent months sinking tons of money into this joint venture under the understanding that it would pay off $500 for every hospitalization prevented. If Betna had initially offered $300, then they would never have taken the joint venture on. But now, it's not clear she can walk away. The investments have been made, and $300 is the minimum price she'll accept and stay in the game.

This is what economists call the "holdup problem." The CEO of Betna "holds up" the CEO of RapidClinic, lowering the price to the minimum that will keep RapidClinic from walking away.

Anticipating this possibility, RapidClinic may have never agreed to the joint venture with Betna in the first place. Even though there is a profitable joint venture here, the possibility of holdup may prevent that joint venture from occurring.

What's the answer? Well, one solution is a vertical merger. Betna could merge with RapidClinic. Then there would be no holdup problem, because a company cannot hold up itself. Vertical mergers not only offer a solution to the holdup problem, they also offer other advantages. The two company's IT infrastructures could be completely merged. The companies would then explore all sorts of creative ways in which investment in the retail clinics might make the insurance side of the business more profitable.

In fact, this made-up example is not entirely fanciful. Aetna is one of America's largest health insurers, and in 2018 it merged with CVS Health, a chain of pharmacies. The merger was driven, in part, to incorporate CVS's MinuteClinics into Aetna's operations. CVS MinuteClinics are small provider offices located in its retail pharmacies.

But there are also tremendous downsides to a vertical merger. The merger takes a lot of resources to consummate. Many workers become redundant and have to be laid off. And, in the end, an enormous healthcare corporation ended up both managing health insurance plans and also pricing bags of chips sold next to the cash register at CVS.

Given those drawbacks to vertical mergers, it's not necessarily surprising that other pharmacy chains have chosen not to merge with an insurer. For example, Walgreens is CVS's largest competitor and has something similar to MinuteClinics—Health Hubs. At the time of this writing, instead of acquiring a healthcare system, Walgreens has chosen to contract with different insurers. That approach risks holdup problems, but it keeps Walgreens flexible. The CEO of Walgreens has not tied the future of the company to a single insurer, and it can focus on its core business, not running a giant insurance company.

All in all, the contrasting examples of CVS and Walgreens are a sign of both where healthcare is going in the United States and also the challenges in getting there. Notwithstanding the failure of ACOs, the business of health-care is still going to become more integrated. More organizations are going to face an incentive to prevent hospitalizations and ER visits, which will lead them to focus on upstream interventions. That, in turn, will mean that pharmacies and clinics will collaborate with insurers and hospitals.

Vertical Spillovers between Insurers

So far we've discussed spillovers in the vertical supply chain: from the pharmacy to the hospital. Decisions upstream, at the pharmacy, affect costs downstream, at the hospital. But there exists another vertical supply chain in healthcare, one that also involves spillovers. Most Americans are on commercial insurance plans through adulthood, and then, when they turn sixty-five, they are covered by Medicare. In a sense, that's another kind of vertical arrangement, a temporal one: commercial insurers upstream and Medicare downstream. And before Americans go on Medicare, they typically transition across a variety of commercial insurers, perhaps from Aetna to Cigna to Blue Cross and Blue Shield. Those transitions also amount to a vertical arrangement, with earlier insurers upstream and later insurers downstream.

Just as decisions at the pharmacy can lead to costs at the hospital, decisions at commercial insurers can lead, later on, to costs for Medicare or other insurers. Take, for instance, Sovaldi. Sovaldi is a treatment for hepatitis C, a treatment introduced by Gilead pharmaceuticals in 2013. Sovaldi is a rare example of a miracle cure: the drug cures roughly 90 percent of hepatitis C cases when patients take a full, ninety-day course. For that reason, Gilead priced the drug very aggressively in 2013, charging a list price of about $1,000 per pill or around $80,000 for a full course of treatment.

That high price immediately generated controversy. There was public outcry and Congress investigated. How dare Gilead charge such a high price? Executives at Gilead defended the price. Look, they argued, the drug is a cure. Without a cure for hepatitis C, most patients suffer for years and eventually require a liver transplant. When all is said and done, $80,000 for the drug might actually be a bargain—the cost of not curing hepatitis C is much higher.

But here's the thing: the costs and benefits of Sovaldi are not evenly distributed. Imagine that there's a patient on a commercial plan in 2013 when the drug is introduced. The commercial insurer reluctantly pays $80,000 for Sovaldi to cure the patient's hepatitis C. As a result, the patient thrives and, fifteen years later, she no longer needs a liver transplant.

Is that a good deal for the commercial insurer? Well, the insurer paid for the treatment in 2013, and much of the financial benefits came later, after the patient had gone to another insurance plan, and then, much later, was on Medicare. The financial benefits accrued to those payers, not the original insurance company that footed the bill.

This is an issue not just when it comes to Sovaldi but for many other new, expensive therapies. Take, for instance, Zynteglo. Zynteglo is a gene therapy that treats beta thalassemia, a rare hereditary blood disorder. Bluebird Bio, the company that makes Zynteglo, prices the treatment at $2.8 million. According to the Institute for Clinical and Economic Review, that price is actually not outlandish. Since the treatment can cure an otherwise debilitating blood disorder, the high price might be roughly similar to the financial benefits of the treatment—because the therapy saves tremendous costs down the line.

But tell that to the commercial insurer that happens to cover a patient who needs Zynteglo. The patient needs Zynteglo, and the commercial insurer may reluctantly pay for it, but the monetary benefits go to other insurers years later.

This is a uniquely American problem. Unlike people in most wealthy countries, Americans are covered by a fragmented collection of payers: fifty-one Medicaid programs, Medicare, and hundreds of commercial insurers spread across the country. It's not clear how such a collection of payers can handle new technologies that cost one payer but then go on to benefit a dispersed group of other payers.

There are, nevertheless, ideas about how to make this spillover work. Some pharmaceutical companies are starting to offer "installment plans" for gene therapies. Instead of paying $2 million all at once, an insurer has to pay for the therapy gradually, over several years. If the patient switches to a different insurance plan, then, in theory, the new insurer pays for the remaining installments.

Some propose having Medicare pay state Medicaid agencies to cover the cost of drugs that may ultimately save Medicare money down the line. Many of the details have yet to be worked out. What if the patient's current insurance plan agrees to the installment plan, but the patient's next insurer does not? How does Medicare make sure that Medicaid uses the money for drugs that actually save Medicare money? What if the savings are greater or less than expected?

A similar dynamic might exist between health insurers and *life* insurers. Life insurers pay benefits whenever a policyholder dies—the longer their policyholders live, the more money a life insurer makes. And so, as a result, life insurers profit if their policyholders receive life-extending treatments. In the same way that there exist spillovers between Medicare and Medicaid or between one health insurer and another, there exists a spillover between health insurers and life insurers (Koijen and Van Nieuwerburgh 2020). Health insurers have to pay for life-extending treatments, and life insurers benefit.

The Bottom Line

We've described complexity along one dimension of the American health-care space, the vertical dimension. A lot of healthcare spending is a matter of upstream decisions and downstream costs. And yet it is difficult for down-stream providers to contract with upstream providers because of the holdup problem. Vertical mergers can address some of the challenges associated with holdup problems, but those mergers often lead to higher prices. Similar con-tracting problems also make it hard for insurers to work together to make decisions that lower total costs and improve patient health.

All of that being said, there is still reason to be somewhat hopeful about vertical mergers in healthcare. Vertical mergers may increase care coordina-tion and increase quality of care. We want upstream and downstream parties to work together in healthcare. Cheap clinic visits can prevent hospitaliza-tions, outpatient providers can make sure people take their meds and so stay out of the ER, and on and on. Vertical mergers might facilitate all of that kind of cooperation.

And so we end up being much more ambivalent about vertical mergers as compared to horizontal mergers, which we discussed in the previous chap-ter. Horizontal mergers are often viewed suspiciously by experts, but vertical mergers are viewed more open-mindedly. Vertical mergers are certainly not perfect—we still worry about their price effects. But higher prices and higher quality of care certainly beat out higher prices and lower quality of care. Or to put it another way, neither horizontal mergers nor vertical mergers are going to address the high cost of healthcare, but at least vertical mergers have the potential to improve quality of care.

References

"ACP Lays out Mechanisms for Better Care Coordination between Primary and Specialty Care to Improve Patient Care." American College of Physicians, April 2022. https://www .acponline.org/acp-newsroom/acp-lays-out-mechanisms-for-better-care-coordination -between-primary-and-specialty-care-to-improve.

Barnes, Andrew J., Lynn Unruh, Askar Chukmaitov, and Ewout van Ginneken. "Accountable Care Organizations in the USA: Types, Developments and Challenges." Health Policy 118, no. 1 (2014): 1–7. https://doi.org/10.1016/j.healthpol.2014.07.019.

Burns, Lawton R., and Mark V. Pauly. "Accountable Care Organizations May Have Difficulty Avoiding the Failures of Integrated Delivery Networks of the 1990s." Health Affairs 31, no. 11 (2012): 2407–16. https://doi.org/10.1377/hlthaff.2011.0675.

Capps, Cory, David Dranove, and Christopher Ody. "The Effect of Hospital Acquisitions of Phy-sician Practices on Prices and Spending." Journal of Health Economics 59 (May 2018): 139–52. https://doi.org/10.1016/j.jhealeco.2018.04.001.

Colla, Carrie H., and Elliott S. Fisher. "Moving Forward with Accountable Care Organizations: Some Answers, More Questions." *JAMA Internal Medicine* 177, no. 4 (2017): 527–28. https://doi.org/10.1001/jamainternmed.2016.9122.

Dafny, Leemore, Kate Ho, and Robin Lee. "The Price Effects of Cross-Market Hospital Mergers." Working Paper 22106. National Bureau of Economic Research, 2016. https://doi.org/10.3386/w22106.

Glied, Sherry, and Adam Sacarny. "Is the US Health Care System Wasteful and Inefficient? A Review of the Evidence." *Journal of Health Politics, Policy and Law* 43, no. 5 (2018): 739–65. https://doi.org/10.1215/03616878-6951103.

Gold, Jenny. "Accountable Care Organizations, Explained." *NPR*, January 18, 2011, sec. Health. https://www.npr.org/2011/04/01/132937232/accountable-care-organizations-explained.

Grumbach, K., D. Keane, and A. Bindman. "Primary Care and Public Emergency Department Overcrowding." *American Journal of Public Health* 83, no. 3 (1993): 372–78. https://doi.org/10.2105/AJPH.83.3.372.

Koijen, Ralph S. J., and Stijn Van Nieuwerburgh. "Combining Life and Health Insurance." *Quarterly Journal of Economics* 135, no. 2 (2020): 913–58. https://doi.org/10.1093/qje/qjz037.

Lewis, Valerie A., Elliott S. Fisher, and Carrie H. Colla. "Explaining Sluggish Savings under Accountable Care." *New England Journal of Medicine* 377, no. 19 (2017): 1809–11. https://doi.org/10.1056/NEJMp1709197.

Liebman, Jeffrey, and Ezekiel Emanuel. "The End of Health Insurance Companies." *New York Times*, January 30, 2012.

Neprash, Hannah T., Michael E. Chernew, Andrew L. Hicks, Teresa Gibson, and J. Michael McWilliams. "Association of Financial Integration between Physicians and Hospitals with Commercial Health Care Prices." *JAMA Internal Medicine* 175, no. 12 (2015): 1932–39. https://doi.org/10.1001/jamainternmed.2015.4610.

O'Malley, Ann S., Amelia M. Bond, and Robert A. Berenson. "Rising Hospital Employment of Physicians: Better Quality, Higher Costs?" Center for Studying Health System Change, no. 136 (2011): 1–4.

Schulman, Kevin A., and Barak D. Richman. "Reassessing ACOs and Health Care Reform." *JAMA* 316, no. 7 (2016): 707–8. https://doi.org/10.1001/jama.2016.10874.

Song, Zirui, Sherri Rose, Dana G. Safran, Bruce E. Landon, Matthew P. Day, and Michael E. Chernew. "Changes in Health Care Spending and Quality 4 Years into Global Payment." *New England Journal of Medicine* 371, no. 18 (2014): 1704–14. https://doi.org/10.1056/NEJMsa1404026.

Starc, Amanda, and Robert J. Town. "Externalities and Benefit Design in Health Insurance." *Review of Economic Studies* 87, no. 6 (2020): 2827–58. https://doi.org/10.1093/restud/rdz052.

Sullivan, Kip, and James Kahn. "Accountable Care Organizations Don't Cut Costs. It's Time to Stop the Managed Care Experiment." *STAT* (blog). August 23, 2021. https://www.statnews.com/2021/08/23/stop-failed-accountable-care-organization-experiment/.

Udalova, Victoria, David Powers, Sara Robinson, and Isabelle Notter. "Most Vulnerable More Likely to Depend on Emergency Rooms for Preventable Care." Working paper. Washington, DC: US Census Bureau, January 2022. https://www.census.gov/library/stories/2022/01/who-makes-more-preventable-visits-to-emergency-rooms.html.

Quality

We are old enough to remember Nokia cell phones. Cell phones used to be plastic candy bars, dominated by hardware buttons and tiny, low-resolution screens. We used to text by tapping on the tiny plastic keys. Tap the "1" button once for an "A," twice for a "B."

Then, in 2007, Apple released the first iPhone. That first iPhone was magical—a columnist for the *Wall Street Journal* called it the "Jesus Phone" (Kedrosky 2007). Really. It had only a few hardware buttons and—for the time—a giant, high-resolution screen. Within a few years, the iPhone made Apple the most valuable corporation in the world. And soon all cell phones looked like the iPhone: no more hardware keyboards, and no more Nokia phones.

The story of the iPhone is the story of the market rewarding a new entrant with a better product. There are other examples. In the 1980s, Toyota and Honda succeeded in the American car market by producing more reliable cars than Ford, Chrysler, or GM. In 2020, Zoom became a billion-dollar company because the COVID-19 pandemic hit and it made the best videoconferencing software.

This is one of the benefits of a free market. Consumers value good, high-quality products, and they vote with their wallets. We bought a Honda, then we bought an iPhone, then we started using Zoom, all because those companies produced the best products.

Does the same thing happen in healthcare? If a new entrant in healthcare provides higher quality care, does it win?

The answer is not obvious. In healthcare, it's hard to measure quality. Suppose that a new hospital is the "iPhone of hospitals"—how would ordinary patients know? After all, patients are not experts. Would they even know that the hospital's care is any better?

Moreover, there are all sorts of frictions in healthcare that might keep a new, high-quality entrant from winning. We are free to sell our Ford and buy a Honda, but our choice of hospital is often limited by our insurer's network. Many patients don't really choose a hospital to begin with, they just visit whichever hospital their physician chooses for them. And the same is true for physicians themselves: how many patients can really spot a good physician from a bad physician? So, a priori, it's unclear whether providing higher quality is actually rewarded in healthcare.

In the Market for Healthcare, Does Quality Even Matter?

A team of health economists sought to answer that question: Amitabh Chandra, Amy Finkelstein, Adam Sacarny, and Chad Syverson (2016). That team designed a simple test to see whether the "iPhone of hospitals" would win. The authors gathered data on about 3,000 American hospitals, and they calculated measures of each hospital's quality in 2008: patients' survival rates, readmission rates, complication rates, and so on. Then the researchers measured the growth in the number of patients from 2008 to 2010. The authors tested whether those two variables—quality of care and later growth in patients—were positively or negatively correlated.

That one statistical test was the authors' attempt to get at the iPhone question. The iPhone was better than all of the phones available when it was introduced, and, sure enough, Apple sold millions of iPhones in the years that followed. This research team set out to test for the same relationship across hospitals. Some hospitals offered especially high-quality care in 2008: in the years after, were those hospitals rewarded?

It's worth noting that the research team published this paper, not at the dawn of health economics, but rather in 2016. At that late date, this very basic research question had not yet been answered: Does the market work for healthcare? That research question was worthy of investigation because, as we've described, it really wasn't obvious what the researchers would find. There are arguments for why the market for healthcare might resemble the market for cell phones, and also arguments for why the two are entirely different.

What did the authors find? They found a robust positive relationship between hospital quality in 2008 and the growth of patient volume from 2008 through 2010. They experimented with a variety of metrics for quality and always reached the same general conclusion: "higher quality hospitals have higher market shares and grow more over time."

The authors described that finding as a "signpost of competition." In the same way that the market "works" for iPhones, it works—at least somewhat—for hospitals.

Moreover, the authors uncovered an interesting dynamic regarding how healthcare improves over time. Physicians are always getting better at treating patients: mortality rates and readmission rates tend to fall over time for many conditions. Most of that improvement is a matter of the progress of medicine: better clinical guidelines, better drugs, better protocols, and so on. But up to a quarter of the improvement over time is a matter of patients shifting from lower quality hospitals to higher quality hospitals. The switching across providers is part of the progress of medicine.[1]

Still, we shouldn't go crazy here. The authors caution that they are just finding a positive relationship between quality and market share—it's just the overall average, just a "signpost." There are still many low-quality providers out there. The iPhone entirely changed cell phones: within ten years of the iPhone being introduced, practically no cell phones had hardware keyboards. The dynamic is not that stark in healthcare—low-quality care is still out there. This one study just proved that quality does matter, at least somewhat, and the market does reward it, at least somewhat. The healthcare world is certainly beset by frictions that keep the market from working as efficiently as it does for other goods. But market forces still matter, even in healthcare.

But Wait—How Do We Measure Quality?

If quality actually matters in healthcare, how do we measure it? When it comes to phones, we might track the number of megapixels the camera captures, the gigabytes stored by the hard drive, and so on. We could also try to do the same thing for physicians, calculating metrics that purport to measure the quality of the physician's care. For each physician, we can calculate a mortality rate, a readmission rate, a complication rate, and so on.

But, doing so, we would immediately hit a problem. To truly measure quality, we need random assignment of patients to physicians. To see that, imagine a careful study of obstetricians, measuring, for each obstetrician, the share of medical problems that their patients have encountered. For instance, sometimes obstetricians delivering a baby via cesarean section will accidentally nick the baby with the scalpel. The technical term for such a mistake is a "fetal laceration"—it happens to about 1 or 2 percent of babies born via C-section (Wiener and Westwood 2002). So we might go out and measure the rate of fetal laceration for each obstetrician. And, of course, we don't only focus on that one bad outcome, but rather, we study all of the bad stuff that can happen when a baby is born: the baby getting nicked, the mother suffering perineal tears, and, most tragic of all, either the baby or the mother passing away. We perform that analysis and then reach a clear conclusion: one obstetrician, in particular, is a disaster. She has the highest rate of babies and mothers being harmed during delivery.

Should we fire that obstetrician?

Well, we pause for a second and look up the obstetrician. Turns out, the doctor whom our analysis has picked out as a terrible physician is actually a high-risk obstetrician, a "maternal-fetal medicine specialist." She is specially trained to handle the toughest cases. No wonder that doctor has the worst record: she only gets the most challenging patients! Our analysis led to precisely the wrong conclusion: it was because this doctor was the best doctor that she had the worst record!

To really measure a physician's quality, we need random assignment of patients to physicians.[2] Without random assignment, it can be very difficult to isolate the quality of the physician from the preexisting health of their patients. In this example, the obstetrician was great—it was her patients' preexisting health problems that led to poor health outcomes.

But how do we find a setting in which patients are randomly assigned to doctors? Randomization doesn't happen very often. After all, what kind of patient would ever agree to such a thing? "Ma'am, before I transfer you to the operating room, I'm just going to flip a coin to choose your attending physician. No need to be concerned, ma'am. If the coin comes up heads, you'll be in very good hands."

And yet, one team of researchers discovered precisely such a practice. Though it sounds incredible, Joe Doyle, Steven Ewer, and Todd Wagner (2008) found a setting in which patients were truly randomly assigned to physicians. The team studied a large, urban Veterans Affairs (VA) hospital that was affiliated with two academic institutions. There were two teams of resident physicians treating patients at this VA hospital: one team was affiliated with one of the nation's most prestigious medical schools and the other was affiliated with a less prestigious institution. For the sake of confidentiality, we are not told which VA hospital the team studied, or which two medical schools were affiliated with the VA hospital. But the researchers tell us that one team of residents came from "one of the top medical schools" in the country, while the other one came from "near the median of medical schools." One is a "Top 5" medical school and the other is a "Top 50" school.

Administrators at the VA had to assign patients to those two teams of physicians. The administrators wanted to assign patients equitably, so that one team was not burdened with more patients or with more difficult patients. For that reason, the hospital administrators settled on a particular strategy for assigning patients to doctors. Patients with odd Social Security numbers were assigned to residents from the more prestigious program, whereas patients with even Social Security numbers were assigned to residents from the less prestigious program.

What's exciting about such a process is that, effectively, patients were randomly assigned to physicians. Whether a given Social Security number is odd or even is truly random.[3] So this is a rare case in which administrators effectively flipped a coin for each patient.

Administrators at the VA hospital stuck to this system for 30,000 patients, not for the sake of research but solely to keep the assignment of patients to physicians simple and fair. Joe Doyle heard of the practice, and he realized that the VA hospital had actually, unknowingly, run a fascinating clinical trial. And so Doyle and his coauthors collected data on the VA's patients and used the setting to learn whether the prestige of physician training actually matters for patient outcomes.

Now, before turning to the results, it is worth pausing and asking what one might expect to see. In our MBA course, we often do so, asking our students which group of patients ought to do better. Our students mull the question over and usually disagree on what they would expect to occur. One student, a practicing physician, hypothesized that the patients assigned to the residents from the more prestigious program might actually do worse. He imagined that those residents would constantly "overthink" every case, and so overtreat patients. Other students make the opposite prediction: the residents from the more prestigious program would save more lives. The more prestigious training, they argue, would make them more effective clinicians.

The actual results lie somewhere between those two hypotheses. Figure 11.1 summarizes the paper's findings. Patients who were randomly assigned to residents from the more prestigious program were in the hospital for shorter spells. That accounts for the zigzag pattern of estimates in the first panel: odd Social Security numbers (those assigned to the more prestigious program) enjoyed shorter lengths of stay. This added up to lower costs: 10 percent lower medical costs for patients who were randomly assigned to residents from the more prestigious program. So physicians from the more prestigious program discharged their patients earlier and, as a result, ordered fewer medical tests, and so cost the system less money.

Then the authors studied two markers of patients' actual well-being after the hospitalization: readmission and mortality. There, they didn't find any statistically significant differences. Patients assigned to residents from the more prestigious program were no more likely to survive or to avoid another hospitalization.

Logarithm of length of stay

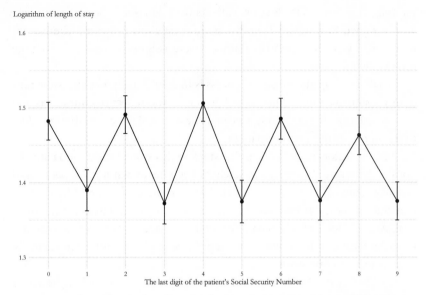

FIGURE 11.1. Average length of stay for patients by the patient's last digit of their Social Security number. Patients with odd Social Security numbers were seen by residents from the more prestigious program (Doyle, Ewer, and Wagner 2008).

All in all, in this rare instance in which we actually observe random assignment of patients to physicians, we see differences across physicians' performance. But the differences are not large enough, in this case, to affect mortality or readmission. Still, we observe large differences in costs. All else equal, if we were the patient, we'd prefer to have a doctor from the "top 5" program. If nothing else, we'd get to leave the hospital sooner.

Measuring Quality Can Lead to Cream Skimming

That study on the VA demonstrates what is, perhaps, an obvious point: the quality of physicians really does vary, at least when it comes to length of stay and costs. So such a finding leads to a natural question: If quality really does vary, why not try to measure it?

Well, as with so much else in healthcare, the problem with such a policy is that the reaction of healthcare providers may undermine the policy. In particular, we might be worried about cream skimming, a topic we first discussed in chapter 2. When doctors know that the quality of their care is being evaluated, perhaps they will choose patients more strategically.

Consider cardiac surgeons in New York State in the late 1980s. For decades, New York's cardiac surgeons had pretty much been left to their own devices, operating on anyone who needed cardiac surgery. Starting in 1989, New York State launched the "Cardiac Surgery Reporting System," which tracked outcomes for bypass surgeons. For the first time, each year administrators measured the share of these surgeons' patients that ended up with complications, or with a hospital readmission, or who died within thirty days of their surgery.

The new reporting system brought transparency to bypass surgery. Before the system, patients could only learn about a surgeon's record if they had a friend at the hospital. Perhaps some patients could ask a surgical tech: "You've seen all of them operate—if you were the patient, which surgeon would you choose?" Maybe some patients had friends who were surgeons and so could give them the inside scoop. But such a state of affairs is clearly inequitable: some patients have access to information and others do not. After the reporting system was put in place, any patient in New York State who needed bypass surgery could look at every surgeon's record.

But how did New York's surgeons react to the new reporting system? Perhaps some worked harder or took on more training or were more careful. Still, others may have reacted in a way that was a bit more insidious.

The change became apparent not in New York State, but over 400 miles away, at the Cleveland Clinic. The Cleveland Clinic is a center of excellence for cardiac surgery, and the center treated patients from New York both before and after the introduction of the reporting system. Researchers at the Cleveland Clinic noticed a striking pattern: after the introduction of the Cardiac Surgery Reporting System in New York, the average health of the patients from New York at the Cleveland Clinic deteriorated (Omoigui et al. 1996). Before the system, about 4 percent of patients referred from New York would die after surgery. After the reporting system was introduced in New York, about 6 percent of patients referred from New York would die after surgery. And there was no similar increase for patients from other states.

The researchers concluded that the tracking of surgery outcomes in New York led surgeons to cream skim. Before the tracking system, if a patient was especially high risk but still needed bypass surgery, the surgeons would happily perform the procedure. Once their outcomes were tracked, however, some of them became hesitant to operate. "Yes, this patient needs the surgery, but there's also a good chance that he'll have a bad outcome. And with this new system, I can't afford a bad outcome. Why not send him to Cleveland?" In chapter 2, we called this kind of behavior "cream skimming." The surgeons suddenly started to choose their patients very strategically.

That behavior is a potential downside of quality-tracking systems. On the one hand, we want to measure the quality of procedure-based physicians, because it is hard to improve what we don't measure. Surely there are some low-quality performers who should get out of the field—measuring surgeons' performance can help us identify them. For that matter, patients simply have a right to know if their surgeon has a bad record. It's not fair to keep the data hidden from patients and their families.

On the other hand, there are two clear, cogent reasons *not* to track surgeons' performance. First, it is difficult to accurately measure quality without random assignment. The best surgeons may be sent the hardest cases, which might, paradoxically, lead us to conclude that they are the worst surgeons. One VA hospital happened to have a system in place that randomized patients to doctors—that's almost never the case. Second, measuring performance can lead surgeons to cream skim. Some doctors may become very selective in which patients they choose, and that kind of behavior would make those surgeons' records look better, but would certainly not be helping the patients. At the end of the day, then, hospitals and local health departments have to decide whether the benefits of tracking outcomes outweigh those costs.

Beta Blockers

In 1983, a group of physicians at the National Heart, Lung, and Blood Institute had an experiment on their hands that was going to change medicine forever. They were experimenting with beta blockers: a class of medications that slow down the heart rate. Beta blockers are performance-enhancing drugs for Olympic sharpshooters—the drop in heart rate improves a sharpshooter's aim. Psychiatrists prescribe beta blockers for people with stage fright—the drop in heart rate is calming to those with a fear of public speaking who nevertheless find themselves in front of a crowd. But, in this case, the researchers wondered whether beta blockers might reduce the damage from a heart attack.

And so the researchers launched a randomized controlled trial ("A Randomized Trial of Propranolol in Patients with Acute Myocardial Infarction" 1983). Nearly 2,000 patients who came into the emergency room with a suspected heart attack received a beta blocker and nearly 2,000 other patients received a placebo. The researchers were planning to run the experiment well into 1982, but they stopped the trial nine months ahead of schedule. Beta blockers proved so effective that it would have been unethical to continue the trial further.

That happened in 1982: definitive proof that beta blockers are remarkably effective at saving the lives of people who have just had a heart attack. What happens next? Here's what one would hope: the next day, all emergency rooms everywhere would start dispensing beta blockers to those types of patients.

Percentage of hospitals

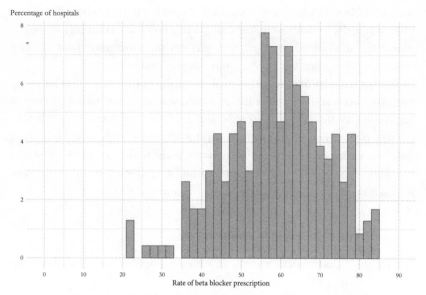

FIGURE 11.2. Rates of beta blocker prescriptions across 243 hospitals (Bradley et al. 2005).

After all, we're talking about a cheap medical treatment that dramatically improves survival rates—it should be everywhere right away.

Unfortunately, that's not what happened. By 1998, about sixteen years after that initial randomized trial, only about half of patients were given beta blockers. And it wasn't half of patients in all hospitals: some hospitals were quick to adopt beta blockers and others took forever (Bradley et al. 2004). The histogram in figure 11.2 comes from a medical study in the late 1990s (Bradley et al. 2005). The researchers documented huge variation in the correct usage of beta blockers across hospitals. Jonathan Skinner and Doug Staiger (Skinner and Staiger 2015), two health economists, call the hospitals that quickly adopted beta blockers "tigers" and call the hospitals that took forever to adopt beta blockers "tortoises." Skinner and Staiger estimated that heart attack patients in "tiger" hospitals were more likely to survive.

Some experts describe the adoption of beta blockers as a "no-brainer" intervention: any physician who looked at the data should have concluded that adopting beta blockers was worthwhile. And yet it took *decades* for the practice to spread.

Why do we fixate on this one particular medical intervention? Medicine is an extraordinarily complex field, with thousands of diagnoses and thousands of treatments. The adoption of beta blockers is one particular example of a broader phenomenon: variation in the adoption of high-quality practices. Research identifies how clinicians should treat patients, and often, as with the case of beta blockers, the research is decisive. But then, some healthcare providers are way too slow to respond. At this point, beta blockers are nearly universally distributed appropriately in American emergency rooms. But it took over thirty years to get here (Akbar and Alorainy 2014).

So this is evidence of some hospitals behaving poorly and others behaving well. We have a context where there's a right way to treat a particular class of patients—give them beta blockers!—and a wrong way. Some hospitals take decades before they switch from the wrong way to the right way, while other hospitals switch much more quickly. In other words, the case of beta blockers is evidence that quality varies across hospitals, and, more broadly, that new research takes way too long to be converted into practice.

Bottom Line

A small town has two barbershops. One barbershop: "$5 haircuts!" The other: "We fix $5 haircuts!"

In other words, the price of a haircut isn't all that matters—we also care about quality. When it comes to barbershops, people might have a good sense of quality. After all, they get a first haircut at a barbershop, and then they know whether or not they ought to come back for a second. For that matter, they can read reviews of the barbershop online, and they can always just see whether other customers leave the barbershop well groomed.

In healthcare, quality also varies. One team of doctors at the VA got their patients through the hospital much more quickly than the other team. Some hospitals adopted beta blockers much more quickly than others.

But even though the quality of healthcare varies, measuring that quality is tricky. To credibly measure the quality of healthcare providers, we need patients to be randomly assigned to those providers. And, what's more, the very practice of measuring quality might change the behavior of those providers in ways that undermine the whole enterprise. If providers respond by cream skimming, choosing to treat only the lowest-risk patients, then perhaps we should not even be measuring quality in the first place.

References

Akbar, Shahid, and Mohammad S. Alorainy. "The Current Status of Beta Blockers' Use in the Management of Hypertension." *Saudi Medical Journal* 35, no. 11 (2014): 1307–17.

Bradley, Elizabeth H., Jeph Herrin, Jennifer A. Mattera, Eric S. Holmboe, Yongfei Wang, Paul Frederick, Sarah A. Roumanis, Martha J. Radford, and Harlan M. Krumholz. "Hospital-

Level Performance Improvement: Beta-Blocker Use after Acute Myocardial Infarction." *Medical Care* 42, no. 6 (2004): 591–99.

———. "Quality Improvement Efforts and Hospital Performance: Rates of Beta-Blocker Prescription after Acute Myocardial Infarction." *Medical Care* 43, no. 3 (2005): 282–92.

Chandra, Amitabh, Amy Finkelstein, Adam Sacarny, and Chad Syverson. "Health Care Exceptionalism? Performance and Allocation in the US Health Care Sector." *American Economic Review* 106, no. 8 (2016): 2110–44.

Doyle, Joseph J., Steven Ewer, and Todd Wagner. "Returns to Physician Human Capital: Analyzing Patients Randomized to Physician Teams." Rochester, NY: SSRN Scholarly Paper, 2008. https://papers.ssrn.com/abstract=1165502.

Kedrosky, Paul. "The Jesus Phone." *Wall Street Journal*, June 30, 2007, sec. Opinion. https://www.wsj.com/articles/SB118308453151652551.

Omoigui, N. A., D. P. Miller, K. J. Brown, K. Annan, D. Cosgrove, B. Lytle, F. Loop, and E. J. Topol. "Outmigration for Coronary Bypass Surgery in an Era of Public Dissemination of Clinical Outcomes." *Circulation* 93, no. 1 (1996): 27–33. https://doi.org/10.1161/01.cir.93.1.27.

"A Randomized Trial of Propranolol in Patients with Acute Myocardial Infarction." *JAMA* 250, no. 20 (1983).

Skinner, Jonathan, and Douglas Staiger. "Technology Diffusion and Productivity Growth in Health Care." *Review of Economics and Statistics* 97, no. 5 (2015): 951–64. https://doi.org/10.1162/REST_a_00535.

Wiener, J. J., and J. Westwood. "Fetal Lacerations at Caesarean Section." *Journal of Obstetrics and Gynaecology* 22, no. 1 (2002): 23–24. https://doi.org/10.1080/01443610120101655.

Drugs

Many businesses could thrive without any help from the government. A restaurant, for instance, could function without much of a public sector. After all, a chef needs a kitchen and some ingredients to get to work. Restaurants don't require a complex regulatory environment in order to function.

The business of developing new medicines is very different. Imagine an intrepid pharmaceutical entrepreneur who wants to develop a new medicine in an entirely free market. It costs roughly a billion dollars to develop a new medicine (Wouters, McKee, and Luyten 2020). (For new types of medicine—biologics or gene therapies—the cost can be much higher.) Our brave entrepreneur spends that billion dollars, hiring scientists, building laboratories, and so on. Eventually, she has a finished product—a new drug that can help people.

But now she has a problem. At great expense, she's developed this miraculous medicine and now wants to sell it at a price that makes the billion-dollar investment worthwhile. However, once a drug is developed and shown to be effective, it's very hard to keep the formulation secret. A team of chemists can reverse engineer her medicine at a cost far below the billion dollars that she initially put in. What is to stop another business from mass-producing her medicine and undercutting her price?

In other words, in a truly free market, she would not be able to make much of a profit on her medicine. As soon as she developed the drug, competitors would swoop in and offer the same drug at a cut-rate price, because they can sell the drug without covering research and development (R&D) costs. Anticipating that eventuality, she would never develop the drug in the first place. Who can invest a billion dollars when they don't anticipate a return on the investment?

The key issue is that the R&D for new medicines is a "public good." To understand what that phrase means, consider the lighthouse. In the centuries before radio signals and satellites, captains could only hope and pray that their ships would not slam into the shore. Without the aid of radar or night vision or GPS, they had few ways of ensuring that their ships were sailing in the right waters. One collision and the ship would be ruined, all of those barrels of New World rum spilling into the ocean.

At the time, there was only one solution: the lighthouse. At night, lighthouses would help guide ships into port and would keep them from crashing against the rocks. But no single captain could afford to build a lighthouse himself.

In theory, a group of captains could get together and decide to split the cost of building a lighthouse. But once they did so, it would be impossible to keep other captains from using that lighthouse. The technical term for this type of product is "nonexcludable": it is impossible to exclude others from using your lighthouse.

In addition, lighthouses are "nonrival in consumption." Any one captain's use of a lighthouse does not impede someone else from using the lighthouse. Most goods are "rival" in consumption: either I eat the cookie or you do— there's no way we can both eat it. But you can use a lighthouse all night long, and that doesn't stop me from using it too.

Goods that are both nonrival in consumption and nonexcludable are called "public goods." Economists argue that only the government can provide public goods. Individual captains cannot take on the difficult work of building lighthouses on their own.

Today, no one cares about lighthouses, because we have GPS. (And, for the record, GPS was a government project.) However, a more relevant example of a public good today is the research and development, the R&D, that leads to new medicines.

Pharmaceutical R&D is, theoretically, like a lighthouse, both nonrival and nonexcludable. At the end of the day, the product is not a physical object so much as a chemical formula. And once that formula is discovered, it is very difficult to keep it secret. That makes the new medicine nonexcludable—the inventor cannot exclude other pharmaceutical companies from making it.

A chemical formula is also nonrival in consumption. If one chemist uses the formula, that doesn't prevent another chemist from using the formula. Much like lighthouses, it doesn't matter how many people are focused on the new medicine. No one can "use up" the knowledge of how to produce a medicine.

And thus, when it comes to the development of new medicines, we've got a problem. The private market, left to its own devices, is not going to work, because the R&D involved is a public good. There is a role for the government in building lighthouses and there is a role for the government in developing new medicines, because free markets can't sustain public goods. Individuals, on their own, won't build lighthouses, because they can't force users to pay for the lighthouse. The same is true of pharmaceutical R&D, and therein lies the problem that only a government can solve.

The first way in which the government can grapple with the "public good" nature of R&D is through the direct public funding of basic research. The National Institutes of Health, the NIH, distributes over 40 billion dollars each year to researchers. (Some of our own research, as health economists, has been funded by the NIH.) Those grants keep labs running, working hard on research projects that may lead to novel treatments only decades later, if at all. The NIH performs this function in the United States—in Europe, it's the European Commission; in Japan, the Society for Promotion of Science; in China, the National Natural Science Foundation.

Second, the government handles the public good of R&D by granting patents. Think of our intrepid entrepreneur, described above. She has to invest a billion dollars in order to produce a new medicine, and without government intervention, she has no incentive to do so. A grant from the NIH cannot solve that problem alone—NIH grants typically cover only a few million dollars in direct costs.

Instead, a patent might solve the problem. A patent is a guarantee: for twenty years, only she can manufacture the drug. For twenty years, she's allowed to charge whatever price she sees fit, and only after the patent expires can anyone else produce the drug. For twenty years, the patent holder will be the only producer of the drug, and it is profits earned during that period that justify the R&D.

In that sense, high prices for drugs are a feature, not a bug. The high prices for the life of the patent justify the initial investment in R&D. Without the patent and the resulting high prices, a for-profit entity would never bother with the R&D in the first place.

What we have then are twin approaches to handling the public good of R&D. The first approach is for the government to directly fund the R&D through NIH grants. The second approach is for the government to grant twenty-year patents on developed drugs. Both approaches are now fundamental parts of the ways in which new medicines are developed.

Typically, the NIH funds "basic" research, the kind of research that generates and improves scientists' understanding of how the human body works. Then, eventually, for-profit pharmaceutical companies pick up the basic research and spend the billions of dollars necessary to fully develop the drug and take it to market.

And the two approaches—NIH grants and patents—complement each other. About half of drug patents cite either a public-sector patent or a research paper that was funded by the NIH (Sampat and Lichtenberg 2011). In other words, half of the work that pharmaceutical companies do is work that started with an NIH grant. But the NIH can't develop drugs on its own—it needs industry.

Dynamic Efficiency

In 2019, Gallup surveyed about 1,500 Americans and asked them whether they approved or disapproved of various industries (McCarthy 2019). The most popular industry: America's restaurants. Only 8 percent of Americans expressed negative views about the restaurant industry. And who can blame them? Who doesn't like the occasional dinner and drinks out on the town?

Also near the top: the computer industry. We've all watched as our laptops and phones have gotten sleeker yet more powerful, year after year. Other favorites included the grocery industry, agriculture, and, perhaps somewhat perplexing: accounting.

At the bottom of the list: the pharmaceutical industry. About 58 percent of respondents expressed a negative view of the pharmaceutical industry, which was more than any of the twenty-four other industries the surveyors asked about.

The pharmaceutical industry is, to say the least, unpopular. To see that, one need only glance at the headlines of op-ed essays about the industry. In the New York Times (2019): "It's Time for Pharmaceutical Companies to Have Their Tobacco Moment." Kevin Drum in Mother Jones (2015): "It's Really Hard Not to Hate the Pharmaceutical Industry."

That said, the COVID-19 pandemic added some nuance to the popular view of the industry. On the one hand, there are many reasons to hate the industry. On the other hand, it did quickly produce vaccines and treatments that prevented millions of deaths from COVID-19.

Our goal here is not to convince you to like the industry. Instead, what we hope to do is review the basic, fundamental principles at play. And to see those basic principles at play, one need only consider a simple way to cut healthcare costs: just force drug prices to be lower. After all, most patented drugs are priced way above the cost of producing them (Yu, Atteberry, and Bach 2018). The government could force those prices down by changing how Medicare pays for drugs. What could go wrong?

The key complication is that high drug prices are how the world lures for-profit companies to invest in drug R&D. To see that in action, consider what happened when Medicare started covering drugs.

Since the 1960s, the Medicare program has provided health insurance for all Americans older than sixty-five. Medicare Part A has always covered hospital stays and Medicare Part B has always covered outpatient care. For decades, that left one important part of healthcare uncovered: drugs.

In the 1960s, when the Johnson administration designed the Medicare program, they didn't bother to include drug coverage as part of the program. Back then, drug spending was about 10 percent of all healthcare spending, but healthcare spending was only 5 percent of GDP. Today, drug spending is still not much more than 10 percent of all healthcare spending, but healthcare spending has more than tripled as a share of GDP. As a result, Americans spend more on drugs today than they spent on all of healthcare in the mid-1960s (Centers for Medicare and Medicaid Services 2020).

For that reason, in 2003 the George W. Bush administration passed the Medicare Modernization Act. That law, which went into effect in 2006, added a prescription drug benefit to Medicare, Medicare Part D.[1] Suddenly, as of 2006, all Americans over the age of sixty-five had drug coverage.

The new drug benefit had a big effect on ordinary Americans. In fact, it may have even lowered mortality rates among the elderly.[2] The program was not perfect, but it enabled more Americans to afford medicine that they otherwise would not have been able to purchase.

For now, though, we are less interested in what Medicare Part D did for its beneficiaries and more interested in what its passage can tell us about the market for drugs. Two researchers—Margaret Blume-Kohout and Neeraj Sood—were curious as to how the program affected drug companies. For drug companies, Medicare Part D meant that many more Americans, *millions*, would be willing and able to buy the medicines that they produced. So, Blume-Kohout and Sood wondered: Would that have any effect on R&D?

It's not obvious, a priori, that an expansion of health insurance would affect drug R&D. After all, new medicines are born from a complex process that extends back to basic research on a lab bench and then culminates in randomized trials overseen by the Food and Drug Administration. Some argue that this complex process of R&D is entirely constrained by "scientific opportunity." They argue that it is only the gradual progress of science—peer-reviewed paper by peer-reviewed paper—that drives R&D. In other words, drugs are only researched and, finally, developed, when scientists have figured out the relevant science. That argument suggests that the passage of

Medicare Part D should have had *no* effect on R&D at all: the key constraint was science, not business.

Of course, there is another view. The other view, pushed not so much by scientists as by health economists, is that incentives matter. Medicare Part D grew the market for drugs that older Americans might take. And businesses should respond to an increase in market size: it means that there exists a larger return on investment, given more customers willing to buy the products that might arise from the R&D.

So Blume-Kohout and Sood (2013) got to work, studying the R&D of drugs before and after the passage of Medicare Part D. As a first step, they focused on two categories of drugs: drugs to treat Alzheimer's disease and contraceptives. They focused on those two categories because they offer a treatment-control comparison. The vast majority of American Alzheimer's patients are Medicare recipients. As a result, the passage of Medicare Part D had a major impact on that category, dramatically expanding the market for treatments related to Alzheimer's. Meanwhile, contraceptives were much less affected: few Medicare recipients take contraceptives.

So Blume-Kohout and Sood decided to study clinical trials for those two types of drugs. Figure 12.1 summarizes their findings. The number of clinical

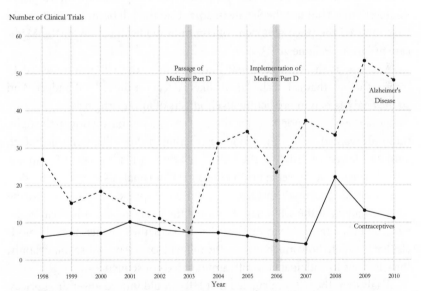

FIGURE 12.1. Number of clinical trials for drugs designed to treat Alzheimer's disease compared to drugs that can be used as contraceptives (Blume-Kohout and Sood 2013). The increase in clinical trials after 2003 for Alzheimer's drugs relative to contraceptive drugs is interpreted by the authors as a reaction to the incentives created by Medicare Part D, which was passed in 2003 and implemented in 2006.

trials related to Alzheimer's disease was declining prior to 2003. Then, with the passage of Medicare Part D, the trend reversed, and clinical trials related to Alzheimer's disease exploded from 2003 through 2009. Meanwhile, the number of clinical trials related to contraceptives remained flat throughout.

Blume-Kohout and Sood started with this one case study, comparing just these two types of drugs. They then turned to all categories of drugs and found a stark relationship. The more elderly the patients for a class of drugs, the larger the increase in clinical trials after the passage of Medicare Part D.

OK, so more people with drug coverage means more clinical trials—so what? Why do we care? We care because this kind of evidence rejects the view that all drug development is exclusively a matter of scientific opportunity. It's clear here that incentives matter: politicians passed a law that gave a certain group of Americans more drug coverage, and pharmaceutical companies responded by developing more drugs for that group of Americans.

Critically, this is about more than just Medicare. This kind of evidence suggests that R&D is a matter of business, that it responds to incentives. So policies that change the amount of money drug companies might earn will, in turn, affect the amount of R&D they do.

As an example, consider the "Elijah E. Cummings Lower Drug Costs Now Act," a bill also called HR3. That proposed law was passed by the House of Representatives but not the Senate in 2019. Had the bill become law, it would have lowered the price of dozens of common medications under the Medicare program (Pallone 2021).

Analysts at the Congressional Budget Office, the CBO, were asked to "score" the bill, that is to calculate its likely effect on the federal budget. And so the analysts had to predict the likely effects of lower drug prices.

Now, the CBO is nonpartisan: the analysts did not have a dog in the fight, they only wanted to do a good job of predicting the law's likely effects. In fact, Tal interviewed for a job at the CBO back during his last year of graduate school. The job might seem boring to some: CBO analysts spend a great deal of time clicking through spreadsheets. But those spreadsheets do fascinating work. Analysts at the CBO have to model the likely effects of legislation. So when a bill is intended to lower the price of drugs, the CBO has to build models that estimate how much money the bill will save. And, more importantly, the CBO has to anticipate the bill's unintended consequences.

Analysts at the CBO calculated that HR3 would indeed lower drug prices, as intended, and so lead to massive savings. They predicted that the law would lower federal spending by $345 billion (Swagel 2019). That's a big drop in federal spending, even in Washington. In some sense, all American taxpayers would benefit from those savings: drugs would be cheaper, and so the cost of providing Medicare would be much lower.

But the analysts didn't stop there. They read the research literature on drug R&D, including the paper by Blume-Kohout and Sood that we just described. The analysts understood that drug R&D responds to incentives. And so a drop in drug prices would mean a drop in the financial return to drug R&D, which, in turn, would mean that there would be less incentive to do drug R&D.

And so the analysts paired their estimates of savings, $345 billion, with one potential cost of the bill. They predicted that the bill would also lead to eight to fifteen new drugs *not* being developed over the following ten years.

It's important to recognize the human cost of eight to fifteen new drugs not being developed. Some of those potential drugs would not have offered much value. Perhaps they would treat superficial conditions or perhaps they would not be as effective as drugs that already exist. But others may have had tremendous value. They may have slowed the growth of cancer or prevented heart attacks. It's not hard to imagine people lying on hospice beds, gasping for breath, and suffering in ways that those potential medicines might have prevented.

And therein lies the central trade-off when it comes to the debate over drug prices. On the one hand, there is the benefit of cheaper drugs. Americans spend more on drugs than the people of any other country—drugs are outrageously expensive here. So cheaper drugs would mean a boost in what economists sometimes call "static efficiency": our well-being today. But, on the other hand, cheaper drugs would reduce the incentive to research the drugs of tomorrow. That would mean a reduction in what economists sometimes call "dynamic efficiency": our well-being tomorrow.

The policies that govern pharmaceutical spending have to grapple with this fundamental trade-off: static efficiency versus dynamic efficiency, that is, cheap drugs versus new drugs. And the key issue is the point we take away from the Blume-Kohout and Sood paper: R&D responds to incentives. Lowering the price of drugs will help us today but hurt us tomorrow. Lower prices will prevent new drugs from being developed.

Now, we are certainly not arguing for the status quo here. There *are* major problems with how Americans pay for drugs. The point is simply that a trade-off exists. It is certainly reasonable to argue that drugs should be cheaper in the United States. But it is unreasonable to argue that drugs should be cheaper and that we can enjoy those cheaper drugs at no cost. There's no free lunch: if you want drugs to be cheaper, then R&D becomes less profitable, and then we'll see less R&D. But perhaps that's a trade-off worth taking.

Advanced Market Commitments

What we've described so far are two ways in which America generates new drugs: NIH grants and high drug prices through twenty-year patents. That system has worked reasonably well for decades. There are now thousands of medicines that are off patent and used daily by physicians around the world to treat disease. And such medicines continue to be developed: the system induces thousands of for-profit pharmaceutical companies to research and develop new medicines.

But the system is certainly not perfect. One problem is that this arrangement tends to reward the development of drugs meant for the wealthy. After-all, companies invest in R&D today so that they can charge high prices for the patented product tomorrow. But if those who need the drug have little money to spend, then the company will never be able to set a high price tomorrow. So why bother with costly R&D today?

Think of diseases that are common only in low-income countries: malaria, schistosomiasis, and other tropical diseases. For a for-profit pharmaceutical company, focusing in such areas is not where the highest return to investment lies.

The problem is not just that those who suffer from tropical diseases have little cash. There's another problem at play here, one that some call a "commitment problem." Imagine that you run a large, sophisticated pharmaceutical company, and your company has a lead on a potential vaccine for a tropical disease that is disproportionately common in one low-income country. Yes, the people who need the vaccine have little income, but there are millions of them. So your accountants put together a spreadsheet: millions of doses at a low price might still be enough money to justify further investment.

A bureaucrat from the Ministry of Health comes to your headquarters and encourages you to continue to develop the vaccine. She emphasizes the benefits of the vaccine, how many lives will be saved, how many children will no longer be orphaned.

Still, there's a nagging worry. "If we do develop this vaccine and bring it to market, can you commit to honoring our patent?" The bureaucrat nods emphatically. "Of course, we will honor your patent. We are a nation of laws. We respect intellectual property."

Is that assurance enough? She is committing to honoring your future patent so that you will continue to invest in R&D today. But is such a commitment *credible*? Once the vaccine is developed, once the R&D is done, it will be very tempting for the Ministry of Health to ignore the patent. This is not to shame the bureaucrat or her government: when millions of a country's citizens are in trouble, it is the responsibility of the government to act. So, if necessary, the Ministry of Health will tear up the patent if doing so will help get the vaccine to where it is needed.

In the early 2000s, Michael Kremer became fascinated with this problem. Kremer, a Harvard economist at the time, wondered whether there might be some way to resolve the commitment problem. If so, the benefits might be enormous. Neglected tropical diseases (dengue, rabies, leprosy, intestinal worms, etc.) affect more than a billion people and kill about 200,000 each year (Centers for Disease Control and Prevention 2019; World Health Organization 2022). If pharmaceutical companies could be attracted to studying potential cures for those diseases the way that they study the diseases of affluence, then much human misery might disappear.

Kremer came up with a particular scheme that, he believed, might resolve the commitment problem. The trick was to make a *credible* commitment to reward a pharmaceutical company if it developed a cure for a tropical disease. And to make the commitment credible, the resources had to be amassed in advance.

So here was Kremer's idea. Think of the hypothetical conversation with the representative of the Ministry of Health. The original conversation would not go well. "We promise to honor your patent" would be followed by "We don't believe your promise." The new conversation would go something like this. "We have assembled a team of donors. The donors have all contributed large sums of money and that money now sits in a Swiss bank account—you can check, the money is there. If you can provide a vaccine that meets certain clinical criteria, the pile of money is yours."

All of a sudden, the commitment is credible. After all, the money is just sitting there. The Ministry of Health is no longer promising to honor a patent in the future, it is instead making a credible commitment by collecting the money in advance. Kremer, working with a team of other researchers, called the plan an "Advanced Market Commitment" (Berndt et al. 2007).

The name "Advanced Market Commitment" should make sense. Normally, the patent system involves a commitment *after* a drug has come to market. A patent is really a promise that the government will allow a company to charge a high price once the drug is developed. This plan is instead about making a commitment in advance of the drug being developed.

Kremer and Glennerster first proposed Advanced Market Commitments in 2004 and then spent years describing it to other experts and policymakers. The idea caught on. In 2007, five countries and the Gates Foundation put together an Advanced Market Commitment worth $1.5 billion. The money was dedicated to induce companies to develop a pneumococcal conjugate vaccine covering strains prevalent in developing countries. In 2010, the pharmaceutical companies GSK and Pfizer were attracted to the deal and each committed to continue developing the vaccine and then supplying 30 million doses annually. "In 2019, a third vaccine developed by the Serum Institute of India qualified for the AMC program" (Kremer, Levin, and Snyder 2020).

It is difficult to measure how much of the development and distribution of those vaccines was due to the Advanced Market Commitment and how much would have occurred otherwise. But most policymakers active in the area believe that the Advanced Market Commitment made a difference. In 2019, Michael Kremer was awarded the Nobel Prize in economics, partly for his work on Advanced Market Commitments.

Gene Therapies, Personalized Medicine, and the Next Frontier

For most of its history, the pharmaceutical industry has produced "small-molecule drugs." Small-molecule drugs are relatively simple chemical compounds that can be synthesized by chemists in a laboratory. Their production has been the norm for decades.

The system we have of patents and NIH grants seems to work fairly well for small-molecule drugs. Take, for example, Lipitor. Lipitor was developed by a Pfizer subsidiary in the late 1980s. The drug proved highly effective at preventing heart attacks and Pfizer made about $10 billion each year from 2003 to 2011 (Pfizer Inc., 2019). In November of 2011, the patent expired and generic producers stepped in. The price of Lipitor for Americans plummeted by 95 percent, from five dollars a pill to about 30 cents a pill (Rosenblatt 2014).

That is a success story. Heart disease is a leading cause of death. The industry was presented with an incentive to research and develop drugs that prevent heart disease. Pfizer delivered, was rewarded, and now *humanity* has an effective and cheap drug that will be useful forever.

More recently, though, the industry has shifted toward two new types of products that don't follow the same rules. First, there are large-molecule drugs. Large-molecule drugs are drugs that are produced from a living organism.[3] For instance, insulin is a hormone produced by the pancreas. Type-1 diabetics cannot produce their own insulin, and so, in the 1920s, scientists figured out how to isolate the hormone in animals. Then, in the 1990s, scientists at Novo Nordisk developed Novolog, a so-called "fast-acting" insulin. Novolog is a modified version of human insulin that can be absorbed by the body more efficiently.

The patent for Novolog expired in the mid-2010s, but patent expiration is very different for large-molecule drugs. In the case of small-molecule drugs, generic producers start producing precisely the same molecule in their own labs. Nearly all consumers switch to the generic options, which are much cheaper and yet "bioequivalent." For large-molecule drugs, the production process is too complex for any other company to replicate the molecule exactly. Novo Nordisk developed a yeast to produce Novolog and that production process is covered by multiple patents and trade secrets.

As a result, there is no "generic" Novolog, in the sense that no company other than Novo Nordisk can produce Novolog. Instead, there exist biosimilars. Biosimilars are approximate copies of large-molecule drugs that have gone off patent. They are approximate, because no other company has Novo Nordisk's yeast: no other company has access to Novo Nordisk's entire production process.[4]

Large-molecule drugs are nearly always more difficult to produce than small-molecule drugs. They require bioreactors and genetically modified yeasts or bacteria that, under just the right conditions, will produce the drug. As a result, it is much more difficult to create a biosimilar than it is to produce a small-molecule generic. And so large-molecule drugs end up being more expensive than small-molecule drugs and patent expiration often does not make them much cheaper.

Finally, there's a third category of pharmaceutical products: personalized therapies—drugs that require a novel development process for each patient. As an example, consider Kymriah, a treatment for one particular kind of leukemia.[5] Kymriah is a form of CAR-T cell therapy. Doctors remove some of the patient's blood cells and then train those blood cells to attack the patient's cancer. This requires a separate procedure for each patient: it's a therapy that is covered by a suite of patents, because it is not just one molecule but rather a multistep, twenty-two-day process for every patient.

Novartis priced Kymriah at about half-a-million dollars. And, yes, half-a-million dollars is an awful lot of money. But, for Kymriah, half-a-million dollars might not actually be a ludicrous price. First, Kymriah is genuinely expensive to produce, since its treatment has to be customized for each patient. A small-molecule drug costs pennies per pill to produce—Kymriah costs much more.

Second, the half-million-dollar price might simply be worth it. Kymriah is a one-time treatment that often *cures* leukemia. The Institute for Clinical and Economic Review (ICER) is an organization in Boston that releases reports on the cost-effectiveness of pharmaceuticals. ICER examined the data on Kymriah and concluded that its high price was "aligned with its clinical value."

Indeed, the British National Health Service performed its own review and decided to cover Kymriah in September of 2018 (National Health Service 2019).

So that's three types of pharmaceutical products: small-molecule drugs, large-molecule drugs, and personalized therapies. One can argue that the healthcare system we have has succeeded when it comes to the first category, small-molecule drugs. The system has created thousands of medications over the decades, and the most useful medicines quickly become very cheap once their patents expire.

Of course, that is not to say that the world of small-molecule drugs is not without controversy. Many small-molecule drugs are very expensive, especially before the associated patents expire. But the current system has the trade-off we described above: lowering prices will lead to less drug R&D. So while experts will debate whether American prices are too high or too low, relatively few argue that the fundamental system is flawed.

For the other two types of products, however, it gets a bit more complicated. Since large-molecule drugs are so hard to produce, it is not clear that biosimilars will be developed that will sufficiently reduce the price once patents expire. For personalized therapies, cheaper alternatives may *never* be developed. After all, personalized therapies are protected by a slew of patents and trade secrets.

All of this is to say that large-molecule drugs and personalized therapies pose a problem with which the American healthcare system must continue to grapple.

The Bottom Line, or, Really, How to Hate Drug Companies

At this point, dear reader, you may be wondering how much consulting money we have collected from pharmaceutical companies. Surely we are paid shills, since everything above seems to simply excuse drug companies for the high prices they charge. Yes, drugs are expensive, we seem to be saying, but that's because we need to preserve the incentive for R&D. *Thank you Pfizer for this new Mercedes!*

OK, well, first of all, neither of us has accepted consulting money from pharmaceutical companies. Neither of us drives a Mercedes. And, more importantly, we are not telling you to stop hating drug companies. But if you do hate drug companies, we want you to hate them for the right reasons.

The pharmaceutical industry is guilty of scandals that cannot simply be waved away as the inevitable result of an economic trade-off. There's Purdue Pharmaceuticals, which pushed a highly addictive drug, OxyContin, on vulnerable populations, causing millions of deaths (Alpert et al. 2022). There's

Turing Pharmaceuticals, which, in 2015, raised the price of an off-patent drug, Daraprim, from about $13 a pill to $750 (Pollack 2015). There's AbbVie, the maker of Humira, that has chosen to protect its US sales of the highly effective biologic with hundreds of patents (Robbins 2023).

All of those scandals are examples of where the system of patents and NIH grants has gone awry. There are, without a doubt, problems here. Too often, companies producing certain generic drugs can dramatically raise prices because no other company happens to be licensed to produce a competing generic. Too often, companies market drugs aggressively, and sometimes that marketing persuades doctors to prescribe drugs when there are actually better, cheaper alternatives. And too often companies can create patent "thickets" to protect their complex products for much longer than the protection a single patent would offer.

But for every scandal, there are many cases in which the industry has created tremendous value: COVID-19 vaccinations, Lipitor, curing hepatitis C, Kymriah, so on and so forth. The challenge here, as is the challenge throughout healthcare, is to somehow excise the bad while preserving the valuable.

References

Alpert, Abby, William N. Evans, Ethan M. J. Lieber, and David Powell. "Origins of the Opioid Crisis and Its Enduring Impacts." *Quarterly Journal of Economics* 137, no. 2 (2022): 1139–79. https://doi.org/10.1093/qje/qjab043.

Berndt, Ernst R., Rachel Glennerster, Michael R. Kremer, Jean Lee, Ruth Levine, Georg Weizsäcker, and Heidi Williams. "Advance Market Commitments for Vaccines against Neglected Diseases: Estimating Costs and Effectiveness." *Health Economics* 16, no. 5 (2007): 491–511. https://doi.org/10.1002/hec.1176.

Blume-Kohout, Margaret E., and Neeraj Sood. "Market Size and Innovation: Effects of Medicare Part D on Pharmaceutical Research and Development." *Journal of Public Economics* 97 (January 2013): 327–36. https://doi.org/10.1016/j.jpubeco.2012.10.003.

Drum, Kevin. "It's Really Hard Not to Hate the Pharmaceutical Industry." *Mother Jones* (blog). 2015. https://www.motherjones.com/kevin-drum/2015/09/its-really-hard-not-hate-pharmaceutical-industry/.

"Form 10-k 2019." 2019. Pfizer, Inc. https://investors.pfizer.com/Investors/Financials/SEC-Filings/default.aspx.

"Historical." Baltimore: Centers for Medicare and Medicaid Services, 2020. https://www.cms.gov/Research-Statistics-Data-and-Systems/Statistics-Trends-and-Reports/NationalHealthExpendData/NationalHealthAccountsHistorical.

Huh, Jason, and Julian Reif. "Did Medicare Part D Reduce Mortality?" *Journal of Health Economics* 53 (May 2017): 17–37. https://doi.org/10.1016/j.jhealeco.2017.01.005.

Kremer, Michael, and Rachel Glennerster. *Strong Medicine: Creating Incentives for Pharmaceutical Research on Neglected Diseases.* Princeton, NJ: Princeton University Press, 2004. http://www.jstor.org/stable/j.cttldr365r.

Kremer, Michael, Jonathan Levin, and Christopher M. Snyder. "Advance Market Commitments: Insights from Theory and Experience." *AEA Papers and Proceedings* 110 (May 2020): 269–73. https://doi.org/10.1257/pandp.20201017.

McCarthy, Justin. "Big Pharma Sinks to the Bottom of U.S. Industry Rankings." Gallup. September 3, 2019. https://news.gallup.com/poll/266060/big-pharma-sinks-bottom-industry-rankings.aspx.

"Neglected Tropical Diseases." World Health Organization. 2022. https://www.who.int/health-topics/neglected-tropical-diseases.

"Neglected Tropical Diseases (NTDs)." Centers for Disease Control and Prevention. February 19, 2019. https://www.cdc.gov/globalhealth/newsroom/topics/ntds/index.html.

New York Times. "It's Time for Pharmaceutical Companies to Have Their Tobacco Moment." February 24, 2019, sec. Opinion. https://www.nytimes.com/2019/02/24/opinion/drug-prices-congress.html.

"NHS England Announces Groundbreaking New Personalised Therapy for Children with Cancer." National Health Service. September 5, 2019. https://www.england.nhs.uk/2018/09/nhs-england-announces-groundbreaking-new-personalised-therapy-for-children-with-cancer/.

Pallone, Frank. "H.R. 3—117th Congress (2021–2022): Elijah E. Cummings Lower Drug Costs Now Act." Legislation. 2021/2022. April 27, 2021. http://www.congress.gov/.

Pollack, Andrew. "Drug Goes From $13.50 a Tablet to $750, Overnight." *New York Times*, September 20, 2015. https://www.nytimes.com/2015/09/21/business/a-huge-overnight-increase-in-a-drugs-price-raises-protests.html.

Robbins, Rebecca. "How a Drug Company Made $114 Billion by Gaming the U.S. Patent System." *New York Times*, January 28, 2023. https://www.nytimes.com/2023/01/28/business/humira-abbvie-monopoly.html.

Rosenblatt, Michael. "The Real Cost of 'High-Priced' Drugs." *Harvard Business Review*, November 17, 2014. https://hbr.org/2014/11/the-real-cost-of-high-priced-drugs.

Sampat, Bhaven N., and Frank R. Lichtenberg. "What Are the Respective Roles of the Public and Private Sectors in Pharmaceutical Innovation?" *Health Affairs* 30, no. 2 (2011): 332–39. https://doi.org/10.1377/hlthaff.2009.0917.

Swagel, Philip. "Effects of Drug Price Negotiation Stemming from Title 1 of H.R. 3, the Lower Drug Costs Now Act of 2019, on Spending and Revenues Related to Part D of Medicare." Washington, DC: Congressional Budget Office, 2019.

Wouters, Olivier J., Martin McKee, and Jeroen Luyten. "Estimated Research and Development Investment Needed to Bring a New Medicine to Market, 2009–2018." *JAMA* 323, no. 9 (2020): 844–53. https://doi.org/10.1001/jama.2020.1166.

Yu, Nancy, Preston Atteberry, and Peter Bach. "Spending on Prescription Drugs in the US: Where Does All the Money Go?" *Health Affairs* (blog). 2018. https://www.healthaffairs.org/do/10.1377/forefront.20180726.670593/full/.

PART III

Other Determinants of Health

Contagion

A "LoJack" is a small piece of black plastic, about the size of a deck of cards. For about $700, you can buy the device and have a mechanic install it behind your car's dashboard. If your car is stolen and you file a stolen vehicle report, the LoJack transmitter will send radio signals to the police so that they can find your car and arrest the thief.

Car owners have to decide for themselves whether or not they want to buy a LoJack. On the one hand, it costs $700. On the other hand, in the event that their car is stolen, it will be quickly returned.

But there's a funny thing about LoJacks: they don't only benefit the car's owner, they also benefit the owners of *other* cars. When a thief steals a car, he typically drives it straight to a "chop shop" where mechanics disassemble the car so that they can sell its parts. The LoJack leads the police straight to the chop shop, where they arrest everyone they find there. In the 1980s and 1990s, LoJacks helped the police break up fifty-three chop shops in Los Angeles alone. And with chop shops closed, there are fewer car thefts overall. Car thieves are either arrested along with their chop shops or else give up on car thefts when they have nowhere to take the vehicles.

This means that there are two benefits to LoJacks. First, the device benefits the car owner: if the car is stolen, it is more likely to be returned. Let's call that the "private benefit." Second, each device benefits nearby car owners: LoJacks lead to chop shops closing and thieves quitting the business. Let's call that second benefit the "social benefit."

When a car owner decides whether or not to buy a LoJack system, the owner focuses only on the private benefit and not the social benefit. After all, $700 is a lot of cash to drop on a plastic device that may never be switched on. But the social benefits of LoJacks still matter. Economists who have done the math—namely, Steven Levitt and Ian Ayres in a 1998 economics paper—argue that, in some neighborhoods, the social benefits of LoJacks are fifteen times greater than the price tag (Ayres and Levitt 1998).

But hold on—record scratch—this is a book about healthcare. What does car theft have to do with healthcare? Well, search and replace "LoJack" with "vaccines."

What benefit is there to a flu vaccine? Like LoJacks, a flu vaccine brings with it both private and social benefits. The person getting the flu vaccine is less likely to get the flu themselves. That's a week of misery that person gets to avoid, the private benefit. But there's also a social benefit. Every needle that pierces a deltoid makes it less likely that a flu outbreak will occur. Everyone at risk for the flu, that is, *everyone*, benefits from each shot delivered. The same is true not just of the vaccine for the seasonal flu but also vaccines for measles, mumps, rubella, COVID-19, and so on.

Levitt and Ayres argued that the social benefits of LoJacks mean that there are too few LoJacks. Car owners buy LoJacks based on the private benefits, not the social benefits, and yet the social benefits are vast. In the same way, there are too few flu shots. People get the flu shot based on the private benefits of the shot, ignoring the social benefits. And therein lies the problem.

Externalities

To truly understand LoJacks and flu shots, we need a technical term: "externality."

An externality is a benefit or harm that is imposed on a third party. LoJacks are an example of a "positive externality," a personal acquisition that benefits a third party. Your neighbors benefit when you buy a LoJack, because *their* cars are now less likely to be stolen. Most transactions, in contrast, involve no externalities. An example: we go and buy sandwiches from a restaurant. Only two parties are affected by the transaction: ourselves and the owner of the restaurant.

In the presence of externalities, the private market, left to its own devices, does not work well. The private market consists of individuals who buy and sell goods based on their own private costs and benefits, ignoring social benefits, meaning ignoring externalities. If we leave the private market alone, then we will end up with too few LoJacks sold and, also, too few vaccines.

And therein lies the rationale for treating products with externalities very differently from other goods. When it comes to LoJacks, Levitt and Ayres concluded that there is room for some type of regulation. LoJacks, they say, are "likely to be dramatically undersupplied by the free market, suggesting a role for public policy."

Similarly, government action is warranted for vaccines, because vaccines also involve positive externalities. When you get vaccinated, not only do you get to enjoy the private benefits, but the vaccination makes an outbreak less likely. With no government action, people will choose whether or not to be vaccinated based on whether or not their private benefit from vaccination justifies the price and the personal hassle of the vaccine. (Yes, many people are socially minded, and so think of the greater good, but many others are not.) So it makes sense for the government to come in and subsidize vaccination—to make the vaccines free.

Even beyond that, there's an economic argument to be made for vaccine mandates. Choosing to be unvaccinated is not simply a personal choice, like choosing what kind of sandwich to buy. It's a personal choice that affects others: the more people who are unvaccinated, the more likely an outbreak.

So: How Do We Get People Vaccinated?

If we can't rely on the private, unregulated market for vaccinations, what can we rely on? How can we convert the social benefits of vaccination into private benefits, so that those hesitant about vaccination will actually agree to get vaccinated?

First of all, vaccines should be free, the way that COVID-19 vaccinations were free in 2021. When vaccines are so heavily subsidized that they are free, the subsidy converts the social benefits of vaccination into a private benefit.

Second, we might even want to mandate vaccinations. American children already need to be vaccinated to go to school. Soldiers need over a dozen vaccinations before they are allowed to enlist in the military. One could argue for more such requirements, not only for vaccinations against old diseases, like measles, but also for new ones like COVID-19.

But free vaccinations and mandated vaccinations are not enough. Vaccine mandates end up challenged in court, and, in any case, not everyone complies with them. Other interventions are necessary.

It's at this point that behavioral economists have something to offer. Consider, for instance, the work of Katie Milkman, John Beshears, James Choi, David Laibson, and Brigitte C. Madrian (2011). That team had an idea for how organizations might encourage people to get vaccinated.

It's hard to convince people to get vaccinated when they are deeply opposed to the practice. The researchers didn't know how to handle adamant antivaxxers. But many people who are unvaccinated are not ideological, they are just unmotivated. After the COVID-19 vaccines were available for ten months, 35 percent of Americans remained unvaccinated (Mathieu et al. 2020). About 7 percent told surveyors that they were not necessarily opposed to getting vaccinated, they just would do it "when they got around to it" (Hamel et al. 2021).

The researchers came up with an intervention they called a "planning prompt." A planning prompt is a remarkably simple intervention, really just a sentence and a little icon. And that one little sentence and icon make a big difference.

Here's how it works. The research team collaborated with a "large Midwestern utility firm." We don't know the identity of the firm. A power plant in Des Moines? A sewage-treatment facility in Peoria? The team had to keep the firm's identity secret for the sake of confidentiality. But we do know that the business had about 3,000 employees, and that managers at the firm were worried that too few were getting their flu shots.

With very few workers vaccinated against the flu, managers were concerned that a really bad flu season could force the utility to shut down. For the company, low vaccination rates were not only a public health problem but a business problem.

The managers arranged for an on-site clinic, so that employees could just walk down the hall one day and get their flu shots. But even that was not enough. Many employees forgot about the on-site clinic or put off visiting it. These are men and women with jobs and families and mortgages to pay—their cars need oil changes, they are worried about dandelions on their lawn, they are struggling to impress their bosses at work. It's not a surprise that many forgot about the clinics, even when the clinic was just down the hall.

This is where the researchers got to work. The team randomly assigned the 3,000 employees into two groups. One group was sent a flyer that announced the flu shot clinic. "YOUR COMPANY IS HOLDING A FREE FLU SHOT CLINIC. Flu shots will be available on site at the following times. . . ." The flyer then listed the precise location of the clinic and its hours of operation.

That was the "control" condition: a pretty boring flyer that just informed employees of the on-site clinic. The other group got the exact same flyer with one, small difference. Their flyer also had a little sentence in the middle: "Many people find it helpful to **make a plan** for getting their shot. You can write yours here." Below that was a tiny picture of a pencil and a little box in which workers might jot down the time that they would visit the clinic (fig. 13.1).

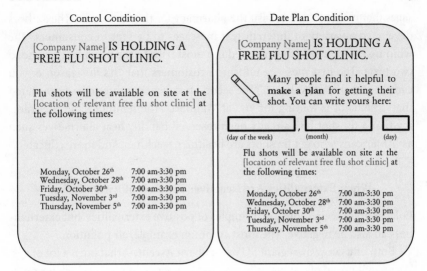

FIGURE 13.1. Flyers distributed by Milkman et al. (2011). The first is the control group's flyer that simply provided information about the location and time of the company's free flu shot clinic. The second is the treatment group's flyer, which suggested that people write down when they would visit the clinic.

That's it! That's a planning prompt: a little nudge to jot down when you plan on actually visiting the clinic. In other words, a planning prompt is just a gentle suggestion to make a plan.

The planning prompt made a difference. About 33 percent of employees who got the ordinary flyer visited the clinic, while about 37 percent of employees who got the planning prompt visited the clinic. Yes, both numbers are small. But, remember, some of those flyers may have gotten lost in the mail or been thrown away, unread. It is hard to change people's behavior. But, that said, flyers are a relatively cheap behavioral intervention, and the planning prompt cost no money to add.

The planning prompt improved the number of flu shots administered by 4 percentage points. For this utility firm with over 3,000 employees, that means adopting the planning prompt got an extra 130 or so employees to be vaccinated. Were the intervention to be adopted by other organizations, it could lead to thousands of additional vaccinations.

Planning prompts are just one example from a growing arsenal of cheap, behavioral interventions. There are many other approaches. For instance, some of these same authors ran a large experiment in 2021 that sent text messages to encourage people to receive a flu vaccine (Milkman et al. 2021). The team randomized 650,000 Walmart pharmacy customers to receive text messages that nudged them to visit the pharmacy for the flu vaccine. The authors developed a variety of different text messages to be sent to consumers. The winning message, which generated the most trips to the pharmacy, included two texts. The first message informed customers that "it's flu season & you can get a flu shot at Walmart." The second text, sent out three days later, stated that "a flu shot is waiting for you at Walmart." The reminder and the framing that a flu shot had already been reserved handily beat alternatives such as "Americans who get flu shots are healthier, wealthier, and more educated."

When Externalities Are Negative: The Case of Air Pollution

LoJacks and vaccinations are examples of positive externalities, but externalities can also be negative. The most common example: air pollution.

Both of us now own giant SUVs—Subaru Ascents—that burn a lot of gas. We are not proud of our gigantic cars, but they can seat seven, which becomes useful when we carpool to our kids' school. Buying the cars was not a simple, one-on-one transaction. It's not just a matter of us giving money to Subaru. When we drive these gigantic vehicles around, we produce air pollution—mostly carbon monoxide, nitrous oxide, and what scientists call "volatile organic compounds." That air pollution drifts off and hurts others while hastening climate change.

There's no way around it: our gigantic cars hurt people. And so there is a role for the government in regulation here. Without regulation, we would buy our Subarus based solely on private costs and private benefits. We would be focused on the convenience of having a third row of seats, ignoring the air pollution that that third row entails.

Economists have a solution for this problem: the gasoline tax. In theory, that tax forces us to pay for the externality of burning gas. Anyone is free to buy a gigantic car, but the gas tax forces them to grapple with the costs of air pollution, because the gasoline tax makes that social cost a private cost: now you have to pay for it: almost 20 cents per gallon.[1]

In practice, the gasoline tax is way too low. Many economists argue that the most important way to combat climate change is to raise the gasoline tax (Mankiw 2009). But that economic imperative slams into the brick wall of politics. The gasoline tax is remarkably salient: ordinary Americans are very sensitive to the price of gasoline. And so American politicians have historically shied away from any policy that might raise the price of gas.

Another challenge with the gasoline tax is figuring out precisely how large it should be. About 20 cents per gallon is certainly too low, but what number would be appropriate? Answering that question requires measuring the negative externality of air pollution. But measuring the economic costs of air pollution is easier said than done.

Suppose that there's a small city with one large, polluting factory. The city, like any city, has both wealthy residents and poor residents. The wealthy tend to settle in the best part of town, the area with the cleanest air, the nicest view, and the most trees. Meanwhile, poorer people can't afford to live in those neighborhoods. So they end up downwind from the big, polluting factory. That alone is a tragic state of affairs: it's unfair that poor people, along with everything else, are the ones that have to endure the pollution of the factory.

But, on top of that, such a state of affairs makes it difficult to study the impact of pollution from the factory. Researchers cannot simply compare the health of neighborhoods downwind from the factory to the health of neighborhoods upwind from the factory. The residents of those two neighborhoods are different, and so it's impossible to isolate the effect of pollution from everything else.

As a result, economists have to come up with clever ways to measure the effects of pollution. In a fascinating 2011 paper, Janet Currie and Reed Walker came up with one such approach. Currie and Walker focused on something that might, at first blush, seem entirely unrelated to pollution. Over the 1990s and early 2000s, American highways switched from manual toll collection to electronic toll collection. Currie and Walker argued that the change from human-occupied toll booths to digital toll booths allows one to isolate the causal effect of air pollution.

Before the switch to electronic toll collection, cars on the highway would line up in front of toll booths. Each toll booth was occupied by an actual human who would collect cash—*cash*—from each driver, give them change, and then wave them through the toll booth. This was a slow process and it meant that there were often many cars idling in front of each toll booth.

Then local governments switched to electronic toll collection. The systems are called "E-ZPass" in the Northeast, "SunPass" in Florida, "PeachPass" in Georgia, "FasTrak" in California, "I-Pass" in Illinois, and on and on. These days, if you own a car, you've probably used one. You buy a little transponder, which you affix to your windshield, and then the toll is automatically collected when you drive through an automated booth.

Before electronic toll collection, cars would have to wait and idle, and that meant a lot of pollution near toll booths. But once the toll booths switched to electronic systems, there were much shorter lines and so much less air pollution. Currie and Walker's idea was to exploit this change as a natural experiment. Lots of Americans live near toll booths. And those Americans faced a sudden drop in the air pollution around them when the shift to electronic toll collection occurred.

Sure enough, that drop in pollution had an effect. Currie and Walker study births born to women who live near toll booths. They measured a clear drop in the number of babies born with low birth weight after electronic toll collection. The shift to electronic toll collection led to a decrease in low-birth-weight babies for those within one mile of the toll booth but to no change for those farther away.

Such a finding is consistent with what scientists know about air pollution. Air pollution dissipates over long distances, so those who live within one mile of a change in air pollution should be much more affected than those who live farther away. In addition, scientists believe that carbon monoxide, in particular, plays a role in birth weight. Exposure to carbon monoxide reduces the availability of oxygen transported to the fetus and so limits the weight of the baby.

Currie and Walker used these estimates to demonstrate, first and foremost, that air pollution really matters for infant health. They found a clear, statistically significant effect of air pollution on low birth weight. Their study is one of many that suggests the gasoline tax should be much larger in order to account for these negative externalities. Just like the decision to remain unvaccinated puts everyone around us at risk, our decision to drive a (polluting) automobile adds to the air pollution that negatively affects the health of the newborn babies in our neighborhoods.[2]

The Self-Limiting Effect

Vaccination and air pollution are two contrasting examples of the same idea. In either case, the private market will not work on its own. And so there is a role for the government to subsidize vaccination and to impose a gasoline tax.

But there are some cases in which externalities exist and yet it's not clear what the government can do. Consider the COVID-19 pandemic before vaccines were available. Without vaccination, the only way to prevent the transmission of COVID-19 was to "socially distance." And yet, that is a decision that is hard for the government to influence.

Take May of 2020, which was a difficult month for us. Then again, it was a difficult month for everyone. COVID-19 had emerged in the United States in March. Barbecues, dinner parties, and playdates for the kids were out of the question. We had to keep our distance.

Both of us have two daughters, and our daughters were all under the age of ten at the time. The social distancing took a toll on them. The kids were used to playdates and soccer games and trips to the mall. As parents, we were also tired of being unable to hire a babysitter, of handling bedtime and week-end afternoons by ourselves. In other words, we were also desperate for a playdate.

And so, we started to wonder: Was a playdate really unsafe? What if it were outdoors? What if the kids wore masks? We consulted the graph, the curve that plotted the number of new cases each day. That summer, all Americans were consulting the graph, checking the trajectory of new cases in their state or in their county.

Tal took a hard look at the graph and decided that an outdoor playdate would be OK. Look, we wanted to do the right thing. We had friends who were ER physicians at the time, we had family members who had contracted COVID. We were not naive. But we looked at the graph: that month, the number of cases in our region was extremely low. So it seemed unlikely that an outdoor playdate would give our kids COVID-19.

That is to say, we performed a cost-benefit analysis. The cost of a play-date was low, because the chance that our friends had COVID was low, since case counts, at the time, were low in our region. The benefits of a playdate, meanwhile, were enormous: we were desperate for social interaction. So why not?

The problem was that everyone else in our community was making the same calculation. When case counts decreased, it became extremely tempting to stop social distancing. After all, with case counts low, the chance of catching the disease was also low. But once people started socializing again, however carefully, then, surely, that would bring the disease back. And it did.

That dynamic is what economists call the "self-limiting effect" of epidemics. Suppose that you have a contagious disease that can only be prevented by costly individual actions. COVID-19 in May of 2020 certainly met those criteria: it was contagious and all we could do was wear masks and keep our distance. Then, when the disease becomes rare, it is rational for people to stop those precautions. That was the calculation we made: given low case counts, why not let the kids have an outdoor playdate? But once many people reach that same conclusion, the disease comes back. Once the disease comes back, people take those precautions again. Those precautions work, and so there is a drop in prevalence, so on and so forth. You can think about the self-limiting effect as a kind of cycle (fig. 13.2).

That cycle is one explanation for why the COVID-19 pandemic came in waves. Once a wave took off, people would become extremely cautious. That reaction would cause the wave to dissipate. But then, after a while, with case

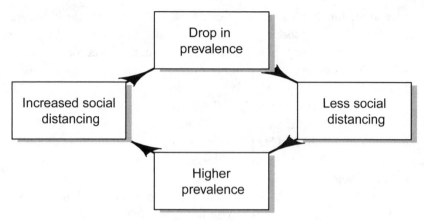

FIGURE 13.2. The self-limiting cycle of disease prevalence. When the disease is prevalent (bottom of cycle), people take precautions (such as social distancing) that lead to a drop in prevalence. This in turn leads people to feel comfortable relaxing their precautions, which in turn leads to greater prevalence.

counts low, it would become tempting to relax. And that would start the cycle yet again.[3]

The self-limiting effect is also relevant for other infectious diseases. Consider HIV. HIV is certainly contagious and the only way to prevent the disease is to take costly precautions: practice safe sex, use clean needles, and so on. (Today, drugs that prevent the transmission of HIV are available, but for many years those were not around.) When HIV is prevalent, more people will practice safe sex. But once the disease becomes rare, some might take a calculated risk and stop using condoms. That decision, taken by enough of the at-risk population, can lead to a resurgence in HIV. Philipson (2000) found evidence for such a dynamic. And, indeed, HIV has never disappeared, even though, in theory, if everyone practiced prevention, it *could* disappear.

The self-limiting effect is also useful in understanding diseases for which a vaccine exists. Take, for instance, measles. Measles is a terrible disease, one that, like COVID-19, is airborne and highly contagious. Children who contract measles experience a high fever and an awful rash. Some lose their vision and some even die.

Fortunately, a vaccine for measles became widely available in the late 1960s. And, all of a sudden, the number of cases of measles plummeted (fig. 13.3). That drop in cases in the 1960s amounts to a great success for modern medicine. Measles vaccination has saved over 17 million lives in just the past twenty years alone (Vanderslott, Dadonaite, and Roser 2019). Vaccines work and vaccines save lives.

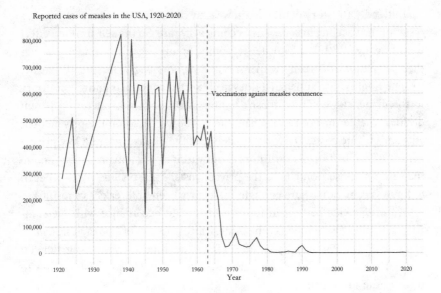

Reported cases of measles in the USA, 1920-2020

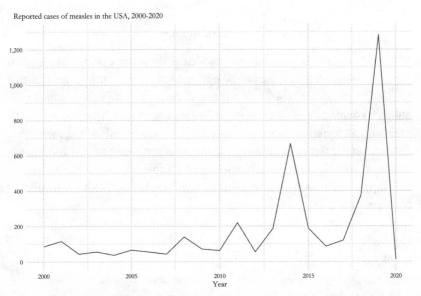

Reported cases of measles in the USA, 2000-2020

FIGURE 13.3. The first graph shows the trend in reported cases of measles from 1920 to 2020 (Vanderslott, Dadonaite, and Roser 2019). The second graph "zooms in" to the 2000–2020 period, which has seen a sharp increase in measles cases.

But, sadly, the story of measles in wealthy countries doesn't end there. As a result of the vaccine, measles has become very rare. So the self-limiting effect went to work. With low prevalence, some parents began to wonder whether the vaccination was really worth it. False rumors began to spread that the vaccine might cause autism. (It does not.) Such a concern is entirely contrary to the evidence—but that doesn't matter. A rational, self-interested parent decides whether or not to vaccinate their children based on the private benefits and private costs. The low prevalence of the disease means a low private benefit of vaccination. And rumors about vaccines and autism—even though they are nonsense—only raise the private costs. And so some parents began to forgo vaccinations. Sure enough, there have been outbreaks as a result.

All of *our* kids have been fully vaccinated in accordance with the standard schedule distributed by the American Academy of Pediatrics. *Reader, you should do the same for your kids!* First of all, there's a real private benefit: you don't want your children to get these diseases. But, also, we should try to think of the social benefit too.

The Bottom Line

Most chapters in this book rely on a hidden assumption: that the transactions we study only affect two parties. We have focused on simple arrangements in which one doctor treats one patient or one company makes a deal with another company. But often the relationships are more complex. That's the case with vaccination: one pharmaceutical company sells a vaccine to one patient, but the rest of us are affected, too. It's also the case for any transaction that leads to pollution. In such cases, there's a role for the government: subsidizing vaccination, mandating vaccination, taxing gasoline, and mandating mufflers, to name just a few.

References

Alexander, Diane, and Hannes Schwandt. "The Impact of Car Pollution on Infant and Child Health: Evidence from Emissions Cheating," *Review of Economic Studies* (February 2022): rdac007. https://doi.org/10.1093/restud/rdac007.

Ayres, Ian, and Steven D. Levitt. "Measuring Positive Externalities from Unobservable Victim Precaution: An Empirical Analysis of Lojack." *Quarterly Journal of Economics* 113, no. 1 (1998): 43–77. https://doi.org/10.1162/003355398555522.

Christensen, Björn, and Sören Christensen. "Are Female Hurricanes Really Deadlier than Male Hurricanes?" *Proceedings of the National Academy of Sciences* 111, no. 34 (2014): E3497–98. https://doi.org/10.1073/pnas.1410910111.

Currie, Janet, and Reed Walker. "Traffic Congestion and Infant Health: Evidence from E-ZPass." *American Economic Journal: Applied Economics* 3, no. 1 (2011): 65–90. https://doi.org/10.1257/app.3.1.65.

Hamel, Liz, Lunna Lopes, Grace Sparks, Ashley Kirzinger, Audrey Kearney, Mellisha Stokes, and Mollyann Brodie. "COVID-19 Vaccine Monitor: October 2021." *KFF* (blog). October 28, 2021. https://www.kff.org/coronavirus-covid-19/poll-finding/kff-covid-19-vaccine-monitor-october-2021/.

Jung, Kiju, Sharon Shavitt, Madhu Viswanathan, and Joseph M. Hilbe. "Female Hurricanes Are Deadlier than Male Hurricanes." *Proceedings of the National Academy of Sciences* 111, no. 24 (2014): 8782–87. https://doi.org/10.1073/pnas.1402786111.

Mankiw, N. Gregory. "Smart Taxes: An Open Invitation to Join the Pigou Club." *Eastern Economic Journal* 35, no. 1 (2009): 14–23. https://doi.org/10.1057/eej.2008.43.

Mathieu, Edouard, Hannah Ritchie, Lucas Rodés-Guirao, Cameron Appel, Charlie Giattino, Joe Hasell, Bobbie Macdonald, Saloni Dattani, Diana Beltekian, Esteban Ortiz-Ospina, and Max Roser. "Coronavirus Pandemic (COVID-19)." *Our World in Data*. 2020. https://ourworldindata.org/coronavirus.

Milkman, K. L., J. Beshears, J. J. Choi, D. Laibson, and B. C. Madrian. "Using Implementation Intentions Prompts to Enhance Influenza Vaccination Rates." *Proceedings of the National Academy of Sciences* 108, no. 26 (2011): 10415–20. https://doi.org/10.1073/pnas.1103170108.

Milkman, Katherine L., Mitesh S. Patel, Linnea Gandhi, Heather Graci, Dena Gromet, Hung Ho, Joseph Kay, et al. 2021. "A Mega-Study of Text-Message Nudges Encouraging Patients to Get Vaccinated at Their Pharmacy." Rochester, NY: SSRN Scholarly Paper, 2021. https://doi.org/10.2139/ssrn.3780356.

Philipson, Tomas. "Chapter 33 Economic Epidemiology and Infectious Diseases." In *Handbook of Health Economics*, 1:1761–99. Elsevier, 2000.

Vanderslott, Samantha, Bernadeta Dadonaite, and Max Roser. "Vaccination." *Our World in Data*. 2019. https://ourworldindata.org/vaccination.

Health Gradients

Noto lives near his office at the University of Chicago. The Hyde Park neighborhood is a nice place to live: racially diverse with good schools and little crime. Life expectancy among the residents of Hyde Park is extremely high: nearly eighty-five years. That's higher than the average life expectancy in any country. And, somehow, the housing is still quite affordable (Robert Wood Johnson Foundation, 2020).

If Noto were to walk a couple miles, though, those numbers would change. The Englewood neighborhood, just down the street, is one of the lowest income neighborhoods in Chicago. Estimated life expectancy there: under sixty-seven years. That's lower than life expectancy in Ethiopia, India, or Indonesia.

That's a difference of seventeen years in life expectancy between two close neighborhoods. The seventeen-year difference is similar to the gap in life expectancy between Japan and Ghana.

That's two neighborhoods close together on a map, and yet light-years apart on a table of health statistics. How can it be that populations that live so close together face such vastly different health problems?

Documenting the Gradient

To rigorously study disparities in health, one needs statistics on people, not neighborhoods. To gather those statistics, we turn to the National Longitudinal Mortality Study, the NLMS. That data set has been compiled by government agencies to provide researchers with a sense of how mortality rates vary by demographics.[1]

We take all people in the survey between the ages of sixty and sixty-four

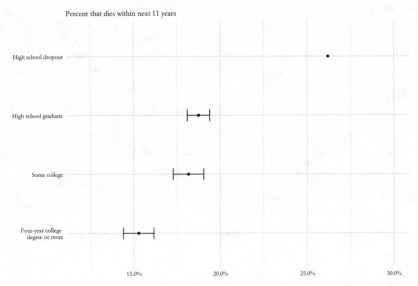

Percent that dies within next 11 years

FIGURE 14.1. The eleven-year mortality rate for American sixty- to sixty-four-year-olds with different levels of education. The "some college" category refers to those who attended college but did not receive a four-year college degree.

and then track the share of them that die within the next eleven years. Figure 14.1 shows the eleven-year mortality rate by level of education. Overall, we see a stark relationship between education and mortality. Among those who dropped out of high school, about 26 percent die within the next eleven years. For those with a high school degree, mortality is much lower: under 19 percent. It is lower still for those who went to college but did not get a four-year degree—just over 18 percent—and even lower for those who have a four-year college degree—about 15 percent.

We can repeat the same exercise with income and reach a similar conclusion: those who make more money face a lower risk of death. Figure 14.2 shows an extremely strong correlation between income and mortality. In almost every case, going up one income bracket is associated with a lower mortality rate. We can use the data to estimate that, on average, a 10 percent increase in household income is associated with a decline in mortality of 2.3 percent.[2] Or to put it another way, the top income bracket has an eleven-year mortality rate that is about 25 percent lower than the bottom income bracket.

There are two things to note right away. First, these are all human beings. It's not as though we are comparing cats and dogs. (Cats live longer.) So such enormous gaps in mortality should be jarring. Second, note that there's a *gradient* here. It's not solely that the lowest-income groups end up dying earlier:

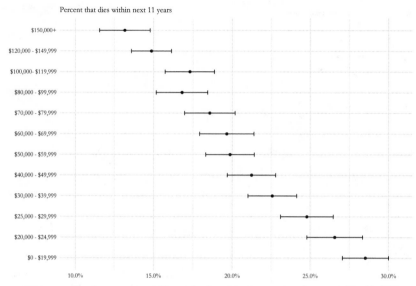

FIGURE 14.2. The eleven-year mortality rate for American sixty- to sixty-four-year-olds with different levels of household income.

there's a strong correlation between socioeconomic status and length of life across the entire spectrum. So it's not simply that "poverty is correlated with mortality." It's more than that—the gradient exists across all education and income groups.

Is This Just an American Thing?

What we've established with some mortality statistics is that there exists a gradient between health and both education and income. As a shorthand, we call that the "health-wealth gradient," even though it's really about more than pure financial wealth—here, "wealth" becomes shorthand for higher socioeconomic status. The higher a person's socioeconomic status, broadly defined, the better their health.

It's natural to wonder whether the health-wealth gradient is driven entirely by the American way. After all, the wealthier Americans are, the more money they can spend on healthy food and better doctors, the more they can enjoy unpolluted air, a more satisfying job, and other benefits. The less money Americans have, the more likely they are to have trouble finding good medical care, to face unemployment, and to encounter other difficulties. Perhaps the health-wealth gradient is solely a troubling consequence of American capitalism.

Remarkably, though, more egalitarian societies still end up with large health-wealth gradients. Take, for instance, Sweden. Swedish socialism is the polar opposite of American capitalism. Swedes enjoy universal healthcare, poverty rates are substantially lower in Sweden than in the United States, and the social safety net there is much more generous than anything in the United States. For instance, when Americans lose a job and apply for unemployment benefits, they can receive those benefits for about six months (Center on Budget and Policy Priorities 2022). In Sweden, the benefits last for nearly a year (Nordic Council of Ministers 2022; Tatsiramos and van Ours 2014). Swedes also enjoy lower levels of air pollution and face a more progressive taxation system (Climate and Clean Air Coalition 2022.).

In other words, if America is a capitalist dystopian hellscape, then Sweden is a socialist utopia. So one might imagine that the Swedish population simply does not exhibit a health-wealth gradient. After all, unlike Americans, all Swedes have access to good healthcare. And while life is always harder for people with less money, the generous social safety net in Sweden surely eliminates much of the risk that America's poor have to face.

It is perhaps surprising then that the correlation between wealth and health is *stronger* in Sweden than in the United States. David Cesarini, one of our graduate school classmates, estimated that correlation after teaming up with a few researchers in Sweden: Erik Lindqvist, Robert Östling, and Björn Wallace. The researchers measured the correlation between a household's wealth and its members' risk of mortality in both countries. In the United States, they found that an extra $140,000 in wealth is associated with an 8.1 percent reduction in the ten-year mortality rate. In Sweden, the same increase in wealth is associated with a 13.3 percent reduction in the mortality rate. So the correlation between wealth and mortality is 64 percent *larger* in Sweden as compared to the United States (Cesarini et al. 2016). That finding is at odds with a couple other studies (Semyonov, Lewin-Epstein, and Maskileyson 2013; Maskileyson 2014), but, regardless, it is clear that the gradient between wealth and health is not at all uniquely American.

Now, to be clear, our goal is not to argue for or against capitalism, socialism, social safety nets, meatballs, or Ikea. The point is to rule out a tempting set of explanations for America's health-wealth gradient. It's tempting for Americans to say: "if only we had more equitable access to healthcare, there would be no health-wealth gradient." Or, similarly, to argue that America's health-wealth gradient is solely a consequence of America's minimal social safety net, or America's rising inequality, or other aspects of American social injustice. The evidence rejects, at the very least, an extreme version of that argument. Countries with much more generous social policies also end up with remarkably stark relationships between socioeconomic status and health. It's not just an American story.

What Drives the Gradient?

So if we can't blame the health-wealth gradient solely on America's unique approach to public policy, then what explains it? Well, the relationship between wealth and health is complex. We can't just say that "wealth causes health" or "health causes wealth." Wealth and health are related through a complicated web of causal relationships.

To start with, being in good health allows some people to become wealthier. After all, those in good health can work longer hours and be more productive during those hours. Our favorite demonstration comes from a famous medical trial: the Multiple Risk Factor Intervention Trial, MRFIT.

First of all, MRFIT is a great acronym. (*A bodybuilder flexes his biceps. Hi! I'm Mr. Fit!*) But MRFIT is more than just a fun name. MRFIT was a randomized trial developed by physicians to study the effects of treatments for heart disease. The physicians took 13,000 men and monitored their health over six years. One group was randomly chosen to receive a variety of interventions meant to lower their cholesterol, lower their blood pressure, and to nudge them to quit smoking. By "interventions," we don't mean fancy, new technologies. Rather, the men were encouraged by their doctors to follow sensible recommendations: stop smoking, improve their diets, get more exercise, and take certain medications, if appropriate.

The combination of those interventions really did improve the men's health. The first panel of figure 14.3 presents some of the estimated effects on health. Men who were randomly assigned to receive the interventions had 2 percent lower cholesterol six years later, their systolic blood pressure was down 4 percent, and so on. To the physicians involved, those results were cause for celebration. Here's scientific proof that the doctors could get these men to be healthier.

And then two economists wondered if there was more to learn from the trial. Mel Stephens and Desmond Toohey wondered whether MRFIT might be a useful setting to study the health-wealth gradient. After all, the MRFIT trial led one group of men to be made healthier. So what happened to their wealth?

Stephens and Toohey analyzed the results from MRFIT with one additional outcome that the physicians didn't bother studying at first: earnings. The doctors were focused on medical outcomes—the economists, naturally,

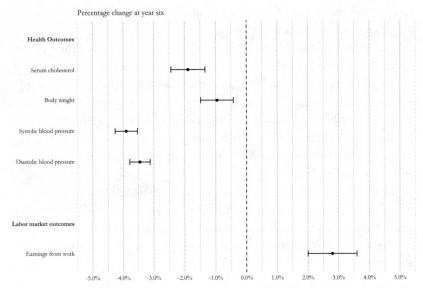

Percentage change at year six

FIGURE 14.3. Changes in health outcomes from the Multiple Risk Factor Intervention Trial (MRFIT) six years after enrollment in the study. The differences represent percentage differences between the treatment and control group and can be interpreted as the causal impact of MRFIT because it was a randomized control trial. The first four rows show that MRFIT improved multiple risk factors for cardiovascular disease: reductions in cholesterol, smoking, body weight, and blood pressure. The final row shows that the treatment group also experienced a significant increase in income from work, which the authors interpret as the causal effect of better health on income.

were focused on an economic outcome. And lo and behold, men who received the MRFIT intervention earned nearly 3 percent more money six years later than men who were randomly assigned to the control group (Stephens and Toohey 2022).

That finding demonstrates that health causes wealth. The doctors running MRFIT made men healthier, and then that made them wealthier. So the health-wealth gradient is, in part, a consequence of health leading to wealth. Some people make more money because they are healthier, and so that, in part, drives the statistics we found in the NLMS.

That said, there's more to the health-wealth gradient than just a single arrow from health to wealth. It also works the other way: those who are made wealthier end up in better health. A famous paper by Adriana Lleras-Muney of UCLA demonstrated that relationship. Lleras-Muney studied compulsory schooling laws in the early twentieth century. Around the 1920s, American states gradually began requiring all Americans to stay in school for longer. For instance, in 1921, New York State switched from requiring six years of schooling for all children to requiring seven years. Many states were making similar changes around the same time. States gradually shifted to longer and longer compulsory school requirements.

Lleras-Muney realized that those law changes are a kind of natural experiment.[3] Normally, a person's level of education is in no way randomly assigned. Typically, the number of years that a person stays in school is a matter of a slew of factors: the education of their parents, whether or not their friends drop out of school, so on and so forth. In this context, some Americans were forced to spend more time in school than others, solely by chance, based on whether or not they were born just after or just before one of these new compulsory schooling laws.

So Lleras-Muney studied Americans who attended more or less school based on when these compulsory schooling laws went into effect. First, she found large effects from the laws on levels of education. When a state shifted to require that kids stay in school for longer, the law actually made a difference, increasing average levels of education. That is to say, the laws had the intended effect: children ended up staying in school for longer.

Then she studied what happened to those Americans' health. She found that Americans who were forced to stay in school longer exhibited a lower mortality rate. An extra year ended up making someone 3.6 percentage points less likely to die during the next ten years. Those who were nudged to have a bit more education, it turned out, ended up living longer (Lleras-Muney 2005).

In other studies, labor economists have established that more education improves people's wealth (Angrist and Krueger 1991; Zimmerman 2014). So, taken together with Lleras-Muney's work that traces a causal relationship between education and health, that suggests that more education leads to more wealth which then leads to better health. And so her work suggests that the health-wealth gradient is partly a matter of wealth leading to greater health.

The Bottom Line

What we are left with here is a complex web of relationships that underlie the connections between wealth and health. MRFIT—again, great name— tells us that better health can lead to wealth. At the same time, the history of compulsory schooling laws suggests that the relationship works in the other direction, too. American kids who were nudged to stay in school for longer ended up living longer. Wealth, it seems, also leads to better health. In other words, the health-wealth gradient represents a mishmash of different forces. And those forces operate even in a wealthy, egalitarian country like Sweden.

That is not to say that the health-wealth gradient should be ignored. A world in which the health-wealth gradient was less steep—where health was less tied to wealth—would be a better world.

It is disheartening that good health seems to be yet another privilege of the wealthy—yet one more thing that comes with money and access. And so we might wonder whether there is something to be done about the health-wealth gradient. Are there ways to help disadvantaged people who end up in bad health? We address that possibility next.

References

Angrist, Joshua D., and Alan B. Krueger. "Does Compulsory School Attendance Affect School-ing and Earnings?" *Quarterly Journal of Economics* 106, no. 4 (1991): 979–1014. https://doi.org/10.2307/2937954.

Cesarini, David, Erik Lindqvist, Robert Östling, and Björn Wallace. "Wealth, Health, and Child Development: Evidence from Administrative Data on Swedish Lottery Players." *Quarterly Journal of Economics* 131, no. 2 (2016): 687–738. https://doi.org/10.1093/qje/qjw001.

"Life Expectancy: Could Where You Live Influence How Long You Live?" Robert Wood Johnson Foundation. March 9, 2020. https://www.rwjf.org/en/library/interactives/whereyouliveaffectshowlongyoulive.html.

Lleras-Muney, Adriana. "The Relationship between Education and Adult Mortality in the United States." *Review of Economic Studies* 72, no. 1 (2005): 189–221.

Maskileyson, Dina. "Healthcare System and the Wealth–Health Gradient: A Comparative Study of Older Populations in Six Countries." *Social Science and Medicine* 119 (2014): 18–26. https://doi.org/10.1016/j.socscimed.2014.08.013.

"Policy Basics: How Many Weeks of Unemployment Compensation Are Available?" Center on Budget and Policy Priorities. August 1, 2022. https://www.cbpp.org/research/economy/how-many-weeks-of-unemployment-compensation-are-available.

Semyonov, Moshe, Noah Lewin-Epstein, and Dina Maskileyson. "Where Wealth Matters More for Health: The Wealth–Health Gradient in 16 Countries." *Social Science and Medicine* 81 (2013): 10–17. https://doi.org/10.1016/j.socscimed.2013.01.010.

Stephens, Melvin, Jr., and Desmond Toohey. 2022. "The Impact of Health on Labor Market Out-comes: Evidence from a Large-Scale Health Experiment." *American Economic Journal: Applied Economics* 14, no. 3 (2022): 367–99. https://doi.org/10.1257/app.20180686.

"Sweden." n.d. Climate and Clean Air Coalition. Accessed August 8, 2022. https://www.ccacoalition.org/en/partners/sweden.

Tatsiramos, Konstantinos, and Jan C. van Ours. "Labor Market Effects of Unemployment Insur-ance Design." *Journal of Economic Surveys* 28, no. 2 (2014): 284–311. https://doi.org/10.1111/joes.12005.

"Unemployment Benefit in Sweden." *Nordic Co-operation*. Nordic Council of Ministers. August 1, 2022. https://www.norden.org/en/info-norden/unemployment-benefit-sweden.

Zimmerman, Seth D. 2014. "The Returns to College Admission for Academically Marginal Stu-dents." *Journal of Labor Economics* 32, no. 4 (2014): 711–54. https://doi.org/10.1086/676661.

Social Determinants of Health

Most of our work as health economists focuses on the *financial* forces that shape healthcare. And, accordingly, we've spent most of this book describing those financial forces. We've discussed the business of health insurance, how pharmaceutical companies are regulated, how healthcare providers are reimbursed for their work, and many more topics.

All of that is important, but it only takes us so far. Financial forces can't really explain why some people are in poor health and others are in excellent health. Sure, part of it may be a matter of the copayments they face or the way in which their doctors are reimbursed. But most differences in health are driven not by financial forces but rather by social forces. Health is a consequence of socioeconomic background, the support people have in the community, their employment, and so on.

Those forces are called the "social determinants of health." People in the medical and public health world discuss social determinants so often that they use an abbreviation: SDOH. The initials are often brought up to remind everyone that health is produced by inputs that include more than just medical care. A child might suffer from severe asthma attacks because her school is near a highway and her home is filled with cigarette smoke and dust. Sure, she can be treated for each episode, but the asthma attacks may damage her lungs enough to remove her from school. What she really needs is help that gets at the root causes of her problems. What really matters is not her medical diagnosis for a particular ER visit but rather the entirety of her life.

Once one recognizes the importance of the social determinants of health, it leads one to wonder whether we all focus too much on medical interventions. Maybe what people really need is not only more medicine, or better medicine, but help that addresses the social determinants of their health.

The Legacy of Institutionalized Racism

Herman Shaw lived in Alabama his whole life, from 1909 until he passed away in 1999. Shaw was a remarkable man. He was valedictorian of his high school class. He raised a family in a house that he himself built. For decades, Shaw farmed cotton and also worked at a textile mill—he would plow his fields in the morning and then work at the textile mill from 2:00 in the afternoon until 10:00 at night.

Back when Shaw was twenty-three years old, he happened to see a paper flier advertising a program that provided free medical care. On a Sunday afternoon, Shaw traveled to a nearby church where a representative from the US Public Health Service described the program. As a participant in the program, Shaw would be given free hot meals and also free medical care: a doctor from the North would visit every three months who the participants would see for free. In return, Shaw simply had to rely on the program for all of his medical needs—he agreed not to seek other care. This was 1932, in the midst of the Great Depression, and it seemed like a terrific deal. Shaw signed up.

The study was called the "Tuskegee Study of Untreated Syphilis in the Negro Male." About six hundred other black men in Alabama were also recruited. Most of them had syphilis, and the goal of the study was to leave the disease untreated and track how it affected the body.

No one told Shaw this when he was recruited. That alone makes the initiation of the study unethical: the participants did not know what they were getting into. But an even more egregious lapse in ethics came about a decade later. In the 1940s, penicillin became the standard of care for syphilis, and yet the Tuskegee researchers chose not to offer proper treatment to participants in the study *for the next thirty years.*

As the years went by, participants in the study got used to a certain routine. Each year, they received a free meal and then a thorough medical examination. Some underwent painful spinal taps—they were told that the spinal taps were a necessary treatment, that they had "bad blood," and so needed the treatment. But actually, the doctors were lying to the men: they were withdrawing spinal fluid solely for the sake of research.

When participants died, the researchers would offer the participants' survivors a small honorarium for a burial allowance, but only if the family agreed to an autopsy. No one mentioned that this was all done for research. And the study was only kept secret from the men who participated in it—the researchers happily published dozens of medical studies over the years.

Finally, in 1972, reporters at the Associated Press, the *Los Angeles Times*, and the *New York Times* published stories on the Tuskegee study. By that point, many of the study's participants had died. Herman Shaw was sixty-three years old and was shocked to learn of the program. He had trusted the doctors. Shaw joined a lawsuit against the government over the Tuskegee study and, eventually, received $37,000 in damages. In 1997, Shaw traveled to the White House, where President Clinton issued a formal apology for the study.

When the world became aware of the Tuskegee study, many people were livid. And rightly so: there are other examples of horrific medical ethics in the United States, but the Tuskegee study stands out.[1] The Tuskegee study was revealed as "the longest non-therapeutic experiment on human beings in medical history" (Geiger 1981). There's never been another study in which patients were harmed for so long.

Nevertheless, Herman Shaw expressed remarkable forgiveness for what happened. At the White House, he stood before the president and said, "In my opinion, it is never too late to work to restore faith and trust."

But is it? What did the Tuskegee study do to black Americans' trust in the medical system? Black men are less likely to be organ donors, less likely to volunteer for clinical trials, and are in poorer health than nearly all other demographic groups ("Final Report of the Tuskegee Syphilis Study Legacy Committee" 1996). Many researchers suspect that that disparity is, partly, the legacy of the Tuskegee study.

Two economists, Marianne Wanamaker and Marcella Alsan (2018), set out to measure the Tuskegee study's "long shadow." Wanamaker is an economic historian and Marcella Alsan is an MD-PhD: she has a doctorate in economics and is also an infectious disease doctor.

Wanamaker and Alsan studied how the public disclosure of the Tuskegee experiment in 1972 affected black Americans as compared to white Americans. They studied trends in a variety of outcomes: mortality, the share of people who have seen a physician in the past year, and so on. One of the most relevant outcomes Wanamaker and Alsan studied was a question in the General Social Survey that asks Americans whether "doctors can be trusted."

Wanamaker and Alsan found a clear divergence in trends in those variables just after the 1972 disclosure of the Tuskegee experiment. Black Americans who lived near Tuskegee, Alabama, became less likely to see a physician, less likely to report that doctors can be trusted, and exhibited a higher rate of mortality. Those results suggest that the Tuskegee experiment alone can account for about a third of the overall gap in life expectancy between black and white men. All in all, the work demonstrated that the Tuskegee study had an enormous effect on the relationship between black Americans and the healthcare system.

The project motivated Marcella Alsan to continue studying the topic. How, she wondered, might the healthcare system change to address the lasting impact of the Tuskegee study? Were there ways that medical care might evolve to be more inclusive, to rebuild trust despite the memory of the Tuskegee study?

To answer those questions, Alsan joined forces with Owen Garrick and Grant Graziani (2019) and sought to measure how the race of doctors affects the behavior of their patients. The team went to barber shops in Oakland, California, and recruited hundreds of black men to participate in a study. The men were paid to visit a clinic for preventive care.

Once they arrived at the clinic, the men were handed an Android tablet. They sat down in the waiting room and worked their way through a digital survey. After some questions about their background, the tablet described the doctor that they were about to see. Importantly, the digital survey included a *picture* of the doctor, so the doctor's race would be clear to the participants. All of the participants in the experiment were black, but only half of them had been randomly assigned to a black doctor.

The survey on the tablet asked the patients to select the preventive services they wanted. The app gave them a checklist.

- Blood pressure measurement
- Weight and height measurement
- Cholesterol screening (requires finger prick)
- Diabetes screening (requires finger prick)
- None of the above

The researchers included those parenthetical warnings ("requires finger prick") in order to make it clear to the patients that some of these preventive services were more invasive than others. Measuring your blood pressure is, perhaps, no big deal, but screenings that require a finger prick—that's a bit more.

The participants chose the tests that they wanted via little digital check marks. Then, after a few minutes, they finally were called in to meet with a doctor. The doctors talked to the patients for an average of twenty minutes. During those twenty minutes, the doctors asked the patients, again, which preventive services they wanted. "You indicated that you only want us to check your blood pressure—are you sure you don't want a diabetes screening, too?"

After about six hundred of these appointments, the researchers sat down and went through the data. The bar chart in figure 15.1 describes some of their findings. Before meeting the doctor, black patients who were assigned to a

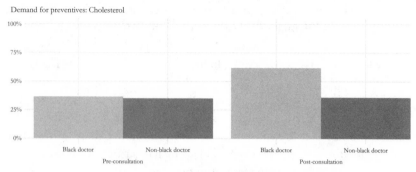

Demand for preventives: Cholesterol

FIGURE 15.1. Share of black men who chose to get screened for high cholesterol after consulting with a randomly assigned doctor. Before their consultation, only about one-third of the patients wanted a screening. After the consultation, if the black men had been randomly assigned a black doctor, then they were more likely to choose a cholesterol screening compared to the black men who were randomly assigned a non-black doctor.

non-black doctor made the same decisions as patients who were assigned to a black doctor. They all saw a headshot of their doctor on the tablet—the doctor's race was made apparent. But just knowing that they had been assigned to a black doctor didn't seem to change their behavior.

After actually meeting with the doctor, however, behavior diverged. Black patients who were randomly assigned to a black doctor were over 20 percentage points more likely to choose a cholesterol test. In fact, the divergence was greater for the more invasive tests: patients were only about 10 percentage points more likely to choose a blood pressure screening when presented with a black doctor. In other words, when black patients were randomly assigned to black doctors, they were more likely to agree to all tests, but the increase was even larger for tests that required a finger prick.

The researchers interviewed some patients during the experiment in order to understand precisely how being matched to a black doctor changed their behavior. One patient made a comment that stuck out. Before seeing his doctor, the patient said that he did not want the flu shot out of "fear of being experimented on." What did he mean by that? Was he referring to the Tuskegee study?

All in all, the study demonstrated that black patients are more interested in preventive care when they can meet in person with black doctors. The researchers could only speculate as to precisely why that is. But it fits with a general pattern across many other studies, and it supports the notion that diversity among physicians helps their patients (Greenwood, Carnahan, and Huang 2018; Hill, Jones, and Woodworth 2020). When physicians look like their patients, their patients are more likely to listen. And yet, only about

4 percent of practicing physicians identify as black (Ly 2022). This experiment in Oakland, along with much other work, suggests that the ongoing discussion about diversity among physicians is very much warranted.[2]

Addressing Social Determinants with
Social Workers and Personal Coaches

Indulge us for a moment in a thought experiment. Imagine two patients: Mr. A and Mr. B. Both men are unemployed, they both have very little money and suffer from serious health problems. And by serious health problems, we mean big problems: "severe congestive heart failure, chronic asthma, uncontrolled diabetes, hypothyroidism, gout, and a history of smoking and alcohol abuse."[3]

Both men cycle in and out of the emergency room and the hospital. When they're in the hospital, they get good, acute care. After all, both men visit large, urban hospitals staffed with well-trained physicians and nurses. But then they are discharged from the hospital, and that's where things fall apart. They don't have a regular primary-care physician and, anyway, it can take months for an appointment to open up. The two men will routinely forget about their medications, and when they stop taking their medications, no one checks on them and asks why. No one checks their blood pressure or blood-sugar levels. They're on their own, and they're not doing well.

Mr. A and Mr. B might qualify for all sorts of benefits: unemployment insurance, disability insurance, food pantries, housing assistance. But they don't know about the programs and, anyway, the paperwork is daunting. There's also the issue of their drinking, smoking, and drug abuse. Alcoholics Anonymous has helped millions of Americans quit drinking, but no one ever encourages Mr. A and Mr. B to go to a meeting. Cheap tools can help people quit smoking cigarettes, from nicotine patches to short training programs, but, again, Mr. A and Mr. B don't bother.

It's unfair to blame Mr. A and Mr. B for their situation. Yes, some of their health problems are a result of decisions they've made: not to exercise, to eat poorly, to drop out of high school. But the two men have grappled with challenges that don't often afflict those from more privileged backgrounds: trauma, abuse, bullying, terrible job prospects, crime, and so on.

Mr. A and Mr. B are identical. But then, all of a sudden, their lives diverge. Mr. A is enrolled in a new program at the hospital. He is matched to someone whom we might call a "personal health coach," although no one ever uses that term. The coach talks to Mr. A for hours and then drives Mr. A home. The coach finds out that there are Alcoholics Anonymous meetings in a nearby church basement and encourages Mr. A to attend. The coach reaches out to local physicians and helps Mr. A book appointments: a regular visit to a primary-care physician, but also a visit to a podiatrist and an endocrinologist. The coach helps Mr. A apply for disability insurance. He even encourages Mr. A to find a talk therapist, to make sense of the childhood trauma that has caused him so much pain.

This is what some experts call a "high-touch intervention." The personal health coach spends a whole lot of time with Mr. A. Some of the work is strictly medical: measuring blood sugar and weight and blood pressure, assuring access to physicians. But much of it is not exactly medical but rather social: finding better housing, enrolling Mr. A in social programs, and grappling with his addiction. In other words, this intervention deals directly with the social determinants of Mr. A's medical problems.

So that's our thought experiment: Mr. A and Mr. B are similar people with similar, severe problems. Mr. A gets a high-touch intervention and Mr. B does not. What happens next?

For that, we turn to evidence on a variety of different interventions. First, there's the Camden Coalition of Healthcare Providers, a program run in Camden, New Jersey. The Camden program matched people like Mr. A and Mr. B to intensive work with physicians, social workers, and registered nurses.

The Camden program was profiled in a 2011 New Yorker article that described the program in glowing terms. The author of the profile, Atul Gawande, wondered whether high-touch interventions like the Camden program might be the holy grail of healthcare reform: interventions that both help people and save money. Finally, politicians wouldn't have to decide between spending more on healthcare and spending more on schools. Spending on programs like the Camden program—the argument goes—pays for itself. "We can have it all—teachers and health care."

So suppose that Mr. A is assigned to be treated by the Camden program—he gets a slew of attention from a team of professionals. Meanwhile, Mr. B gets the usual treatment: discharge from the hospital to uncoordinated, fragmented care. Which one of the men would be first to be readmitted back to the hospital?

Now, based on Atul Gawande's New Yorker article, the answer is obvious. If Mr. A gets all of that attention, then he should be much better off. Six months later or twelve months later—Mr. A should be doing better and Mr. B should be back in the hospital.

After Gawande's New Yorker article came out, a team of researchers—Amy Finkelstein, Annetta Zhou, Sarah Taubman, and Joe Doyle—approached the people running the Camden project. The team had read the New Yorker profile, and they wanted to study the program. But they didn't want to just interview participants in the program, they wanted to run a randomized controlled study. They wanted to randomize some patients to the Camden program and randomize others to a control group.

The Camden program was founded and run by a physician named Jeffrey Brenner. Brenner agreed to run a randomized trial. That decision was brave, because Brenner had, by that point, invested years in the program. Once you start a randomized trial, there's no way to know whether or not you'll like the trial's results. For that reason, there are organizations that shy away from evaluating their work—they don't want to receive bad news. But Brenner, a true physician scientist, wanted to know.

And so the team worked with Brenner to implement a randomized trial. It took them four years: to set up the infrastructure, to get approval from human-subjects review boards, to secure research funding. But eventually, they recruited 800 patients in Camden hospitals: 399 were randomized to receive a high-touch intervention via the Camden project and 401 were randomized to receive no treatment.

The researchers ended up with results that were quite contrary to what one might expect from Gawande's *New Yorker* profile. Despite all the hype, Mr. A was no less likely to end up back in the hospital after six months than Mr. B. Despite so much personal attention from social workers, physicians, health coaches, and nurses, hospital readmission rates did not budge.

Those results were a huge wet blanket thrown on top of tremendous excitement for high-touch interventions. Some argue that high-touch interventions attack not just medical problems but the social determinants of health. So if we spend the time and money to address those fundamental problems, the argument goes, only then will we see medical benefits. Well, this study didn't find any evidence to support such an argument.

The research team also found an interesting pattern that speaks, more broadly, to studying vulnerable patients like Mr. A and Mr. B. Figure 15.2 comes from the study—it plots the number of hospital admissions for men randomly assigned to the intervention (Mr. A) and those randomly assigned to standard care (Mr. B). For both groups, the risk of hospitalization went way up just before the experiment: from about 0.3 admissions per person two quarters before the experiment, to triple that just before the experiment. But then, after the intervention, the risk of hospitalization went way down, even for those who did not receive the treatment.

What can possibly explain such a pattern? This is an example of what statisticians call "regression to the mean." Regression to the mean works in the following way. Imagine that we were to pick out the best students in a first-grade class: the kids who had all gotten the highest scores on a standardized

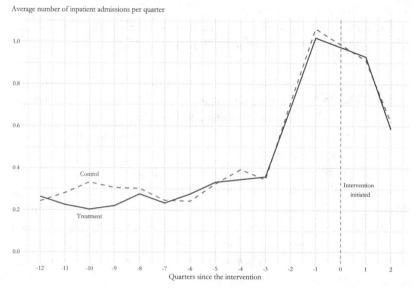

Average number of inpatient admissions per quarter

FIGURE 15.2. Average number of inpatient hospital admissions in the treatment and control group in the Camden experimental study.

test. Then we follow those students to see how they did the following year, in second grade. On average, those kids would have lower scores, as compared to their classmates, in second grade. That finding is not a matter of the kids' motivation or a question of how teaching works—instead, it's a statistical phenomenon. Whenever two variables are positively correlated, an extreme sample based on one variable is less extreme based on the other variable. So students who have very high test scores in first grade tend to have lower test scores in second grade.[4]

Regression to the mean makes it very tricky to study interventions in healthcare without randomized trials. If we just compare patients before and after they go through the Camden program, they are going to end up healthier. But that's not because the Camden program made them healthier—it's because the program deliberately selected troubled patients. And, on average, people with the worst problems one month tend to look better the following month. The issue is that when you only select the toughest cases, those cases improve, no matter what, on average, since, by definition, you were catching them when the patients were at their worst. That's why we need a control group, why we need randomized controlled trials.

And, lo and behold, when the authors studied the Camden program with a randomized control group, they found no effect. Now, that's only one particular study. That one study is certainly not the final word on high-touch interventions. The topic is too important to drop after just one set of disappointing results.

In fact, other interventions seem more promising. Take, for instance, the work of Shreya Kangovi and David Grande, two physicians who run high-touch interventions on patients in Philadelphia—just a twenty-minute drive from Camden. Kangovi and Grande (2014, 2017, 2020) run randomized trials to assess what happens when expensive and difficult patients in a hospital are matched to health coaches upon discharge.

So far, they have found some encouraging results. In one study, Kangovi and Grande found no effect on their "primary outcome" but did find an effect on "secondary outcomes." They expected to see an improvement in self-rated health and did not, but they found that health coaches reduce hospitalization rates. That kind of mixed result is common in this area. When carefully measured, health coaches don't work like magic on every outcome. And, so far, there's no sign that these types of programs pay for themselves. Health coaches are expensive, and even if they lower healthcare costs, the savings don't outweigh the initial expense. But, that being said, the work has suggested that some high-touch interventions can reduce hospitalization rates and improve clinical outcomes.

So what do we learn here about high-touch interventions that address the social determinants of health? First of all, we need randomized trials. Regression to the mean suggests that simple before/after comparisons are going to mislead us. Patients with big problems tend to get somewhat better, on average, anyway. And so every study needs a good control group.

Second, as the Camden study shows, just because a high-touch intervention *sounds* helpful, doesn't mean that it actually works. It is difficult to help people. There are plenty of medical interventions that doctors once believed were helpful but that actually do nothing. The same is true of complex, high-touch interventions like these. We need good evidence—we can't just rely on our intuition.

Third, it is worth emphasizing that these kinds of interventions are important, and more research on them is warranted. Think of our made-up Mr. A and Mr. B—a single, new pharmaceutical is not going to help them very much. What could help them, perhaps, is serious, time-intensive work by a professional who cares about them.

Addressing Social Determinants by Sending Nurses into Homes

Maybe the problem with interventions like the Camden program is that they try to help people once it is too late. Once people have faced adversity for decades, it can be hard to help them. So what if, instead, we intervene early on, before those decades of adversity.

A variety of interventions try to do just that, by intervening during the very first months of life. The Nurse-Family Partnership is one example. The program pays nurses to visit young, low-income, first-time mothers. The nurses visit the young mothers about every couple weeks, starting during their pregnancy and ending when their newborn becomes a toddler.

The program is designed to address the social determinants of health. The first-time mothers develop a close relationship with the nurse assigned to them, so that the nurses become a trusted resource. The nurses teach the moms how to change diapers, how to breastfeed, and the many ways to protect and encourage the baby's development.

One mother who went through the program commented: "Many women don't have support. Yes, I was young when I got pregnant and I felt like people were quick to judge me. Nurse Stephanie being there for me made me feel like I could do it" (Nurse-Family Partnership 2018).

The Nurse-Family Partnership has been around since the 1970s. Over the years, it has been evaluated through several randomized trials. In Elmira, New York, in 1977, four hundred low-income mothers were randomly assigned either to be part of the Family-Nurse Partnership or else to be in a control group (Olds, Henderson, Chamberlin, and Tatelbaum 1986; Olds, Henderson, Tatelbaum, and Chamberlin 1986). A couple other, similar studies followed. Those trials suggested that partnering with a nurse led to some benefits: higher birth weight and some evidence that the kids ended up more prepared for school (Kitzman et al. 2010).

More recently, though, results have been less encouraging. In 2022, the largest randomized study of the Nurse-Family Partnership was published in the *Journal of the American Medical Association* (McConnell et al. 2022). The study dwarfed previous evaluations of the Nurse-Family Partnership: 3,319 mothers were randomly assigned to a nurse and 1,647 were randomly assigned to the control group.

Unlike previous, smaller randomized evaluations, the 2022 study found no statistically significant effects on adverse birth outcomes. The researchers looked at incidence of low birth weight, neonatal morbidity, stays in the neonatal intensive care unit, and other signs of newborn health. There was no difference between the babies whose mothers had been visited by a nurse and those whose mothers had not. Nearly 27 percent of mothers randomized into the Nurse-Family Partnership experienced an adverse birth outcome, compared to just over 26 percent in the control, and that difference was not statistically significant.

That 2022 study focused only on newborn health. It's possible that benefits to the children will appear later. And, indeed, the researchers are still working to test for early childhood outcomes. But, for now, we are left with something of a mixed bag. Early evaluations of the Nurse-Family Partnership found benefits—this larger, more recent study found none.

The conclusion, though, is not that newborn health is impossible to improve. We know that's not the case. Consider the Earned Income Tax Credit, the EITC. The EITC is a tax benefit for low-income, working families. The EITC is one of the largest antipoverty programs in the United States. It provides about $2,000 or so in additional cash to low-income families that they otherwise wouldn't have.

Researchers have demonstrated that the EITC improves birth outcomes: higher birth weight, lower incidence of low birth weight, lower incidence of preterm birth, and a higher birth weight for gestational age (Hoynes, Miller, and Simon 2015). The researchers even found improvements in APGAR scores. When low-income families receive more money from the EITC, an extra thousand dollars or so, their babies are born healthier.

This evidence on the EITC then suggests a useful benchmark for interventions like the Nurse-Family Partnership. The Nurse-Family Partnership costs about $6,000 per family over the two years of the program. (Nurses are expensive.) We know from the EITC that just giving low-income families money can improve the health of their newborns. So expensive interventions need to be effective—otherwise, we should just give the cash directly to the families rather than hiring them nurses. And this is the hurdle that most economists would like to set for new programs that address SDOH. The program has to be at least as helpful as just giving the money to the families directly.

The Bottom Line

Many lament the fact that America's healthcare system spends so much money on medical interventions and so little on social interventions. Insurance plans will pay a million dollars for a heart transplant, but won't pay a dime for thirty minutes with a social worker. And that despite the fact that so much of health is socially determined.

There is much to that argument. Perhaps the healthcare system would benefit from a shift away from expensive surgeries and toward approaches that might improve food security, housing, employment prospects, family dynamics, and so on.

And in such a shift toward social interventions, let us recognize the legacy of institutionalized racism. The Tuskegee syphilis experiment, along with so much else in America's history, has led to disparities in health across race.

We've described a couple interventions that *seemed* helpful: the Camden program and the Nurse-Family Partnership. Large, preregistered, rigorous studies of those interventions have found few tangible medical benefits. Why is this? Is it that nurse home visits never work, or don't work in this particular context? Are more complementary inputs needed? We don't know. But, for the time being, we should not act as though addressing social determinants is automatically, unquestionably worthwhile.

Finally, absence of evidence is not evidence of absence. Perhaps tomorrow a team of researchers will unveil an intervention that is marvelously effective at helping people and keeping them out of the hospital. Maybe it'll even save money in the long run, as the up-front investment leads to lower healthcare costs in the long run. Certainly, research in this area ought to continue, and we hope that such an intervention one day exists. But, that said, it is difficult to help people. A person lives a hard life for forty or fifty years: How much can we expect from an intervention that lasts for a few months?

References

"About Us." Nurse-Family Partnership. August 2022. https://www.nursefamilypartnership.org/about/.

Alsan, Marcella, Owen Garrick, and Grant Graziani. "Does Diversity Matter for Health? Experimental Evidence from Oakland." *American Economic Review* 109, no. 12 (2019): 4071–111. https://doi.org/10.1257/aer.20181446.

Alsan, Marcella, and Marianne Wanamaker. "Tuskegee and the Health of Black Men." *Quarterly Journal of Economics* 133, no. 1 (2018): 407–55.

"Final Report of the Tuskegee Syphilis Study Legacy Committee." Tuskegee University: Tuskegee Syphilis Study Legacy Committee, 1996.

Finkelstein, Amy, Annetta Zhou, Sarah Taubman, and Joseph Doyle. "Health Care Hotspotting—a Randomized, Controlled Trial." *New England Journal of Medicine* 382, no. 2 (2020): 152–62.

Gawande, Atul. "Finding Medicine's Hot Spots." *New Yorker*, January 16, 2011. http://www.newyorker.com/magazine/2011/01/24/the-hot-spotters.

Geiger, H. Jack. "An Experiment with Lives." *New York Times*, June 21, 1981, sec. Books. https://www.nytimes.com/1981/06/21/books/an-experiment-with-lives.html.

Greenwood, Brad N., Seth Carnahan, and Laura Huang. "Patient-Physician Gender Concordance and Increased Mortality among Female Heart Attack Patients." *Proceedings of the National Academy of Sciences* 115, no. 34 (2018): 8569–74. https://doi.org/10.1073/pnas.1800097115.

Hill, Andrew, Daniel Jones, and Lindsey Woodworth. "Physician-Patient Race-Match Reduces Patient Mortality." Rochester, NY: SSRN Scholarly Paper, 2020. https://doi.org/10.2139/ssrn.3211276.

Hoynes, Hilary, Doug Miller, and David Simon. "Income, the Earned Income Tax Credit, and Infant Health." *American Economic Journal: Economic Policy* 7, no. 1 (2015): 172–211. https://doi.org/10.1257/pol.20120179.

Kangovi, Shreya, and David Grande. "Don't Throw Cold Water on Health Care's Hot Spotters." *Health Affairs* (blog). 2020. https://www.healthaffairs.org/do/10.1377/hblog20200205.342657/full/.

Kangovi, Shreya, Nandita Mitra, David Grande, Hairong Huo, Robyn A. Smith, and Judith A. Long. "Community Health Worker Support for Disadvantaged Patients with Multiple Chronic Diseases: A Randomized Clinical Trial." *American Journal of Public Health* 107, 10 (2017): 1660–67. https://doi.org/10.2105/AJPH.2017.303985.

Kangovi, Shreya, Nandita Mitra, David Grande, Mary L. White, Sharon McCollum, Jeffrey Sellman, Richard P. Shannon, and Judith A. Long. "Patient-Centered Community Health Worker Intervention to Improve Posthospital Outcomes: A Randomized Clinical Trial." *JAMA Internal Medicine* 174, no. 4 (2014): 535–43. https://doi.org/10.1001/jamainternmed.2013.14327.

Kitzman, Harriet, David Olds, Robert Cole, Carole Hanks, Elizabeth Anson, Kimberly Arcoleo, Dennis Luckey, Michael Knudtson, Charles Henderson, and John Holmberg. "Enduring Effects of Prenatal and Infancy Home Visiting by Nurses on Children: Follow-up of a Randomized Trial among Children at Age 12 Years." *Archives of Pediatrics and Adolescent Medicine* 164, no. 5 (2010). https://jamanetwork.com/journals/jamapediatrics/article-abstract/383202.

Ly, Dan P. "Historical Trends in the Representativeness and Incomes of Black Physicians, 1900–2018." *Journal of General Internal Medicine* 37, no. 5 (2022): 1310–12. https://doi.org/10.1007/s11606-021-06745-1.

Mansour, Hani, Daniel I. Rees, Bryson M. Rintala, and Nathan N. Wozny. "The Effects of Professor Gender on the Postgraduation Outcomes of Female Students." *ILR Review* 75, no. 3 (2022): 693–715.

McConnell, Margaret A., Slawa Rokicki, Samuel Ayers, Farah Allouch, Nicolas Perreault, Rebecca A. Gourevitch, Michelle W. Martin, Annetta Zhou, Chloe Zera, Michele R. Hacker, Alyna Chien, Mary Ann Bates, Katherine Baicker. "Effect of an Intensive Nurse Home Visiting Program on Adverse Birth Outcomes in a Medicaid-Eligible Population: A Randomized Clinical Trial." *JAMA* 328, no. 1 (2022): 27–37.

"Nurses and Mothers: Transformational Relationship Creating 2-Gen Change." Nurse-Family Partnership. 2018. https://cchealth.org/fmch/pdf/NFP-Nurses-Mothers.pdf.

Olds, David, Charles Henderson Jr., Robert Chamberlin, and Robert Tatelbaum. "Preventing Child Abuse and Neglect: A Randomized Trial of Nurse Home Visitation." *Pediatrics* 78, no. 1 (1986). https://publications.aap.org/pediatrics/article/78/1/65/54135/Preventing-Child-Abuse-and-Neglect-A-Randomized.

Olds, David, Charles Henderson Jr., Robert Tatelbaum, and Robert Chamberlin. "Improving the Delivery of Prenatal Care and Outcomes of Pregnancy: A Randomized Trial of Nurse Home Visitation." *American Academy of Pediatrics* 77, no. 1 (1986). https://publications.aap.org/pediatrics/article/77/1/16/79560/Improving-the-Delivery-of-Prenatal-Care-and.

Conclusion

When we first started putting sticky notes on the walls of our offices, one for each chapter, we added one more for a conclusion. And then we spent a great deal of time wondering what to put in that conclusion. After all, what we've tried to do in these pages is provide a tour of health economics. There's no conclusion to that. The field continues to evolve as health policy evolves alongside it. A conclusion implies an ending, but here, there is no ending. Policymakers will continue to reform how pharmaceutical companies are paid, how healthcare providers are paid, how this country stumbles its way toward universal health insurance coverage. There is no end in sight—the work of health economists will never be done.

It is tempting, in writing a conclusion, to list . . . conclusions. "If only Americans were to realize that healthcare is [fill in the blank], then the healthcare sector would improve." We can't give into that temptation because, at the end of the day, so much of healthcare is a matter of trade-offs. Yes, we could lower the price of drugs, but that would probably reduce the number of new drugs developed (chap. 12). Yes, we could lower physician salaries, and there is some money to be saved there, but it is a small part of the overall healthcare sector, and some unintended consequences may arise (chap. 6). Yes, we can shift from fee-for-service payments to value-based purchasing, but that would shift us from the induced-demand problem to the problems of cream skimming and stinting (chap. 8). And on and on.

Our point is not that such policy changes are necessarily bad ideas, but rather that they—like all policy changes—involve trade-offs. In healthcare, there are virtually no free lunches—virtually no changes in policy that would benefit everyone without any downside. Now, that certainly does not mean that we should stick to the status quo, only that we ought to be aware of the downsides. Let's remember the dolphin-and-tuna conundrum: there is no way of catching tuna that does not snare at least some dolphin.

The healthcare sector poses remarkable challenges. We believe that the Affordable Care Act made many positive changes, and that future reforms may as well. But healthcare is a collection of hard problems and there are no easy solutions.

Acknowledgments

We are deeply grateful to the many students, colleagues, friends, family members, and acquaintances who helped turn a series of poorly formatted Google Docs into an actual book.

Chad Zimmerman of the University of Chicago Press provided incredible guidance through the entire process, from proposal to printing.

Nettie Silvernale served as the research assistant for this book and we are grateful for her tremendous work creating figures, fact checking, wrangling references, and analyzing data.

Emily Austin is a real writer, and she assured us that, one day, we might be real writers too. She graciously agreed to give us feedback on early drafts.

We are grateful to the many Good Samaritans who read early drafts of chapters and provided feedback, but especially to Marcella Alsan, Sherry Glied, Josh Gottlieb, Jon Gruber, Emily Oster, Alex Boyarsky Pratt, Maria Polyakova, Jim Rebitzer, Christina Starks, and Richard Thaler.

Lastly, we would both like to thank our families. For Noto: Jenny, Leah, and Kate. For Tal: Sydney, Sally, and Nora.

Notes

Introduction

1. Either it's that dolphins are cute, or that they're smart, or both. On a trip to Hawaii, Noto learned that dolphins have been shown to pass the mirror test: they recognize that the image in the mirror is a reflection. Tuna do not.

2. It's really not clear how long health economics has been around, but many pin the start of the field to the publication of "Uncertainty and the Welfare Economics of Medical Care" by Ken Arrow, published in 1963.

Chapter One

1. Noto grew up in Columbus, Ohio, so he was (and is) a fan of the Ohio State Buckeyes. Like many kids in Columbus, he didn't have a baseball team to root for. Some of his friends chose either the Cleveland Indians or the Cincinnati Reds, or just picked whichever team was doing better that season. At the time Noto and Jenny bought their table, Noto had lived in the Boston area for several years, and he had adopted the Red Sox as his favorite team. In fact, he spent the better part of graduate school working with the team on ticket pricing and eventually became a season ticket holder. So betting against the Red Sox did not come easy.

2. Noto placed the bet right before the World Series, when the odds were close to 50-50. For the sake of simplicity, we round the numbers a bit here. In the end, the Red Sox won the World Series that year. So, after the fact, Noto and Jenny would have been better off had he not placed the bet. But that is the nature of insurance: you don't know if you'll need it until it's too late.

3. When you really think about it this way, health insurance (and gambling) are tools of science fiction. We only observe one timeline, one reality. But health insurance allows us to transfer resources across timelines, even though only one of them ever becomes realized.

4. This is a direct quote from Finkelstein, Mahoney, and Notowidigdo (2018). Not exactly a textbook, but close enough.

5. Note: you should not use gambling in this way. We are professionals. Do not try this at home.

6. Our favorite memory during this bleak time period: we compiled a giant data set of cricket games. It started like this—we thought about the notion of *morale*: that one win might

motivate people for the next challenge. Now studying morale is tricky: it's rarely randomly assigned. Psychologists have lab experiments that are designed to test how morale affects behavior, but it's difficult to isolate morale outside of the laboratory.

And that's where we had an idea: in certain sports, coin tosses influence which team wins the game. A little Googling taught us that the coin toss in American football doesn't matter so much, but that the opening coin toss in cricket games *does* matter. The cricket team that wins the opening coin toss is 5 percent more likely to win the game.

And so our idea was to test whether winning a cricket coin toss made a team more likely to win the *next* game. This seemed like a neat way to isolate the importance of morale: the outcome of the coin toss is randomly assigned, and so it would allow us to measure whether having won one game improves your chances of winning the next game.

We found a website that listed the results of cricket games dating back to the nineteenth century. Noto wrote a Perl script to scrape the site and, after running the script overnight, we had a data set with 80,000—*80,000*—cricket games.

Then we ran some regressions. Sadly, those regressions did not lead to a compelling finding. We confirmed that the opening coin toss really affects which team won that game, but we found no effect of that coin toss on the *next* game. We had hoped for a more interesting result, a demonstration of the importance of morale. Instead, we ended up with a pretty uninteresting one, and so we never wrote up the findings.

7. For simplicity, we are only describing Chapter 7 bankruptcy here, not Chapter 13. In practice, consumer bankruptcy is a bit more complicated.

8. Senator Elizabeth Warren was a law professor at the time and wrote several influential papers on bankruptcy and healthcare costs. She and her coauthors argued that most bankruptcies are driven by healthcare costs. But there was some question as to whether her papers were based on an unreliable methodology. See, for instance, a paper by Dranove and Millenson (2006) that critiqued her work.

9. Since the bankruptcy filing rate was about 1 percent during this time period, our results imply that a 10 percentage-point expansion of Medicaid eligibility would reduce the bankruptcy filing rate from about 1 percent to 0.92 percent. That may not sound like a large effect, but it implies a meaningful share of consumer bankruptcies are genuine "medical bankruptcies," where the difference between filing and not filing depends on access to health insurance.

10. Noto's father defaulted on his credit card bill when Noto was in his teens. To this day, Noto's mother still gets calls from collectors asking for the debt to be repaid.

11. Technically, there is an increase of about $200–$300 in unpaid medical bills for those with health insurance at the time of the hospitalization. The key point is that this is substantially smaller than the increase for the uninsured ($200–$300 compared to $6,000). The unpaid medical bills for the insured could come from consumers not paying the out-of-pocket costs associated with the hospital visit (e.g., copays or coinsurance).

12. Bhash Mazumder and Sarah Miller (2016) studied the Massachusetts healthcare reform prior to the ACA. They like to call the program "Romneycare," since Mitt Romney was the governor of Massachusetts at the time the reform took place, and to emphasize its broad similarity with the "Obamacare" Affordable Care Act that came to the entire country years later. Using survey data and similar credit report data, Mazumder and Miller found clear evidence that low-income households in Massachusetts gained health insurance coverage and that this both reduced bankruptcy filings and substantially reduced the probability that households would accumulate thousands of dollars of unpaid medical bills (Mazumder and Miller 2016). These

findings come from two complementary research strategies: (1) comparing Massachusetts to other states in the Northeast before and after the reform, and (2) comparing areas within Massachusetts that had many residents who gained coverage to other parts of the state that were less affected. The fact that the results are similar in both approaches gives confidence that the estimates really represent the effects of the healthcare reform and not some other confounding factor. Another study that found similar results is the Oregon Health Insurance Experiment discussed below (Finkelstein et al. 2012). That team of researchers also gained access to consumer credit report data and found that individuals who gained access to Medicaid had lower out-of-pocket medical costs and fewer unpaid medical bills than otherwise similar individuals who remained uninsured. These results are particularly convincing given that the study was set up as a randomized experiment (the so-called gold standard of evidence). More recently, a team of researchers studied Obamacare directly by comparing states that did expand Medicaid to "nonexpansion" states, also using credit report data, and these authors found evidence that unpaid bills sent to collection agencies decreased in expansion states relative to nonexpansion states after the ACA (Hu at al. 2018).

13. In fairness, there had been some other studies that suggested the same conclusion: health insurance coverage leads to greater utilization. Tal cowrote two such studies, suggesting that health insurance coverage leads to more ER visits and also more inpatient visits (Anderson, Dobkin, and Gross 2012, 2014).

14. Economists often send out letters to test how information affects people's behavior. Recently, Noto—along with Finkelstein—sent out letters to older adults in Pennsylvania (Finkelstein and Notowidigdo 2019). The letters informed people that they were eligible for food stamps. Before this study, other researchers had sent letters to provide information about the Earned Income Tax Credit (Bhargava and Manoli 2012), Social Security Disability Insurance (Armour 2018), and enrolling in college (Bettinger et al. 2012; Barr and Turner 2018; Dynarski et al. 2018).

Chapter Two

1. Chad is named after our editor at the University of Chicago Press. Chad, you're #3 when it comes to Aaron through Zack, but to us, you'll always be #1.

2. This quote comes from an article where Paul Krugman uses an imaginary economy that only produces hot dogs and buns to say something interesting and important about international trade (Krugman 1997).

3. We follow here a convention that we were exposed to as graduate students: male names for the workers and female names for the managers. To quote the mathematical economist Martin Osborne, if this convention "diverts some readers' attention from the subjects discussed in this book and leads them to contemplate sexism in the use of language . . . then an increase in social welfare will have been achieved."

4. To be more formal, we could say that Aaron is risk averse, which means that he is willing to pay more than his expected healthcare costs for insurance. But he is not *that* risk averse. We might assume that all of these men are willing to pay 20 percent more than their expected healthcare costs in order to be insured. Under that assumption, Aaron is willing to pay up to $1,200 for health insurance. He's willing to pay more than $1,000 because insurance will take care of the nightmare scenario in which his healthcare costs one year soar beyond his baseline average. But $13,500 is just way too high for him. He'd rather take his chances and remain uninsured.

5. The age of onset varies. In some rare cases, the symptoms can begin in childhood or, at the other extreme, in a person's eighties.

6. Ultimately, this research shows that availability of genetic testing leads to adverse selection in the market for long-term care insurance. Huntington's disease, however, is so rare that the adverse selection does not affect insurers' operations that much. It's an interesting open question whether the future of genetic testing will generate many more examples like this case study, where consumers learn about their future healthcare needs and change their insurance appropriately. If that happens, then adverse selection could end up destabilizing more markets.

7. Another example of a selection business: lenders. If a credit card company signs up customers who will all default on their balances, never paying off their credit cards, then that kills the lender's profits.

8. In reality, there were several plans. We simplify the story a bit here. But the full version is available in the paper that Sarah Reber and David Cutler eventually wrote (Cutler and Reber 1998).

9. Again, we're simplifying here a bit. The subsidy depended on the employee's salary.

10. Sarah was using Stata version 3. We started graduate school a bit later than her—we started with version 7. In 2021, the Stata corporation released version 17.

11. If you're curious about the early effects of the Massachusetts healthcare reform, see work by Miller (2012) and Kolstad and Kowalski (2012).

Chapter Three

1. Specifically, the Emergency Medical Treatment and Active Labor Act (EMTALA) requires that hospitals provide emergency medical treatment to all patients.

2. Tal has a cousin who moved to Los Angeles in her twenties to pursue her dreams of becoming a musician. She joined a band and took on odd jobs to make ends meet, but she was never insured. When Tal asked her what she would do if—*heaven forbid*—she needed medical care, she explained that there was a Catholic hospital nearby, and she had heard that they would treat her.

3. This puzzle of low take-up is not just observed in health insurance. It's also observed in long-term care insurance. The fact that individuals "know" that, if they require long-term care, the state—say, through the state Medicaid program—will cover long-term care for them may lead many individuals to decide that long-term care insurance just isn't worth it.

Chapter Four

1. One of the first times the term "moral hazard" appears in the economics literature is in a 1968 paper in the *American Economic Review* written by Mark Pauly. The paper was written as a comment on the pathbreaking paper by Kenneth Arrow published in 1963 in the same journal. In that paper, Arrow wrote that the "special economic problems of medical care can be explained by adaptations to uncertainty." (Many economists give Arrow credit for launching the study of health economics as a separate area of research within economics with this paper.) In his comment on Arrow's work, Pauly notes that in addition to the issues of risk and uncertainty, insurers also have to anticipate how consumers will respond to the change in the price of healthcare caused by insurance. He describes how the term "moral hazard" comes from the medical insurance literature and discusses how insurance writers viewed the individual response to insur-

ance as a "moral or ethical problem." Insurance writers described moral hazard as reflecting the "hazard that arises from the failure of individuals who are or have been affected by insurance to uphold the accepted moral qualities." However, Pauly then writes that the "response of seeking more medical care with insurance . . . is a result not of moral perfidy, but of rational economic behavior." Given this history, it's a bit of a shame that the term "moral hazard" subsequently became the standard term used throughout economics, since it's not a moral failure to respond to economic incentives. But we'll use it throughout the chapter, anyway, since it continues to be the standard term used to describe this type of behavior in both academic research and policy discussions.

2. There were actually a few groups. We are simplifying here. For more detail, see Manning et al. 1987.

3. The authors tested for differences by household income, and, for the most part, they found that the key research findings didn't really vary by income.

4. We are adjusting the estimates to 2021 dollars. Economists prefer to work in real rather than nominal units, and we try to follow that convention here.

5. A fun study on this: Jaime Rosenthal called up about a hundred hospitals and told them that her grandmother was uninsured and wanted to pay for a hip replacement out of pocket. Only ten of the hospitals could give her a single price.

Chapter Six

1. Tal took a sociology class in college in which the faculty member laid out this particular strategy.

2. This statistic comes from the paper by Gottlieb et al. (2020), which we describe below.

3. This hypothetical is partly inspired by Paul Krugman's 1997 *Slate* article on the role of "playful theorizing" in economics. The article begins: "Imagine an economy that produces only two things: hot dogs and buns. Consumers in this economy insist that every hot dog comes with a bun, and vice versa. And labor is the only input to production." Krugman then goes on: "One of the points of this column is to illustrate a paradox: You can't do serious economics unless you are willing to be playful." The broader point of the hot dog parable is to illustrate why economists are skeptical that productivity growth in a single sector is unlikely to reduce employment in the economy as a whole.

4. The fact that one of us (OK, it's Tal) is entirely bald and so never visits a hairdresser somehow makes this scenario even more fanciful.

5. Actually, in many states, it *is* illegal to sell haircuts without a license (Kleiner and Krueger 2013)!

6. Economists largely think the bulk of these restrictions are excessive. The Council of Economic Advisers under the Obama administration put out a report in 2015 highlighting the costs of excessive occupational licensing. It stated that when there are too many barriers, licensing can reduce employment opportunities—particularly for disadvantaged workers—by making it more difficult to enter a profession (Department of the Treasury Office of Economic Policy 2015).

7. Angoon, Alaska, is used as an example in the recent article "Dental Care Where There Is No Dentist" to discuss the role of dental therapists in providing dental care to Alaska Natives (Otto 2019).

8. The term "minimum efficient scale" refers to the fact that some businesses require a certain number of customers or sales in order to cover their fixed operating costs. In healthcare, a

dental practice may need a certain number of patients to be financially sustainable, and if the local population is too small to meet this minimum efficient scale, the dentist will have to pull in patients from nearby towns, or possibly choose to locate elsewhere, leaving some small villages to carry on as so-called dental deserts.

9. As of 2022, dental therapists have been authorized to work in only thirteen states (Mizzi Angelone and Corr 2022).

10. Of course, how much lawyers earn varies a lot. Corporate lawyers tend to earn a lot more money than public defenders, for example. This kind of calculation is inherently rough—it lumps all lawyers together and then large groups of physicians together. The point is simply that the average lifetime income is a lot higher for physicians than lawyers, even after adjusting for the amount of training required.

Chapter Seven

1. We are inspired here by an old saying in health policy: "asking your doctor how much medicine you need is like asking a butcher how much meat you should buy."

2. See, for instance, a paper published in *JAMA* in 2018, "Hip and Knee Replacements: A Neglected Potential Savings Opportunity" by Vanessa Lam, Steven Teutsch, and Jonathan Fielding.

3. Two other examples from recent literature in health economics include Clemens and Gottlieb (2014) and Ho and Pakes (2014). Clemens and Gottlieb (2014) study a policy reform in 1997 that consolidated the regions Medicare used to set prices. This policy generated sharp changes in physician payments in some areas but not others, which allowed the authors to study how physicians' financial incentives affect their healthcare decisions. The authors find a large effect of financial incentives on the provision of healthcare, particularly for elective procedures like cataract surgery and less so for healthcare that's less discretionary, like cancer treatments and repairing fractured hips. They even find that the increased physician payments spurred the adoption of more expensive medical technologies like MRI machines. Ho and Pakes (2014) study how the financial incentives created by fixed (capitated) payments to physician groups leads physicians to refer patients giving birth to low-cost hospitals. Interestingly, this doesn't appear to affect quality of care or health outcomes, but the hospitals tend to be farther away for the patients, so the financial incentives in this case lead physicians to make decisions that are less convenient for the patients.

4. When the system was first developed there were 467 DRGs. In 2008, the system was modified to the MS-DRG system, with about 750 MS-DRGs. Each DRG belongs to a Major Diagnostic Category (MDC). Below each MDC is a set of DRGs that include specific symptoms and/or conditions. After determining the MDC, the doctors treating the patient categorize the condition as either a surgical or medical condition, and, based on the procedures that the doctors are planning to do, the doctors then indicate a specific DRG. For example, the Respiratory System MDC includes the following DRGs: pulmonary embolism, infections, neoplasms, chest trauma, pleural effusion, pulmonary edema and respiratory failure, chronic obstructive pulmonary disease, simple pneumonia, RSV pneumonia and whooping cough, interstitial lung disease, pneumothorax, bronchitis and asthma, respiratory symptoms and other respiratory diagnoses (Center for Medicare and Medicaid Services 2019).

5. There was another key to hospital profitability: hospitals were more profitable the higher the rates they could negotiate with private payers. We discuss that part of the business in chapter 9.

6. That last case, amputation of the wrong body part, seems especially horrific. Consider Googling "wrong testicle removed" to learn of an awful situation that was horrific for a patient in New Jersey and, less so, his urologist.

Chapter Eight

1. Tal had a student get confused on an exam and discuss the "stinking cream." The student confused "stinting" and "cream skimming," probably due to our failure to enunciate in class.

2. We totally should not be telling this story. Then again, Noto has tenure.

3. Both of them made many other contributions to economics besides the paper we discuss in this chapter. In fact, Paul Milgrom won the prize in 2020 for a completely different area of economic theory—auctions instead of contracts. We do not pretend to understand how the Royal Swedish Academy makes its decisions, but these were two of the most obvious choices to win the prize during our professional careers.

Chapter Nine

1. A long-standing argument among health economists is how to define a hospital market. The results we discuss in this section are based on a market definition that counts up the number of hospitals within fifteen miles of each other. For some types of healthcare (e.g., certain types of specialty care) this market definition is too narrow. If you have an unusual type of cancer, for example, you might get referred to a hospital that's farther away but has more expertise in treating your condition. On the other hand, if you are going in regularly for treatment for a common chronic disease, you might not be willing to travel fifteen miles each time for your treatment. Away from those extremes, the authors' fifteen-mile radius is probably a decent approximation of the set of hospitals patients consider for their treatment. In our own research with Craig Garthwaite (Garthwaite, Gross, and Notowidigdo 2018), we borrowed a definition from economists and sociologists who study labor market outcomes—commuting zones, or CZs (Tolbert and Sizer 1996; Autor and Dorn 2013). What we liked about this definition is that CZs are based on commuting patterns, how far workers are willing to drive for work. It seemed to us that this was a good proxy for how far people would typically be willing to drive for healthcare as well.

2. This statistic comes from the work of Eliason et al. (2020), who cite DaVita's 2004 Annual Report.

3. We are describing here other researchers' peer-reviewed study. It's worth pointing out that the authors describe a few alternative explanations. One key issue is that the composition of patients at dialysis clinics might change after an acquisition. Perhaps the patients who visit the leaner clinic after acquisition are sicker and more likely to die in any case. It's difficult to fully rule out that alternative explanation, but the authors try their best by controlling for characteristics that they can observe in their data. Ultimately, the authors argue that the weight of the evidence suggests a deterioration in average quality of care following acquisition.

4. For instance, Oscar Health started offering Medicare Advantage plans in 2020, as did Devoted Health in 2018 and Bright Health in 2018. These companies have been able to raise substantial amounts of money from venture capital firms that see a lot of potential.

5. Sometimes, it's not the FTC that's involved but state or local healthcare authorities. The Department of Justice is sometimes also involved.

Chapter Ten

1. The American College of Physicians released a report in 2022 stating that "a better system of collaboration between . . . physicians has the potential to . . . use health care resources more efficiently and improve patient access to care" ("ACP Lays out Mechanisms for Better Care Coordination," American College of Physicians 2022).

Chapter Eleven

1. Macroeconomists believe that this kind of productive reallocation is one of the key drivers of economic growth in the economy overall. More productive and efficient firms tend to grow and less productive and efficient firms tend to shrink—which both contribute to the overall growth of the economy.

2. Random assignment solves the problems we are describing because, if patients are randomly assigned to physicians, and each physician sees a large enough number of patients, then any differences in downstream health outcomes can be reliably attributed to differences in physician decisions and skills. If all of the physicians were identical, then the health outcomes would be similar, on average, because random assignment ensures that each physician gets the same distribution of patients. Some patients are sick and some are healthy, but each physician gets the same share of sick and healthy patients on average.

3. In fact, the last four digits of everyone's Social Security number are effectively randomly assigned. When the federal government gives out stimulus checks to stimulate the economy during a recession, the checks are often distributed over time to spread out the distribution of federal funds. To make things fair, the groups who receive the checks earlier are groups defined based on the last two digits of their Social Security numbers.

Chapter Twelve

1. Part C is Medicare Advantage, which we discuss in chapter 8.

2. See the work of Huh and Reif (2017), published in the *Journal of Health Economics*.

3. OK, listen, we are simplifying here. The term "large molecule" does not necessarily mean a biologic, and not all biologics are produced by a living organism. In providing a broad overview of the pharmaceutical industry, we believe it's useful here to think of three, mutually exclusive categories: small-molecule drugs, biologics, and gene therapies.

4. Occasionally, regulators will deem a biosimilar to be equivalent to an original large-molecule drug, and so insurers will force beneficiaries to switch to the cheaper option. But, more often, the biosimilar is similar, not equivalent, and so there is less of a shift away from the expensive, original product.

5. Kymriah is the brand name—the actual name is Tisagenlecleucel, and if you can pronounce that, you should skip this chapter.

Chapter Thirteen

1. Economists tend to think about three main reasons for taxes: (1) to raise funds to pay for public goods like roads, police, and national defense, (2) to redistribute income, and (3) to address externalities like pollution. What's different about (3) is that the government does not

actually need to use the money raised through externality-reducing tax for anything in order to make everyone better off. The money can be used to cut other unpopular taxes and (in theory, at least) make everyone better off.

2. Since we've only been briefly summarizing papers throughout the book, you are forgiven if you are a bit skeptical of these results. Do we really know that air pollution is bad for infant health? How do we know it's really air pollution and not some other factors? For many years, we shared this skepticism. Research is hard, and there are plenty of "false discoveries" in both the natural sciences and social sciences. For example, a very prominent science journal published a paper claiming that hurricanes with female names are more deadly than hurricanes with male names (Jung et al. 2014). If that sounds too crazy to be true, it's probably because it is (Christensen and Christensen 2014). But we have seen the finding that air pollution negatively affects infant and child health replicated again and again in many different settings all around the world. As a result, our skepticism has been gradually (and soundly) defeated. One final example we can't help ourselves from discussing is a recent paper that found clear evidence of car pollution's effects on infant health by cleverly using the Volkswagen (VW) emissions scandal (Alexander and Schwandt 2022). You may have heard about this scandal: Volkswagen intentionally programmed its diesel engines to activate their emissions controls only during laboratory testing. As a result of this negligence, 500,000 VW cars were sold in the United States that caused much greater pollution than practically any other car on the market at the time. The authors were able to track where the cars were sold and found that, in areas that bought more of these cars, the air pollution got measurably worse. Moreover, the authors found that the increases in air pollution from these cars led to increases in the incidence of low birth weight and infant mortality.

3. To our knowledge, epidemiologists are not sure why the COVID-19 pandemic came in waves. There are biological and genetic explanations for those waves, based on the genetic variants of the disease. This is another explanation, involving how people change their behavior as the disease spreads. There may not be one, single explanation.

Chapter Fourteen

1. In order to access the data, we had to agree to include the following sentences in this book: "The National Longitudinal Mortality Study is a collaborative effort between the US Census Bureau and the National Heart, Lung, and Blood Institute (NHLBI), National Cancer Institute (NCI), National Institute on Aging (NIA), and the National Center for Health Statistics (NCHS). The views expressed in this book are those of the authors and do not necessarily reflect the views of the Census Bureau, NHLBI, NCI, NIA, or NCHS."

2. We calculate this statistic by estimating the semi-elasticity of the mortality rate with respect to income by running a regression of the mortality on log income. This requires us to impute income for each household, since we don't observe actual income (we just observe which "bucket" the individual's income is in, as shown in fig. 14.2). The coefficient on log income is 0.047, and the average mortality rate in the sample is 20.5 percent, and the ratio of these two numbers gives the percentage change in mortality for a 1 percent change in income.

3. The idea of studying compulsory schooling laws was originally pioneered by Alan Krueger and Josh Angrist in a famous 1991 paper. Thirty years later, Josh Angrist was awarded the Nobel Prize in economics. Alan Krueger would have almost certainly shared the Nobel Prize alongside Angrist, but he tragically committed suicide in 2019. Mental illnesses affect every-

one regardless of their education, income, or social class. Please visit Mental Health America's website (mhanational.org) if you or anyone you know is struggling with mental illness. If you or anyone you know is experiencing a mental health crisis, please call the Suicide Prevention Lifeline at 988.

Chapter Fifteen

1. Want other egregious examples? James Sims, a famous doctor in the 1800s and the "father of modern gynecology" experimented on enslaved black women. He would operate on them without anesthesia and they would have to be forcibly restrained. But, sadly, we don't need to go back to the 1800s to find horror stories. Fannie Lou Hamer was a civil rights organizer. In the 1960s, she scheduled a procedure to have a tumor removed from her uterus, but the doctor actually performed a hysterectomy without her knowledge or consent.

2. The same thing happens in schools. When students are randomly assigned to teachers of the same race or gender as themselves, the students end up doing better. To take just one example, Mansour et al. (2022) study undergraduate women taking freshman and sophomore math and science courses. Female students randomly assigned to female professors end up more likely to stay in the field long term. Diversity really matters.

3. This list of medical problems comes from the *New Yorker* article by Atul Gawande, further described in the text.

4. Regression to the mean is a powerful statistical force, but it's important to know when to apply it. In this study, by selecting the experimental sample based on recent healthcare utilization, it's likely the case that you have ended up with a mix of people who are chronically ill and people who just temporarily had high utilization. The latter type of individuals are likely to "regress to the mean" whether they are in treatment or control groups (i.e., their high utilization was temporary and would be expected to fall whether they are in the program or not). An example of where you would not want to use "regression to the mean thinking" is selling stocks after they've gone up a lot (thinking that they are bound to come down eventually). That's actually one of the most common mistakes that retail investors make. There's no "regression to the mean" in the stock market; our financial economist colleagues can tell us that as best as they can tell, the stock market behaves like a random walk, which is one of the statistical processes that does not display regression to the mean behavior.

Index

Page numbers in italics refer to figures and tables.